Information Technology and Authentic Learning

The last decade has seen a steady increase in the presence of computers in the classroom. What the effects of such computer-based learning might be has often been left to conjecture. The National Curriculum has stipulated the use of IT as a tool throughout the curriculum for all children wherever appropriate. Yet certain questions remain: how can a teacher judge what appropriate use of IT is and use it to ensure optimum learning? Realistically, what should a teacher be looking for in a child's work, attitude and skill development as a result of using IT?

From word processing to on-line multimedia, this book takes a realistic look at the role of the computer in the National Curriculum and offers practical help to students and teachers wishing to incorporate IT into their day-to-day teaching. It covers all curriculum areas and examines issues such as pupil's perceptions of their own learning, of literacy and 'new literacy', problem solving, collaborative learning, data handling and homework.

The book is aimed at trainee and practising teachers looking for support in building their own understanding and their teaching skills using IT. It is essential to all primary school teachers and trainees who wish to maximise the positive effects of computers in the primary classroom.

Information technology and authentic learning

Realising the potential of computers in the primary classroom

Edited by Angela McFarlane

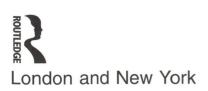

London and New York

First published 1997
by Routledge
11 New Fetter Lane, London EC4P 4EE

Simultaneously published in the USA and Canada
by Routledge
29 West 35th Street, New York, NY 10001

Typeset in Adobe Garamond by Keystroke, Jacaranda Lodge, Wolverhampton
Printed and bound in Great Britain by Biddles Ltd, Guildford and King's Lynn

British Library Cataloguing in Publication Data
A catalogue record for this book is available from the British Library

Library of Congress Cataloging in Publication Data
Information technology and authentic learning: realising
   the potential of computers in the primary classroom / edited by Angela
   McFarlane.
      p. cm.
   ISBN 0-415-14701-8 (alk. paper)
      1. Computer-assisted instruction—Great Britain. 2. Education,
   Elementary—Great Britain—Data processing. 3. Information
   technology—Great Britain. I. McFarlane, Angela, 1957– .
   LB1028.43I5393   1996
   372'.0285–dc21   96–39901
                                                              CIP

Contents

Figures

Contributors

Michael Bonnett is a senior lecturer in the philosophy of education and author of various articles on the nature of understanding and structuring children's learning. He is the author of a book entitled *Children's Thinking*, Cassell, 1994.

Peter Cunningham is a senior lecturer in history education and an established author.

Libby Jared is an ex-head of mathematics at a secondary school and now senior lecturer and college IT co-ordinator. Libby has produced IT study packs for initial training covering all aspects of IT in primary schools and is involved in the induction of students and teachers into the applications of computing in children's learning.

Avril Loveless is a senior lecturer in education at the University of Brighton. She is the author of *The Role of IT: practical issues for primary teachers*, Cassell, 1995.

Anne Thwaites is senior lecturer in mathematics and mathematics education involved in many aspects of the initial and inservice training of primary teachers. Her expertise with IT applications in the teaching of mathematics ranges from infant and primary school children to mathematics undergraduates and number theory.

Linda Webb is a senior lecturer in science education and has been published in Physics Education on the use of spread sheets in science.

David Whitebread is a former primary deputy head teacher, and senior lecturer in the psychology of education. His publications include various articles on children's learning. He edited *Teaching and Learning in the Early Years* for Routledge (1996).

Preface

The initial impetus for this book was the recognition of a lack of suitable reference material for students on the B.Ed. and PGCE, and in-service training, courses within Homerton College. These courses highlighted the need for reference material on learning outcomes related to the use of computers in the primary classroom. No existing volume offered a clear vision of what effects on learning a teacher might reasonably expect when children are given access to different types of computer-based resources across the curriculum. And yet teachers are required by the statutory orders in all subject areas in the National Curricula for Scotland, Northern Ireland, England and Wales, to make judgements on the 'appropriate use' of Information Technology in every context. If a teacher does not have a well-developed understanding of the teaching and learning objectives that particular models of computer use can facilitate, she cannot be expected to manage the integration of these resources in a way which will optimise their impact. Furthermore, she has no guiding criteria against which to evaluate the success of her strategies.

This book has been planned to assist anyone who wishes to maximise the positive effects of information technology in her classroom: to use these technologies to facilitate *authentic learning*, that is, learning which has personal meaning and substance for the learner. It seeks to offer practical help to students and teachers planning work schemes for children. There is advice on task management and examples of classroom practice which have known positive outcomes. The book interweaves this practical advice with the theoretical basis behind the scenarios described, raising issues which are of concern to every reflective practitioner. As the use of computers in schools continues to increase in the coming decade, these fundamental issues will have continuing relevance.

The late 1980s and early 1990s have seen a steady increase in the presence of computers in the classroom. During that time there has been a strong emphasis on informing teachers how to operate the machines, and some input on how different types of computer use could be integrated into the curriculum. The current recommendations for a National Curriculum for teacher training place a strong emphasis on developing student teachers' IT skills. Many useful and highly accessible books and information packs, referred to here, will tell the teacher what to do with a computer, and how to do it. What the effects of such computer-based learning might be has, however, often been left to conjecture. Much of the evidence which does exist is the result of academic research in pilot studies, often in rather artificial conditions with small groups of children. The results are scattered through the academic literature. An additional factor which confounds the novice reader is that much work refers to computer use as though it is some kind of uniform activity, failing to differentiate between activities as diverse as programming in LOGO and writing a story with a word processor.

The only large-scale survey of long-term use of IT in UK schools found little evidence of impact on learning, possibly owing to a low level of pupil access to computers in their case-studies. In the last two years more positive evidence has begun to emerge as the levels of resourcing have risen steeply in some schools, providing suitable populations of children for observation. The National Curriculum has stipulated the use of IT as a tool throughout the curriculum for all children 'wherever appropriate'. How can this use then be managed to ensure the optimum learning outcomes? Realistically, what should a teacher be looking for in a child's work, attitude and skill development as a result of using IT? What sort of learning situations and desired outcomes are best enhanced by the use of a computer? When is it better not to turn to the screen and keyboard?

This book addresses these questions. It informs the reader of known outcomes, where these exist, collated from the literature and original work by the authors, and makes practical suggestions for classroom practice. The areas covered include the main strands of IT in the National Curriculum for Key Stages 1 and 2, and the uses within core and foundation subjects where there is good evidence of positive effects on learning outcomes. There is also a chapter on the use of multimedia and on-line services which are only just entering the primary classroom but which are likely to have a major presence in home and school. Finally there is an epilogue looking at what we might reasonably expect to see in terms of the impact of IT on classroom culture in the near future, including a consideration of integrated learning systems. This book concentrates not on *how* IT should be used, but *why* IT should be used, and in doing so it touches on the fundamental concepts of what effective education is, and challenges teachers to re-examine the objectives underlying their teaching.

Acknowledgements

I would like to extend my thanks to the teachers and children who have allowed us into their classrooms over the years, and whose work has informed the contents of this book. I am also grateful to Margaret Smith, Head of the Cambridgeshire Schools Library Service, for allowing me to use material developed by the service in Chapter 11. Carol McDonnell, an Arts Council Research Fellow at the University of Brighton, kindly provided illustrations for inclusion in Chapter 9. These were gleaned from her work with children in a number of schools.

As in the case of any edited volume, this book owes much to the colleagues who have contributed chapters, and I would particularly like to thank Mike Bonnett for the hours he spent reading and commenting on the book as a whole.

Angela McFarlane, Homerton College
August 1996

Chapter 1

Where are we and how did we get here?

Angela McFarlane

The computer generation

It is worth remembering that in 1980 the only experience of computers children had was confined to the realms of science fiction. The desk-top personal computer was a new invention and yet to become a consumer product. No computers of any kind had any significant presence in British schools. The 'teaching machines' developed during the 1960s and 1970s in the United States, using a mini-computer with networked terminals, never gained a foothold in the more child-centred UK school culture. However, in less than a generation the microcomputer has become ubiquitous; it has found a place in every classroom and workplace and a good many homes. It has also become more powerful, easier to use, smaller and cheaper – a trend which is not yet exhausted.

The evolution of the microcomputer has been as rapid as its dispersal. In the time it takes a human child to develop to maturity, the personal or micro-computer has gone from a box which was good at sums, could make beeps and whistles and draw pictures which looked as though they had been built from Duplo bricks, to an all-singing all-dancing maturity which can play Beethoven in full digital stereo, show television-quality moving pictures and which can calculate at least thirty times faster than before. Almost unbelievably, this can all be achieved on a machine that can fit comfortably into a briefcase. Possibly more significant than the competence with which the computers of the nineties can perform these operations, is the fact that this power can all be harnessed by pointing and clicking at pictures on the screen. This makes the technology far more accessible to the non-specialist user. The earlier machines required a knowledge of sequences of characters, often bizarre ones, which had to be remembered and typed in to get the computer to perform the simplest task. Finally, perhaps even more amazing than the increased power and ease of use of the modern computer is the fact that the price of a state-of-the-art personal computer has stayed more or less the same, which represents a significant drop in real terms when you allow for inflation.

It is worthwhile remembering that despite this rapid expansion of technology, there are still large sections of the population who have remained personally unfamiliar with computers. As a consequence they have a rather hazy view of the personal computer and the tasks of which it is capable, and may be unaware of the role played by computerised components of everyday technology such as microwave ovens or photocopiers. Consider the way computers are still referred to in the popular media. They are often attributed human characteristics or given powers far beyond the currently possible, for example the reasoning and speaking computers frequently found in television programmes. It is easy to forget that the current generation of computers are purely reactive machines, albeit rather complex ones. They can only execute instructions they have been programmed with, including errors in-built by users and programmers who may not have foreseen every consequence of the interaction of algorithms they put into the software. As programs become bigger and more complex these cumulative errors seem inevitable. Most large commercial word processors, for example, will crash from time to time. The easier to use point-and-click user interface has its drawbacks too. It is very easy to click on something unintended and produce an unexpected outcome, which may prove irreversible. When this happens, it is common to hear even the experienced user complain that the computer 'did something'. This apparent tendency to autonomy on the part of the machine is understandably unsettling to the user, and does much to maintain the feeling of mild unease the loss of control engenders in many users.

The time-scale of computer evolution means that the experience of adults and children varies very widely. Anyone born before 1970 will not have seen a microcomputer as a primary school child. In fact surveys of students entering higher education in the late 1980s suggest that few of them had any significant exposure to computers in school at all (see for example Blackmore 1992). In contrast today's children have never known a world without computers. To the present schoolchild a computer is a natural part of her culture, to be explored, played with or ignored as required. Children, unused to having mastery of much in their world, are not intimidated by the computer and its idiosyncrasies and are happy to learn here, as elsewhere, by trial and error. Parents and teachers, used to a degree of competence in dealing with the world around them, may still see the computer as a recent invader, unfamiliar and often unpredictable. The world has changed from a place where children thought they knew more than their parents into a world where they often really do. This is especially so where children meet computers in infant or junior school and parents do not use them either at home or in the workplace. The consequences of this generation gap could be more far-reaching than any created by the so-called sexual revolution of the 1960s.

Whatever this has done for the parent–child relationship, it has often shaken up the teacher–pupil dynamic, especially where computers have been placed in classrooms irrespective of teachers' own perceived needs. The attitudes and experience of teachers and student teachers vary enormously. There are many teachers who have embraced the technology eagerly, and some who have integrated its use into the curriculum to enhance and extend children's learning.

There are many more, however, who are nowhere near this. The reasons for this lack of engagement are many, and usually interlinked. Lack of resources – computers and suitable software – are undeniably important. However, a shortage of appropriate training in the effective use of IT may be the critical missing link. Although levels of resourcing in schools continue to climb steadily, if slowly, levels of use of IT in the classroom do not (DfE 1995e). The following incident, witnessed in a busy classroom, is telling; a child of 9, previously regarded as none too bright, who had a problem with LOGO looked up at his teacher and said, 'Miss . . . . Oh no, you won't know the answer to this.' The fact that he was right was very sobering for his teacher. It is not that teachers knew everything before, it was just that they usually knew more about the task they had set than the average 9-year-old pupil. The presence of computers, and a statutory requirement to use them, has often changed that. The growth of large electronic databases, and the ease of access to them which optical storage media, such as CD ROM, and on-line services such as the Internet provide, are likely to accelerate this change as children gain competence in the 'new literacy' of the information age, and teachers risk being left behind. This may even force a change in the criteria which are used to accredit educational success.

When, ultimately, pupils have access to major archives at the touch of a button, what will be the value of memorised information? The majority of current assessment systems, particularly those administered on a national scale, rely heavily on testing the memory of pupils and their ability to produce certain facts on demand. Already this is of questionable value, given the rate of growth of knowledge. The ability to find, interpret and evaluate information is far more important, as are the skills relating to problem-solving and critical thinking. This skills-based, child-centred approach to learning has of course been at the heart of primary education in the UK for some decades. Recent legislation has tried to force schools away from this towards a more 'traditional' curriculum, which is governed by tests of students' knowledge at regular intervals. The apparent prominence given to skill development has been undermined by the relatively minor role it plays in the formal assessment process. It seems that the political and technological tides are running in conflicting directions, and it is hard to see how this will be resolved. One thing is certain, however; the technological tide will not go away. It is driven by international commercial forces far greater than national politics or education policies. Perhaps the deciding factor will be that those people who will find gainful employment in the next century will be the ones who are flexible, independent learners capable of finding the information they need and applying it to the problem in hand. All these skills have been shown to be enhanced through the judicious use of information technology in the classroom. The school leavers who can simply write neatly, spell, and recite their tables will be joining the dole queues.

Schools may look to newly trained teachers to bring them up to date with computer use. However, data on the competence and confidence of trainee teachers suggest this cannot be relied upon. Youth or recent training are no guarantee of classroom expertise with computers, any more than maturity and experience preclude it. With the increase in time student teachers spend in schools, trainees look increasingly to qualified teachers for advice on the use of computers in the classroom. Since recent surveys suggest that up to 75 per cent of primary teachers do not make regular use of the computer in their teaching they are not in a position to help the newcomers to the profession (DfE 1995e).

How did computers get into schools?

From the earliest days of the microcomputer, there was a ground swell of opinion among some, often very vocal, educationalists and politicians that computers in schools would be 'a good thing'. Not surprisingly, they had different views on why that might be so. Interestingly, the first UK government initiatives to put computers in schools were not from the Department of Education and Science, as it then was, but from the Department of Trade and Industry. Computers would fill the world of work, so children had better learn about them; computer studies was born.

The lobby of educationalists which saw computers as deliverers of curriculum content, via drill and practice software that would in part at least replace human teachers, was small in the UK and gained little credibility in schools. However another lobby of pro-computer educationalists took a very different approach. The most well known is probably Seymour Papert, the inventor of LOGO. He believed that the use of LOGO would revolutionise education. This computer language, which may look pretty arcane in today's world of computers driven by mouse clicks, was a piece of cake compared to anything that had gone before. It opened the world of computer programming to children. They could make the computer do things they wanted it to do, starting with drawing and moving simple shapes. This may seem very tame to today's computer game acolytes, but in its time it was pretty heady stuff. It is one measure of the impact of LOGO that it remains the only computer language ever to have been referred to by name in the UK National Curricula.

Opening up this new world of personal expression and empowerment to children was going to revolutionise the classroom; it was even predicted by some to lead to the end of schools. Papert and his followers underestimated the ability of schools to resist change. Computers were absorbed and their use controlled. Whether or not LOGO ever was the tool to change the face of education beyond recognition is debatable. One thing is certain; it never got the opportunity if only because in mainstream schools no one ever had the money to provide enough machines to have children all sitting using LOGO, or any other software, day in and day out. Even though the UK government education departments spent some £189 million on IT between 1981 and 1994, and the money spent on computers has at least been matched by school and parent funds, 1995 still found us with only one computer for every eighteen children in the average primary school. The advent of the truly personal portable computer is likely to make a significant impact on this situation in the near future. The value of these machines in schools has been shown unequivocally by the National Council for Educational Technology's national pilot evaluation, funded by the DfE (Stradling *et al.* 1994). The smallest and cheapest are equivalent in price to a new bicycle or electronic game system. There are already indications that where parents are aware of the contribution these machines can make to their child's education, and the school cannot provide one for exclusive individual use, some of them are buying a portable for their child to use in school. In time, the problem of inadequate central provision of computers is likely to be overtaken by the personal ownership of portables by the majority of pupils. Schools will only need to supply machines for those unable to provide their own, rather as in the case of calculators today.

We have been promised by many pundits since the early 1980s that schools would never be the same after the information revolution, but this has not happened yet. Political change in the shape of the National Curriculum, and changes in teachers' terms of employment have done far more to affect the day-to-day world of someone who has been a schoolteacher or pupil during the 1980s and 1990s. However, computers are slowly and surely invading every classroom. The support for computers in schools in the UK, especially as provided through local education authority advisory staff during the 1980s and early 1990s (before their recent decline) promoted a computer-based pupil-empowerment culture. This is still present in UK schools; it is even embedded – albeit somewhat disguised – within the National Curriculum Information Technology Capability requirements, which are a statutory part of the curriculum for all pupils aged from 5 to 16. The requirements dictate that pupils must have exposure to the computer as a tool: learning to use it, for example, to communicate effectively and to collect, handle and interpret data. Knowledge of these powerful processes can be very effective in the development of so-called higher-order thinking skills, as later chapters will discuss. Using these processes can promote flexibility and independence in the learner.

By law, teachers have to teach IT, which is given the status of a separate subject in the National Curriculum. Although IT can be taught as a separate subject, and certain elements often are, there is in addition a requirement to incorporate its use into the curriculum 'where appropriate'. Whether teachers feel sufficiently well resourced or competent to do this is another matter. In 1995 the DfE proudly announced that 90 per cent of teachers had had 'initial awareness' training in IT. They were quieter about the fact that 75 per cent had had nothing more. It would be an over-simplification to suggest that shortage of computers and software were the only reasons that children are not having more experience of information technology in schools. (There are instances where a single computer can support an activity, as evidenced here in Chapters 2, 3, 6 and 7.) But whilst there has been an effort to supply resources and basic awareness training to teachers, there is still little information readily available on what constitutes valuable computer use in educational terms, and even less on how we may recognise the positive outcomes of these experiences. Word processing is the most common use of computers in schools by a long way, yet this can all too often mean typing in a story written by hand so that a child has a neat copy with correct spelling. It is hard to see what revolutionary learning gains the child may make as a result of this experience. Computer use alone, without clear objectives and well-designed tasks, is of little intrinsic value. It is entirely reasonable that many teachers are sceptical about computer use in the absence of sound evidence that it is of proven value, or clear guidance as to what that value is.

What do computers do best?

It may be helpful at this point to sketch some of the main uses of the computer, and categorise the types of activity they might support, particularly in the classroom.

Handling information

Computers are very good at searching, sorting and displaying information in a wide variety of forms. Text, numbers, pictures, sound, animated sequences and now even video can be stored and manipulated using a computer. Moreover, because they can do this manipulation very fast, very large collections of information can be handled.

This information might have been provided by a publisher or collected by the children in the school, collectively or individually. It could be as diverse as a commercially published collection of pictures, text, and sound clips on the exploration of space, a story written by a child, or a collection of weather data made by a class. The advantage of having the space exploration information on a computer is that it can be searched and viewed according to the interests and present needs of the user. This makes it easier for you to find relationships between items, make your own cognitive links, and so build personal knowledge. In a well-designed title it should also be possible to extract information and incorporate it in a composition of your own. It may even be possible to add information to the existing collection, so personalising the database. However, what you can do with the information will depend very much on the quality, quantity and format in which it is available. It must be remembered that someone has made decisions about what to include and what to leave out of the collection, no matter how large it is. These can imply a variety of value judgements, real or apparent. Informed use of the material, as with any other information source, must take this into account. Chapter 5, 'IT and thinking skills in humanities' and Chapter 10, 'Computers in the classroom: some values issues' explore these ideas further. Chapter 11, 'New technologies' also explores the use of IT tools and resources in the development of children's learning skills.

In the case of a story the advantages are rather different. Clearly there is a relatively small amount of information, so the speed of handling is less important. However, a story in computer-readable form can be reworked: edited, extended, reordered, with very little manual effort and without compromising the appearance of the finished work. The impact that this facility can have not only on the development of children's writing but also on their thinking is explored in Chapter 8, 'Thinking about writing'. New possibilities are presented by the current generation of computers, which can be used to view, produce and manipulate high quality images, as well as words and numbers. The processes of developing and refining an idea are as relevant when working with visual information as with written text. Processes previously only found in the studios of artists and designers are now practical in the school room. Chapter 9, 'Working with images, developing ideas', considers the role of IT in visual education.

The weather data reveals another aspect of the flexibility of use possible when information is stored in a computer. The measurements can be collected by the computer, using sensors, over a period of time even when the children are not there. They can be viewed in tables or a variety of graphs to help find patterns and relationships. (Chapters 6 and 7, 'Investigating science' and 'Developing graphing skills' examine some practical possibilities.) Through telephone links these data can be swapped with measurements made in other schools, possibly even in other countries. In addition, systems which monitor the prevailing weather and control heating and ventilation accordingly can be modelled. (Chapter 11 examines the use of E-mail to swap data and Chapter 3 looks at sensing and control systems.)

Reacting to the user

As well as simply handling information, and displaying it, computers are also good at responding to input from a user. If a child is reading a book and comes across a word she does not know, she has a number of options. These include skipping over it, trying to sound it out, asking someone what it is, referring to a dictionary. Text on screen can be programmed to offer some of these alternatives directly without leaving the task; clicking on a word may give you the pronunciation, or a definition, or both. It may also offer you alternative information on other topics related to that word. These are very simple examples of responses to the user. At the other end of a very wide spectrum are the complex microworlds, from adventure games to simulations of nuclear reactors. Here, as a process unfolds, the whole course of events can be changed as a result of choices made by the child. This can provide an ideal stimulus for the development of skills relating to problem-solving and genuine collaboration. This area is explored in Chapter 2, 'Developing children's problem-solving: the educational uses of adventure games'.

In simple terms then, the computer offers access to information in a flexible format, which can be manipulated and explored by the child. It also offers scenarios where events are altered as a result of a child's actions. These aspects of flexibility and responsiveness are at the heart of the legitimate role of the computer in the primary classroom. These activities can provide tools to think with, frameworks for making the abstract tangible; this is a theme developed in Chapter 4 'Understanding and using variables in a variety of mathematical contexts'.

Another variety of reaction to the user is offered by the drill and practice type programs which can tell the child immediately that the answer she has picked is wrong, show her the right answer and, ideally, explain why. The more sophisticated systems, known as Integrated Learning Systems (ILS) can go on to select appropriate tasks for individuals depending on their level of performance. This offers a significantly different experience to the equivalent traditional activity where a child may work through a sheet of problems, reinforcing her misconceptions, before having it corrected. Whether children then understand, or remember what they were doing, when they get the corrected version, is an interesting point. Use of these ILS type systems is considered further later in Chapter 10 'Computers in the classroom: some values issues' and Chapter 12 '. . . and where are we going?'.

So what is it about computers?

So what is it about computers that makes people as different as Seymour Papert and Kenneth Baker (Conservative Minister first for Trade and Industry and then for Education in the 1980s, responsible for computers in schools initiatives in both jobs) believe that they belong in a classroom? Obviously the view that children must be prepared to inhabit the computer-rich environment they will live and work in as adults is a strong political motive. However, it goes much further. There has always been a belief, increasingly supported by experience, that computers can enrich the processes of education.

In the early days of computers, in the 1960s and 1970s, educationalists in the US were trying out the so-called teaching machines. These were big computers which serviced individual terminals. Pupils sat at a keyboard and monitor, and did drill and practice exercises in things like arithmetic and spelling. This fitted very nicely with a prevailing behaviourist view of education in the US: you challenged pupils' misconceptions by telling them they were wrong until they gave in. Whenever they got a question wrong, the computer told them and gave them more problems until they got them right. The program then moved on to the next bit of content. It seems incredible now that these systems were hailed by some enthusiasts as the technology that would replace the teacher. Needless to say it did not, and in the UK it did not even raise its head. However as shown later, in Chapter 12, their more sophisticated descendants may finally have made the trip across the Atlantic, in response to the misguided belief that they can teach basic skills more cost effectively than any other method.

In the late 1970s, up until the present time, rather different models of learning have been used to inform teaching strategies in most UK classrooms. We currently believe that children must construct a view of their world, and that this is largely a social process. By working with ideas, materials and objects learners come to a point where they develop certain beliefs. For example, by manipulating Cuisinaire rods children may come to the view that seven is a quantity which can be made up from seven ones, or two threes and a one; that seven and three make ten; that two sevens make fourteen and so on. They build a concept of the 'seven-ness of seven'. This is very different from recognising that when they see '3 + 3 + 1 = ' they must hit the 7 key.

One reason that pro-computer educationalists in the UK have always been unhappy with their use for drill and practice exercises is that this seems a somewhat trivial use of a scarce resource. For example, because computers are powerful and flexible machines they can be used to help children have experiences of manipulating information of many types, which can help them construct personal knowledge in ways analogous to the manipulation of the Cuisinaire rods. Moreover these interactions with computer-based information and software can go beyond that physically possible within a school context. Children can perform these manipulations as individuals, or (and this is often more powerful) as a group. It is important to remember that a computer is a many-faceted instrument. We tend to talk about them collectively: 'Computers can . . . , computers can't . . . '. This linguistic shorthand masks a variety and complexity possibly unparalleled in any other medium. It is even more misleading than talking about watching television as a uniform activity. Certainly there are similar elements which remain constant; a television viewer sits or stands, watching moving images and listening to sounds. Children in particular may respond verbally or physically, but the television set is impassive. However no one would disagree that watching 'Blue Peter' or 'Sesame Street' is a significantly different experience from watching a violent or otherwise pornographic film.

The range of experiences available to a computer user is far greater than that of the television viewer. The differences between the mental processes involved in word processing a story, manipulating a simulation of the local gas supply system or navigating a multimedia database on mammals far outweigh the similarities. Each requires you to look at a screen, tap keys or use a pointing device, but there all similarities become questionable, with one notable exception. What links computers, via the programmed instructions that work them, is that they are reactive. They may on occasion even be interactive. (The term interactive is used very freely to describe software which gives users some choice in the order in which they access content. However, true interactivity only comes when the user can interact with the content and change or add to it in some way.)

When a child makes an input to a computer, by pressing a key or clicking a mouse button, or pointing on a touch screen or concept keyboard, or much more rarely by making a noise or gesture, the computer may react. The extent to which this reaction is predictable will vary enormously (and this does not refer to software glitches or hardware failures, although these do of course occur occasionally). In a word processing program, pressing the A key usually puts a letter *a* on the screen, and this is comfortingly predictable. In the gas supply simulation the effect of turning on half your customers' ovens while increasing the gas pressure by a third is not so easy to predict.

The fact that the computer behaves differently when the user does something can create a powerfully motivating response. In a child, used to a world where things are largely beyond her control and whose attempts at new things are usually only met with at best partial success, the reactions of the computer may elicit wonder, excitement, and a rare feeling of empowerment. In an adult, used to a world she largely understands and often controls, the reactions of the computer, particularly where they are not easily predictable, may cause frustration and a sense of helplessness. A mixture of children and an adult experiencing these reactions simultaneously in a classroom, can cause considerable discomfort – to the teacher, that is.

So why risk it?

Why should we ask teachers to welcome these machines into the classroom? The answer is that when that excitement, wonder and empowerment of children is harnessed and focused by informed practitioners, the intellectual development it facilitates is worth the initial angst. The use of IT tools can help to make learning more accessible, and can reveal the underlying processes implicit in the task. The result is that the skills they are developing are made more explicit to the child and the teacher, and the resulting outcomes have greater relevance to the learner. The key, however, lies in the harnessing and focusing. Just how do you employ computer-based activities in the classroom to maximise the chance of a beneficial educational outcome? Which types of computer activity, and models of use, are worthwhile in terms of learning? How can a teacher develop a teaching schedule which includes effective computer use, not just for some children but for all?

A key to answering these questions must be that the starting point in planning any activity is a clear understanding of the learning outcomes the teacher wants to achieve, and the processes involved in making them *explicit* to the learner. Then, and only then, can the question be asked, 'Is there a way some form of IT can help the children to achieve this?' In all that follows in this book, it is the learning objectives that are driving the process, not the use of the computer. Once those objectives are clear in the teacher's mind, the related IT tools can be employed to make the process more accessible, and the outcomes more readily achievable. The end result is a learning experience that has more meaning for the child, and therefore increases the chances of building an *authentic* understanding, that is, an understanding related to the children's own existence, achieved through a personal evaluation of what they learn and with a degree of authorship of their own understanding (Bonnett 1994 and in Chapter 10).

However, this can only be achieved where the teacher is capable of making informed and timely input. As with any learning scenario, effective teaching is pivotal to the process of learning: knowing what to ask, and when to ask it is essential. The presence of the computer does not change the role of the teacher as facilitator of learning simply because it may become the primary source of information.

It is becoming easier to find examples of classroom activities relevant to the curriculum which integrate computer use into the task. What is more problematic is identifying what this use does in promoting children's knowledge and skill development and more critically, perhaps, how these enhancements can be recognised in the outcomes. In many cases the use of computer-based approaches can facilitate the development of skills which are difficult to promote using non-computer-based methods. This can also have implications for pupils' view of themselves and the world around them. In this book the authors have collected together evidence on significant use of computers in primary schools that has been shown to have positive outcomes in terms of enhanced learning. Each chapter provides a synopsis of that evidence in a given context and translates the findings into descriptions of effective classroom practice. Outcomes in learning and attitude are also considered.

The issue of equal opportunities is referred to throughout the fabric of this book. It is not considered as a separate issue but rather as an important aspect of the management of access to technology as a whole. However it is worth stating here that gender and out-of-school experience are both important factors relating to a child's access to IT. Less assertive members of the class, such as some girls and members of certain ethnic communities, may need a degree of positive reinforcement to encourage them to claim their share of time at the computer. Equally important, over-assertive members of the class may need to be restrained. Ideally those children who have an IT-rich home background can help to develop their own understanding further by teaching their less experienced classmates. Every teacher knows that trying to teach something is a good way of identifying the gaps in your own understanding! There is a caveat here, however, in that it requires very well-developed social and co-operative skills for a child to help another without dominating or de-skilling her would-be pupil. Peer teaching is therefore something which needs careful monitoring, and here as with any other learning scenario, it can be counter-productive simply to leave a group of children at the computer without supervision.

Chapters 2–9 look at a variety of uses of information technology in the curriculum. They cover a range of curriculum areas and types of computer-based interaction with different types of software and data. The strands of National Curriculum IT capability are addressed within the core subjects, and reference is made to foundation subjects. Desired outcomes in terms of attitude, motivation, skill development, and knowledge are highlighted. Illustrative examples are drawn from the primary sector, although the principles addressed often apply across the compulsory school age range. Chapter 10 considers the way that the use of a computer can change the nature of a task, and the value judgements involved in the decision to employ a computer in the classroom. Chapter 11 examines the role of new technologies: multimedia on CD ROM and via on-line services, and E-mail. Evaluations of these systems carried out to date are reviewed, and likely use in the future, in school and at home, is considered. The development of study skills and the likely impact of the use of electronic sources are also considered.

Each curriculum-orientated chapter identifies known learning, cognitive or developmental difficulties and discusses how the use of IT can help to enhance learning and child development in this area. Mention is also made, where appropriate, of the limitations of the computer, and where alternative teaching strategies are likely to be more effective. Extensive reference is made to published research material, and the bibliography provides for follow-up study.

In summary: it is clear that computers are very much a fact of life in schools and in the home, and that the role they play is set to carry on growing. The teacher is faced with a number of key issues in deciding how best to integrate the many possible uses of the computer into the learning experiences she provides for children in her class. She must make decisions relating to the type of computer-based activity that is relevant in a given context. This requires some understanding of the range of possibilities the available computers and software can provide. This knowledge must also be moderated by an understanding of the kinds of learning that using such applications can support. She must then examine the implications for the management of learning, and the effects on pupils' attitudes and perceptions of the task. Such considerations are the central focus of the chapters that follow.

Chapter 2

Developing children's problem-solving
The educational uses of adventure games

David Whitebread

There is currently considerable interest within education in developing children's abilities to apply their knowledge and to solve problems. The important role of problem-solving approaches across the curriculum is widely recognised (see Fisher 1987) and enshrined within the National Curricula for the UK. Teachers, however, often find this kind of approach difficult to organise and manage within the classroom. Inspection reports currently find that in science and mathematics, for example, areas concerned with specific content are taught well, but that areas concerned with using and applying mathematics, or developing scientific processes, are causing teachers more difficulty. What I want to argue in this chapter is that many of the difficulties facing teachers in this area can be overcome by using computer-based problems and, in particular, by using problems set in the context of so-called 'adventure games'.

Computer games have often been dismissed as being at best purely recreational and at worst positively harmful in the context of children's education and development. However, I want to argue that in the case of adventure games the opposite is the case. All the evidence we have from psychological studies of children's learning, and from research directly focused on children working at computers, is that adventure games offer powerful opportunities for children's learning and the development of their problem-solving abilities.

When computers were first introduced into primary school classrooms in the early 1980s there was an emphasis on games and puzzles. Over the last decade, however, as computers have become a more established part of primary school education, and IT has become part of the National Curriculum, the focus has shifted away from puzzles and games towards computer uses that are paralleled in the adult world of work (word processing, managing databases, etc.). Adventure games have been explicitly included in the National Curriculum framework throughout, but have tended to be narrowly defined as an aspect of 'modelling', which has been until fairly recently a relatively neglected aspect of IT within many primary school classrooms. In a recent SCAA publication (SCAA 1995), for example, work with an adventure game is provided as an illustration of modelling at Key Stage 1, although there is recognition of the role of such programs in developing children's speaking and listening skills.

What this chapter attempts to demonstrate is that good adventure games have a much broader impact and significance for children's learning. They make the organisation of problem-solving manageable within primary classrooms and are ideally suited to helping children sustain and learn from problem-solving activities. In the final section of the chapter various issues are discussed which the class teacher needs to consider in order to use this approach to its best advantage.

The organisational advantages of adventure games

Difficulties in organising and managing problem-solving

While there is undoubted enthusiasm for, and commitment to, developing problem-solving approaches in primary schools, there are large organisational and management difficulties for a class teacher attempting this with a class of thirty or so children. Here is a list of some of the key difficulties:

- Problem-solving, to be worthwhile, has to be challenging, and so it often requires the teacher's help and support in a fairly intensive way.
- Children's approaches to problems are inevitably varied; the sheer variety of directions and activities embarked upon may be difficult to manage and resource.
- Problem-solving is difficult to timetable; time taken to carry out particular tasks can be highly unpredictable, and it is often difficult to stop quickly in the middle of a particular part of the process.
- Problem-solving is often about trying out ideas and seeing if they work; through lack of experience children can sometimes pursue ideas doomed to failure for a long time, and then experience severe disappointment when the moment of truth arrives after all their hard work.
- Because solving problems requires hard work and commitment from the children, to be effective, problems have to engage their interest and imagination; 'off the peg' problems often suffer as a result in comparison with spontaneously devised 'real' problems. The latter, however, require a huge organisational and imaginative effort from the teacher. While many able teachers manage to create these kinds of authentic opportunities (see, for example, Atkinson 1992, in the area of mathematics and Fisher 1987, for examples across the curriculum) it is not something that is easy for a class teacher to sustain as a regular part of her provision.

Providing help and support

Using computer-based problems in the context of adventure games alleviates a number of these problems. Because of the interactive nature of these games, for example, the computer itself provides feedback, help and support to the children. While they may still need some guidance occasionally from the teacher, this need is often much reduced by the use of software which can react contingently, depending upon the child's behaviour (a feature which also, of course, makes playing computer games of this type highly motivating). The importance of this reactive quality of computers has been discussed in the introductory chapter of this book.

Coping with a variety of responses

Further, in well-designed games, a good variety of possible responses by the children is catered for and dealt with appropriately. As we shall see, the range of responses permitted by different games is, in fact, a key element in determining their level of cognitive demand. Games vary from the simplest, aimed at the youngest children, where very constrained 'yes/no' type of choices are offered and only one response is allowed (any other response produces either nothing or a message saying something like 'oh yes, you do!') to the most complex; here the child types in messages and the computer is able to respond to a reasonably large vocabulary, several possible decisions can be made at any time and, in some cases, problems can be solved in a variety of ways. From a negative perspective this 'prescribed' feature of possible solutions in adventure games can be criticised for limiting children's creativity. More positively, however, it can be seen as a supportive feature which enables the teacher using adventure games to provide children with a progression in level of difficulty. As I will review below, there are also plenty of opportunities for more open-ended activities, off computer, stimulated by the exciting challenges posed within these games.

Using time efficiently

The difficulties of timetabling problem-solving activities are to some extent also alleviated by well-designed computer games. When children finish a particular session on the computer they are not faced with the problems of clearing up the debris or storing their half-finished construction and the pieces that are half-made. When they resume, they do not have to remember what they had done and which point they had reached. They do not have to find all their bits and pieces from the last time and redo the bit that has got lost or squashed. Most well-designed games allow individual 'adventures-so-far' to be saved at any point and returned to at a later date. In terms of thinking time, computer games are very efficient. If the children have a 30-minute slot, they will spend the vast majority of that time working on the problems posed by the game, not wandering around looking for the glue. I don't wish to imply that more practical types of problem-solving are not worth doing, far from it. They are clearly an important element in any child's educational diet and offer experiences which cannot be simulated on a computer. But it is important to recognise the different but equally valuable experience computer-based problems can offer.

Providing for trial and error learning

The fourth area of management difficulty relates to the trial and error nature of much problem-solving. I was first alerted to the particular strength of computers in this area when working with young children using a computer graphics program. At the press of a key the child could rub out anything she didn't like (and without making a nasty smudge or a hole in the paper!), could change the thickness of a line, or the colour of a shape, and so on. The opportunities for experimentation were boundless in a way that paint or chalk or crayon cannot really offer to a young child. The same is very much the case with problem-solving. In an adventure game, you can try out one possibility, see that it doesn't work, and try out another, all in a matter of moments. In real, practical problem-solving in science or design technology it is very much more difficult to provide for this kind of trial and error learning. In practical work children can very easily spend a lot of time and effort on an idea before it becomes clear to them that it will not work. In an adventure game probably the worst that can happen is that you are splatted by the aliens, or eaten by the wicked witch, but you always miraculously survive to have another go, and you have learned what not to do the next time!

Engaging children's interest

Finally, there is the issue of engaging the children's interest and commitment. This is one of the real strengths of the adventure game format. By placing everything in the context of a compelling fictional world, these games are able to offer children 'off the peg' problems but in a way which makes them real and living. The one feature of adventure games that I have noticed every time I have used one with children is how involved they have become in the story. The most successful of these games become like well-loved books; the children want to play them again and again.

How adventure games help learning

Research from developmental psychology and classroom studies of children working at computers suggests that adventure games contain a number of features which make them ideally suited to helping children learn the skills of applying their knowledge and solving problems.

To begin with, an analysis of the intellectual work involved in playing such games reveals that they involve children in many of the significant skills and processes involved in solving problems of any kind. Further, adventure games provide a context for problem-solving which supports and enhances children's learning. Thus they encourage a playful approach to learning, they place problems in 'meaningful' contexts and they lend themselves to collaborative work and discussion.

In this section, I want to review each of these elements in turn. Together they give adventure games the potential to help children learn in powerful and important ways. A number of specific adventure games are referred to here and details of the suppliers of these are to be found in the Appendix of Software.

Developing problem-solving skills and processes

Problem-solving is a complex intellectual process involving the co-ordination of a range of demanding and interrelated skills. These skills include:

- understanding and representing the problem (including identifying what kinds of information are relevant to its solution);
- gathering and organising relevant information;
- constructing and managing a plan of action, or a strategy;
- reasoning, hypothesis-testing and decision-making;
- using various problem-solving tools.

I want to say a little about each of these. Many adventure games provide opportunities for practising a number of these skills. In some cases, however, some forms of software are more helpful in relation to particular skill areas.

Understanding and representing the problem

A number of researchers have established that the ways in which a problem is understood and mentally 'represented' has a major effect on the likelihood of it being solved. Children and adults who are better problem solvers have been found to spend longer encoding and representing the problem to themselves before they start out on a solution. Within mathematics, for example, children commonly have difficulty recognising which computational procedure they are required to do to solve word problems; this is known as the 'Is it an add, Miss?' syndrome, and will be recognised by all teachers of primary-aged children. This is linked to a second area of development, which is the ability to use existing knowledge. Children's abilities to solve problems can be significantly enhanced if they are simply required to review what they already know that might be relevant to the new task. This is particularly the case where children are being asked to transfer what they know to a new context or use what they know in a slightly different way.

Adventure games are helpful here in at least two major ways. First, the fact that the problems are embedded in 'meaningful' contexts, as I will discuss below, helps children enormously, and particularly helps them to see what is relevant and what is irrelevant. Second, however, adventure games can serve as examples of the same kinds of problems arising in apparently very different contexts, which is vital in helping children to learn to transfer ideas and processes. With some adventure games, this feature is built in. Perhaps the best current example is the excellent 'Crystal Rain Forest' where children solve a series of problems by writing progressively more sophisticated LOGO 'programs'. Instead of just moving a screen turtle around a blank screen, however, the children are engaged in guiding a robot through a temple maze, reconnecting broken wires in a control box, mending rope bridges and so on. All these problems look very different, but have the same underlying structure (see Figures 2.1a, 2.1b).

The same progression of developing similar problem-solving skills but in different contexts can be achieved by using different games with the same underlying structure. This is relatively easy to achieve because there are a number of basic structures common to many adventure games. For example, there are several at different levels of difficulty, which are essentially sequencing problems placed in the context of a search. You are searching for an object in an environment consisting of different rooms or locations. Some of the very simplest games aimed at children in the early years of Key Stage 1 are constructed in this way (e.g. 'Darryl the Dragon', 'Albert's House' and 'Animal Rescue' all contain this element). The opening problem in 'Granny's Garden' is a good example. You must enter the Woodcutter's House and find the first lost child. In order to do this you must go into the rooms in the correct sequence and make the correct decisions about whether to take the apple, what to throw at the snake, and so on. If you get the sequence wrong the witch catches you and you go back to the beginning again.

This kind of sequencing task is present again at a slightly more challenging level in 'The Worst Witch' game, which Sherston has developed from the

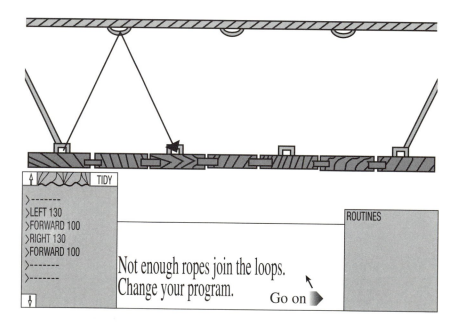

Figure 2.1a LOGO problem from 'Crystal Rain Forest'

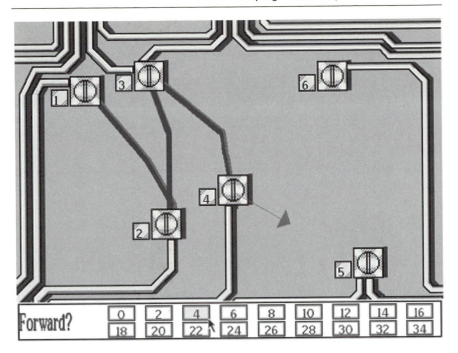

Figure 2.1b LOGO problem from 'Crystal Rain Forest'

popular children's books, and taken even further in games like 'SpaceX', 'Lemmings' and 'Discworld' (based on the Terry Pratchet books), where highly complex sequences of moves have to be discovered and carried out.

All these games have certain common features, and involve common problem-solving skills, but are couched in visually and imaginatively very different environments. Giving children the experience of applying skills and ideas they have learnt in one context to a new context that is superficially very different is enormously beneficial in helping them to learn how to tackle new problems. They learn to look for analogous problems they have encountered before, or things they know about which might be relevant. They also learn to analyse problems by their underlying structure rather than by their superficial characteristics. All this is highly significant in helping children to understand and represent new problems effectively.

Gathering and organising information

Very much part of understanding the nature of a problem is recognising what information is relevant to its solution. The essence of many real-world problems is a lack of information. Children need to develop the skills of gathering relevant information and of organising it in ways that will help them solve problems.

Once again, this is a central feature of many adventure games. At its simplest, this may consist of being presented with particular pieces of information quite explicitly and being told you need to remember this. It might be a password to get on to the next stage of the adventure, or information about the effects of different kinds of magical spells you can use when faced with particular problems. Typing 'WHOOSH' into the computer at the right moment can make you invisible and help you get past the evil troll!

At a more advanced stage, information is discovered in different locations and needs to be remembered and used to construct the kinds of sequences of actions I was discussing above. This is where children are being required to become aware of the information they need and to search for it systematically. For example, they may discover that they cannot enter the Wizard's house because they do not have the golden key. When they find the goblin with the golden key, he will only give it to them in exchange for a bag of corn. And so on. Gradually, as more information is collected it is constructed into a sequence of moves. When all the information is in place and correctly organised, the problem can be solved, the lost princess is found, and Good triumphs over Evil yet again.

There is a special kind of software which may not seem to fall into the category of 'adventure game', but which should be included because it shares a number of key features, particularly in relation to this issue of gathering and organising relevant information. These pieces of simulation software are actually just databases constructed as hypertexts, but they are set up so that the front end or user interface presents the data in an imaginative or 'real world' context within which each user has his or her own unique adventure (for a discussion of the nature of hypertexts, see Chapter 11 of this book). One good example is 'Number 62, Honeypot Lane' which presents data on the events in a house over a calendar year by enabling you to set the date and time and then explore the house (see Figure 2.2). Another good example is Usborne's 'Exploring Nature' CD ROM which presents natural environments within which you can go on a simulated nature walk or field study, equipped with a notebook into which you can paste text and a camera with which you can take snapshot pictures of discovered flora and fauna. (For some reservations concerning this type of simulation see Chapter 10.)

As Scrimshaw has pointed out: 'most adventure games are basically hypertexts with fixed links and a built-in dictionary to enable the program to respond appropriately to the keyboard entries of the user' (Scrimshaw 1993: 173).

Or to put it another way, an adventure game is just a set of information where the pathways you can take through it have been pre-limited and the questions you can ask have been predetermined. One of the main ways in which these games vary in level of difficulty and sophistication is in the number of possible pathways, and the complexities of the answers to the predetermined questions or problems. Programs such as 'Number 62, Honeypot Lane' and 'Exploring Nature' are just at the more sophisticated end of this spectrum. They are

Figure 2.2a The lounge, Christmas Day, from 'Number 62, Honeypot Lane'

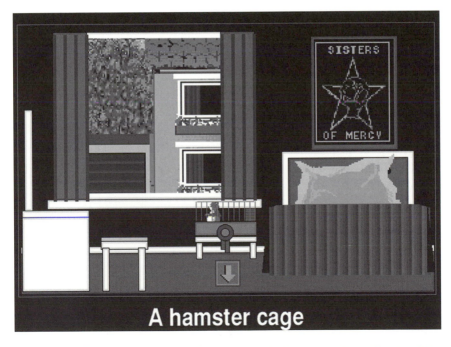

Figure 2.2b A new arrival in one of the children's bedrooms, from 'Number 62, Honeypot Lane'

inevitably more limited as sources of information than the real world which they attempt to simulate, but within these limitations problems to be solved can be constructed by the user, rather than being predetermined, and there is total freedom in the order in which the user views and collects information. For children learning to distinguish relevant and irrelevant information in relation to any particular problem, and devising strategies for collecting relevant information, these programs therefore have a particular value.

A huge variety of different problems can be devised, for example, in relation to the events at Number 62, Honeypot Lane, and different problems will require different search strategies for relevant information. To take just one event, which is the arrival of the new baby: a whole range of different kinds of questions might be posed, as follows:

- What special event takes place on 3 February? Find out as much as you can about this event.
- What begins to happen at one end of the bedroom on 21 January? Why does this happen?
- What is the baby's typical daily routine in July, and how is it different in October? Why do you think it changes?
- Where does the baby sleep in the afternoon, and for how long? Does the baby always sleep in the same place in the afternoons?

To answer some of these questions you have to start at a particular date and search the whole house. For others, you can start in a particular room. Some require you to go through the whole day, while for others you can concentrate on particular times. Some answers require only a limited number of pieces of information to be collected, while much more is needed for others.

Being able to recognise what information you need to solve a problem thus becomes of central significance when working with this kind of more open 'adventure', and the need for this gives this kind of program a particular value.

Planning and strategies

Being aware of the kind of information needed to solve a problem is also fundamental to being able to construct a plan of action. The ability to plan ahead is one of the great achievements of the human intellect. It is a highly complex skill, relying largely upon our ability to form mental representations or models, and then make them explicit.

Children's planning abilities develop in two ways. First, they become able to construct and carry out plans which contain longer strings of 'moves' or elements. Second, their plans become more complex in structure, progressively containing subgoals, subroutines and strategies developed in other contexts and applied to the new problem. For example, it is sometimes necessary to take an action which appears to be moving you further away from the problem goal or solution, but is actually necessary to set up a situation from which you can proceed to a final solution. The classic problem of getting a dog, a cat and a mouse over a river using a boat that will only hold two of them at once is a case in point. The key move, which young children find very difficult, is to bring the cat back across the river to the starting point.

Being able to construct and use plans of action is a fundamental life skill. At the simplest level the organisation of our daily lives depends upon it. Being a parent or a primary school teacher (or both!) necessitates a very high level of skilful planning. In commerce, science or industry it is equally vital. Artists plan their painting, their concerto or their sculpture.

The fundamental skills of constructing plans and devising strategies can be very effectively practised through adventure games. We have already discussed above the common structure of many games, which essentially involves discovering a successful sequence of moves through an environment that will reveal the necessary information and objects in the right order to allow problem solution. This is pure planning.

Another type of program that I want to include under the heading of 'adventure game' also presents planning and strategy challenges of a particularly acute and motivating kind. This is the type of program where a sequence of moves has to be constructed and carried out under time pressure. Perhaps the pre-eminent example suitable for primary-aged children is the excellent 'Lemmings'. This kind of program is sometimes dismissed as just an 'arcade' game, but it could not be more different from the relatively mindless 'splat the aliens' type of program usually implied by this term. In 'Lemmings' each level sets the user a new challenge, and each new challenge is a mini-adventure in itself. The progressive development of skills and strategies through the different levels gives the program a similar structure to that of 'Crystal Rain Forest' discussed above.

The basic problem scenario in 'Lemmings' is that you have to get a certain proportion of a set of lemmings safely from the door where they enter the scene to another door where they leave (see Figure 2.3a for one of the simpler examples). From the moment you start the game lemmings keep coming through the entrance door and, although you can control the rate of their entrance to some extent, you have limited control of the speed at which they move and there is a time limit to solve the problem. At each level you are faced with a new scene through which the lemmings must travel. These scenes contain all kinds of obstacles and dangers. When a lemming hits an obstacle it simply turns round and walks back in the opposite direction. When it reaches a hole or a yawning chasm it simply walks off the edge and plummets to its death.

To enable the lemmings to travel across the scene safely, you may transform any of them into different kinds of lemmings, which each perform particular tasks. These special lemmings can climb, dig holes, bash through obstacles, build bridges and even parachute. A lemming transformed into a 'blocker' becomes an obstacle and stops any more lemmings getting past that point. This can be a very useful strategy to give the climbers, diggers and builders time to construct

Figure 2.3a A simple problem from early in 'Lemmings'

Figures 2.3a and 2.3b are reproduced with kind permission of Psygnosis Limited, ©
Psygnosis Limited, who reserve all rights. Psygnosis and Lemmings are trademarks of
Psygnosis Limited.

a safe route before the rest of the lemmings get to that part of the scene. When
all is prepared, you then, sadly, have to blow up the 'blocker', but his sacrifice
is rewarded by all the other lemmings walking resolutely to safety through the
exit door, and taking you on to the next level!

'Lemmings' and other programs of similar design are a powerful agent in
teaching children how to plan. At each level you can look at the problem scene
before you start the lemmings and try to work out what to do. Once the
lemmings start you try to put your first idea into action and the consequences
are immediately obvious. The lemmings all plunge over the gap you have
forgotten about, and so you work out how to deal with that. And so on until
all the problems are solved and a safe route is devised. As the levels become
increasingly harder you can use strategies devised at simpler levels to help solve
part of the problem. There are all kinds of these strategies. I have mentioned the
holding strategy using blockers. A strategy for long drops where there is solid
ground at the bottom is to parachute a lemming down, turn him around (this
might need you to parachute a second lemming down to become a 'blocker')
and transform him into a builder to build a ladder back up, which the other
lemmings can then walk down. This strategy is useful for the problem called
'A ladder might be handy' (see Figure 2.3b).

Parachuting would not be so useful, however, for a long drop with water at
the bottom. This will need a different strategy, probably involving digging down
diagonally through the cliff, coming out near the bottom and then building a

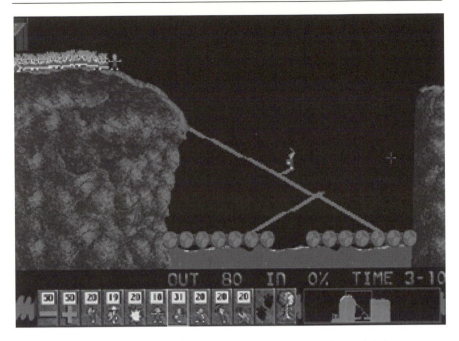

Figure 2.3b The 'A ladder might be handy' problem, from 'Lemmings'

bridge from there. The range of possible combinations of the different kinds of lemmings means that many different strategies can be constructed, and many problems can be solved in a number of different ways.

What we see in all this is the opportunity for children to practise a number of key problem-solving skills. They are devising strategies which they then have to apply appropriately in different contexts and which they have to adapt and co-ordinate together to build a plan of action. The computer-based adventure game context is a powerful tool for learning these skills because it provides motivation and, probably to a unique extent, the opportunity for rapid trial and error learning.

Reasoning, hypothesis-testing and decision-making

Information is not simply just gathered by the human intellectual processing system. Constructing a plan, or deciding to use a particular strategy, is dependent upon a number of active and more fine-grain reasoning skills, which enable us to integrate separate pieces of information into new knowledge. These skills include those of making inferences and deductions, generating and testing predictions or hypotheses, and of making decisions. Crucially, they are about applying what you already know to new situations.

As Loveless (1995) has pointed out, adventure games provide a wealth of opportunities for children to practise these vital reasoning skills. At the simplest level, this can be a matter of making decisions about which direction to choose for the next move. If we chose to go north last time we reached this point, and were faced with a dead end, or a fearsome monster, then we might deduce that going south this time might be worth trying. In this instance, the children are being asked to apply knowledge gained about the particular adventure. Often, however, opportunities are provided for the children to apply their real-world knowledge to a problem, such as when they are asked which piece of equipment they wish to use to help them solve a particular problem.

Different kinds of adventure game provide opportunities for different kinds of reasoning. The kind of adventure game that is essentially concerned with constructing a sequence of moves involves the children in making predictions about what will happen next if a particular move is made. Thus the children make hypotheses and then test them. In 'The Worst Witch' drinking a potion of a particular colour makes you invisible. The children might then predict that they will at last be able to get past the troll who is guarding the trapdoor, and so it turns out!

The kind of game more concerned with exploring a less pre-structured database lends itself more to making inferences and examining cause and effect. 'Number 62, Honeypot Lane' is a very good example of this kind of opportunity. Partly because you only see static 'snapshots' of the various parts of the house on each hour and partly because you never actually see most of the people living in the house (apart from the odd arm or back of a head), you have to make deductions about events largely from the changing location of objects. Thus the baby's daily routine in its early months can be partly inferred from the location of the pram, which is in the hall when the baby is in the cot, outside in the garden when it contains the baby, and nowhere to be seen when the baby has gone shopping with mum. The opportunities provided by this program for reasoning and discussion are consequently enormous.

Using problem-solving tools

One of the main reasons why adults can solve problems that are difficult for children is that we learn to use a range of problem-solving tools. Essentially, these consist of ways of recording information and constructing plans when problems become complicated and difficult to manage just in our heads. They might consist of notes, diagrams, measurements, maps, scale models and so on.

Many adventure games, for example, make use of maps. 'Granny's Garden', 'Dinosaur Discovery' and 'Crystal Rain Forest' are just three examples of this, at differing levels of sophistication (see Figures 2.4, 2.5, 2.6). 'Dinosaur Discovery' offers the interesting variation of gradually revealing the map as different areas are explored. Other programs, such as 'The Worst Witch' , 'Number 62, Honeypot Lane' or 'SpaceX' involve the exploration of an environment, but do not

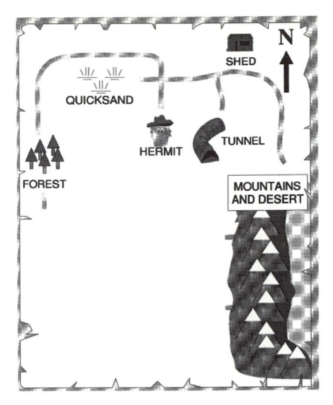

Figure 2.4 Adventure game map, from 'Dinosaur Discovery'

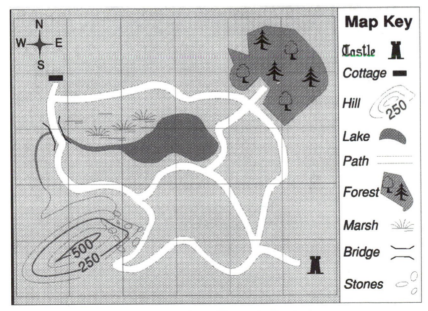

Figure 2.5 Adventure game map, from 'Granny's Garden'

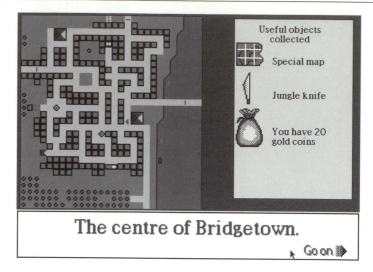

Figure 2.6 Adventure game map, from 'Crystal Rain Forest'

offer a map as such within the program. Quite a useful progression is clearly to give children the experience of using a program with a map, and then helping them to construct their own map of an environment for which one is not provided.

Other programs clearly require note-taking of a fairly systematic nature, so that information can be recorded for later reference. This can be structured in such a way that it fits in with the nature of the adventure. When I used 'SpaceX' with a Year 6 class, for example, as this program involves making 'flights' over an alien planet I prepared 'logs' for each group to complete about each of their 'missions' (see Figure 2.7). Because these fitted into the imaginative context of the program, they were eagerly completed by the children and provided them with a systematic record of information gathered at the various locations.

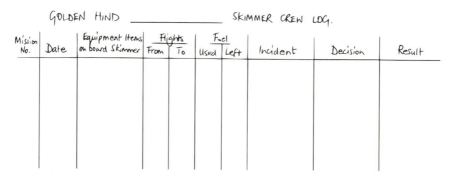

Figure 2.7 Mission log, used with 'SpaceX'

Here is a typical section of dialogue recorded showing the use of this kind of problem-solving tool:

Tim So, where are we?

Mike 0509

Tim Right, so let's go there (points to new location 0912 on screen). We haven't been there, have we?

Helen Yes we have, that's where we went into that fog and crashed.

Tim No it isn't, that was when we were there (points to another location on screen).

Helen No, it wasn't, it was 0912.

Mike I wrote down about the fog. Let's look it up (flicks through log). Here we are. Flight number 11. 0509 to 0912. Hit fog and crashed. Helen's right.

Tim I think you wrote it down wrong.

Eventually all was happily resolved to everyone's satisfaction. The log entry turned out to be correct, and valuable lessons were learned.

Providing a context for learning

Analysis of the intellectual work involved in playing adventure games thus reveals that they involve children in many of the significant skills and processes involved in solving problems. The other great asset of the adventure game format is that it presents these challenges in ways which support and enhance children's ability to learn from them. There are many elements to this, but I want to briefly pick out three. Computer-based adventure games:

- encourage a playful approach to learning;
- place problems in 'meaningful' contexts;
- stimulate collaborative work and discussion.

The role of play in learning

It would be easy to dismiss adventure games on the grounds that they merely engage children in play. What is now well established amongst developmental psychologists and well understood by teachers of young children, however, is that play is one of the most powerful and effective mediums for children's learning. Many psychologists and educators have studied children's play, but perhaps some of the most influential and important work has been carried out by Jerome Bruner, who has shown that play is fundamental to human learning (see Bruner *et al.*1976). Humans are distinguished from other species by their unique ability to think flexibly and to devise new ways to solve new problems. Bruner has argued that our long period of biological immaturity, when we are being cared for by our parents, enables us to play far more and for much longer than any other species, and it is through play that we learn to be flexible and innovative in our thinking, and to become effective problem solvers. Play is an opportunity to try out different possibilities, to combine elements of a problem or situation in novel ways, to see what would happen if . . . all in complete safety.

Bruner's and other research has demonstrated that, for children and for adults, initially being given open-ended, exploratory and 'playful' tasks enhances problem-solving capability far more effectively than being introduced to a new area with carefully broken down, 'closed' tasks, where the object at each stage is to produce the 'correct' answer. The relevance of adventure games in providing playful opportunities for trying out different possibilities and developing flexible thinking is clear.

Other research has concerned different kinds of play (see Moyles 1989, for a review of work in this area). Within the literature a distinction has often been drawn between unstructured and structured play. In unstructured play children simply play in any way they like with the materials available. In structured play, often through some kind of adult intervention, children are posed problems, exposed to new possibilities, and so on. Overall, the evidence is that unstructured play is particularly valuable in enhancing emotional and social development, while structured play enhances intellectual development. Inasmuch as adventure games are examples of relatively structured play, this is further confirmation that they are likely to be useful in fostering intellectual growth.

The importance of meaningful contexts

The study of the development of children's problem-solving really began with the work of Jean Piaget. He argued that children pass through different stages of development. At each stage there is a different set of problems (such as his famous 'conservation' problems), which they are capable of solving because they have acquired a more sophisticated set of logical operations, or understandings. (For a review of Piaget's work see Wood 1988.)

This basic position that children become better problem solvers because they become more logical has, however, as Wood (1988) reviews, been seriously questioned by subsequent research. The problems young children have with Piaget's experiments appear to be more to do with their abstractness, or what has been called their 'disembeddedness'. As a consequence of their lack of experience children are particularly dependent upon the context within which a task is placed. Where they are presented with a task which bears no relation to anything they already know and understand, they have great difficulty in making sense of it and seeing which aspects of the task are relevant and which irrelevant to the problem posed. However, when tasks are placed in contexts meaningful to the child they are often able to demonstrate reasoning powers very similar to those evidenced by adults.

This recognition of the overwhelming significance of meaningful contexts for children's understandings and performance has led to new approaches to teaching in a number of curriculum areas. For example, the recent moves to engage children more with 'real books' as part of their early reading diet, the 'emergent writing' approach to children's early literacy development, and the recognition that children need to write for a variety of real purposes are all born of a recognition that children learn more effectively if the tasks they are set are meaningful from the child's perspective (see Hall 1989). Similar moves towards the use of real problems in mathematics are also beginning to take hold (see Atkinson 1992).

The advantages of an adventure game approach to computer-based problem-solving flow just as directly from this aspect of children's performance. Rather than being faced with arid and obviously artificial problems of the 'if two men can dig a hole in three days' variety, children playing adventure games become involved in a compelling story with Goodies and Baddies, with crises and setbacks and triumphs and, eventually, a satisfyingly happy ending. The children are involved in the adventure because they alone can help the King and Queen find their lost children, or they alone can save the planet, or help Darryl the Dragon find the items he needs to make his breath fiery again.

Such fictional contexts imbue the problems contained within them with real human motivations and purposes. This helps children understand the nature and meaning of problems, and thus enables them to maximise the use of their reasoning powers and learn from the experience most effectively. So, for example, in the award-winning 'Crystal Rain Forest' children are progressively taught to write programs in LOGO, but what they are actually doing is solving a series of problems to outwit the Cut and Run Sawmill Gang and save the Rain Forest by finding the magic crystals.

The meaningful contexts provided by adventure games also, of course, help to make them highly motivating. My own first experience of using adventure games was with a class of top infants and first year juniors (now Year 2/3) using 'Granny's Garden' when it first came out as a program for the BBC in the early 1980s. I followed up some of the suggestions in the Teacher's Handbook and the children and I developed some of our own, and I was bowled over by the enthusiasm of their response. Children in this age-group are, of course, very excited about fairy stories with witches and dragons and elves, and the program tapped into this area of interest very effectively (see Figure 2.8). But it was the problem-solving element of the program that seemed to really enthral them. The whoops of glee when each of the lost children was discovered were electric. If all the tasks we set children in school elicited the level of involvement and perseverance that I have consistently seen with adventure games then we would have long since said good-bye to any problems of discipline, motivation, disruption, truancy and boredom.

Figure 2.8 The witch, from 'Granny's Garden'

The value of collaborative problem-solving

Recent research concerned with children's learning has also emphasised the significance of social interaction, either between adults and children, or between groups of children. This research derives from the writings of the Russian psychologist, Lev Vygotsky, and has been influenced also by the work of Jerome Bruner on the role of language in learning (see Wood 1988, for a review). Two key aspects of the way in which language helps learning in the context of social interaction have emerged. First, it is clear that we come to understand ideas better through articulating them in social or group problem-solving situations. Second, language is used in social contexts to 'scaffold', support and guide problem-solving processes and procedures. This kind of research has been partly responsible for a resurgence of interest during the last few years in the use of collaborative group-work in primary classrooms (see Dunne and Bennett 1990).

In this context, it is interesting to note that, although initially thought of in connection with individualised learning, computers have generally been used by groups in classrooms, and the view of many teachers is that learning to work in groups is one of the main advantages of computer use in schools (Jackson *et al.* 1986). Crook (1994) has recently reviewed the extensive range of work now being carried out in schools involving collaborative learning with computers.

The effectiveness of group-work in children's learning, however, is dependent upon the quality of the talk and interactions generated. In relation to work with computers, recent evidence suggests that, not surprisingly, the pattern and quality of interaction between children is dependent upon the kind of software used. Significantly, the richest discussion has been found to be promoted by adventure games (Crook 1987).

Alongside this, there is now quite a range of research showing that children's development of effective problem-solving strategies is enhanced by working in pairs or small groups on computer-based tasks. Blaye *et al.* (1991), for example, conducted a study with 11-year-olds tackling a typical adventure game which required the children to retrieve a king's crown while avoiding pirates and bandits (see Figure 2.9). The game involved the key problem-solving skills, discussed above, of collecting and organising information and of constructing a plan of action. Blaye *et al.* found that the adventure game format stimulated constructive discussion and debate between the children, which helped them to clarify their understandings of the problem and what information was relevant to its solution. They also found that the problem-solving situation, involving a 'mouse' to control actions on the screen, and a map on paper to help the children discuss and conceptualise the problem, lent itself to a helpful role differentiation. Pairs of children typically took responsibility for either the mouse or the map, producing a problem-solving team similar to a couple attempting to navigate their way by car through a strange town, with one doing the driving and the other reading the map. This role differentiation helped structure the dialogue about the task in ways which supported and 'scaffolded' the children's joint efforts to manage the information provided by the computer and the map, and to construct a plan to solve the problem.

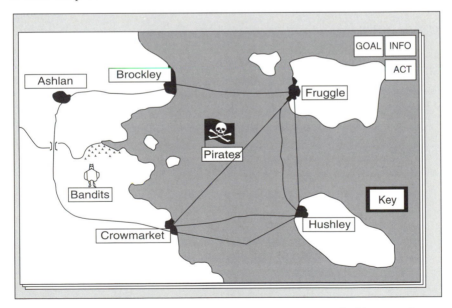

Figure 2.9 The map in the 'king and crown' adventure game in Blaye *et al.* 1991

My own experiences with 'Granny's Garden' and many other games support this view that children working in collaborative groups are provided with a powerful environment that helps them to develop their problem-solving skills. The use of language to clarify ideas and understandings, and to support and guide problem-solving processes, has been very evident. 'Granny's Garden' stimulated enormous amounts of talk and discussion amongst my Year 2/3 class. This enabled them to persevere at and solve the various puzzles much more effectively than they could have managed as individuals. They reminded one another about important information, provided a more varied selection of ideas and strategies and constantly checked one another's reasoning. They also shared out the work that needed doing, making it possible to manage the task in a way which any one of them would have found too demanding. Thus, while one read the on-screen instructions, another manipulated the keyboard and a third made written notes of important information (e.g. discovered passwords, list of helpful animals). The impact on the children's teamwork and communicative skills in the few short weeks of this project was stunning.

Collaborative problem-solving and computers: some classroom issues

The educational potential of computer-based adventure games is immense. To maximise their benefit for the primary school child, however, a number of issues need to be addressed.

Making the context meaningful: on- and off-computer activities

As I have argued, one of the key strengths of adventure games is the way in which they fire the imagination of young children. This will not be achieved nearly so effectively if the program is just left on in a corner of the room, and children play the game at odd moments, unconnected to the rest of their classroom work. Ideally, an adventure game should be used as the central stimulus in a work topic or theme. The work the children do with the game should be intimately related to a series of off-computer activities.

As an illustration, I recall a half term's work I carried out with a Year 6 class in the mid-1980s based on the 4Mation program, 'SpaceX', to which I have referred earlier. This program is of the type where you have to find a correct sequence of moves. Essentially, the story is that you are on a space mission to the faraway planet of Persephone, which is inhabited by a species called Kleptoes. You have to retrieve small shiny objects that they have stolen from your spaceship before the ship will be able to take you on your return journey to Earth. You have to explore the environment of the planet, represented by a grid (see Figure 2.10), solve various puzzles and retrieve all the objects. Because you only have limited fuel, however, you have to find the most efficient route. There are various tools you can take with you which you will need to solve the

	01	02	03	04	05	06	07	08	09	10	11	12	13	14	15
13			*												*
12									*						
11															
10												*			
09					*										
08															
07	*							*				*			
06															
05				*											
04															
03							*								
02	*														
01														*	

Figure 2.10 Grid map of the planet Persephone, from 'SpaceX'

various puzzles, but you can only carry so many at once and have to return to base at some point to swap tools. Each time you make a wrong decision you are splatted and have to start all over again. The game requires a very systematic approach to gathering information and then using that information to construct a correct sequence of moves.

The Year 6 children were just as entranced by this as my earlier class of Year 2/3 children had been with the simpler challenges of 'Granny's Garden'. This time they worked in 'patrols' of four. Instead of writing stories about witches and goblins, they wrote space adventures. Each patrol designed its own space cruiser, its own logo and uniforms. They actually made their patrol hats and often wore them while they were at the computer on their next 'mission'. Alongside this went a serious topic about space and astronomy. As the children learnt about the real extra-terrestrial world, so they enthusiastically incorporated new information into their fantasy world of Kleptoes. It was hard to escape the feeling that here was learning of real quality, and that this would not have been anything like as rich an experience without the computer adventure game.

Many adventure games lend themselves very naturally to this style of organisation, and are, indeed, written with the idea of supporting a school topic in mind. The various history-based packages, such as Sherston's ArcVenture series, are a good example of what is currently available. With imagination, however, it is possible and always profitable to use adventure games in this way. Sue Underhay (1989) has provided an excellent account of a class project based on the program 'Flowers of Crystal'. The off-computer work generated included artwork, scientific and mathematical investigations about crystals, descriptive and informational writing for real purposes (e.g. travel brochures advertising the delights of the planet Crystal), movement work based on the characters in the story, and so on.

Organising collaborative work

A common arrangement when using an adventure game in a primary classroom is to have the children working in groups. This makes good sense in terms of organisation, and, as discussed above, can make a valuable contribution to children's learning.

It is not sufficient, however, simply to put children in random groups and let them get on with it. Composition of groups has been shown in a wide range of research to be crucially important in affecting the amount and quality of verbalisation and discussion that occurs (see Dunne and Bennett 1990). Factors which are likely to affect the success of group-work include size of group, the mix of abilities and gender. All these factors are only significant, however, inasmuch as they affect the quality of talk in the group and the extent to which each individual is genuinely involved in group discussions and decision-making. Underwood and Underwood (1990), for example, found that verbalisation of plans, negotiation between group members and joint decision-making were crucial. Blaye *et al.* (1991) pinpointed the issue of dominance in groups, finding that the most productive groups were ones where one child was not dominating others (which involved predictable gender issues!). In successful groups there was much evidence of turn-taking and teamwork with the task divided up into different roles (e.g. controlling the mouse, reading on-screen text, interpreting the map, making notes). There are clear pointers here to the quality of inter-action for which we should be looking and the kinds of skills and attitudes we should be attempting to encourage.

Teaching problem-solving skills

The final issue, however, concerns the skills that are central to my case about the importance of adventure games as a resource for the primary school teacher. These games, as I have argued, provide a rich opportunity for children to practise a range of problem-solving skills. For these opportunities to be fully realised, however, the teacher's role is crucial. As with any other aspect of children's learning, their experiences need to be mediated by a skilled teacher, who has a number of vital tasks to perform. These include:

- analysing the skills, understanding and knowledge that children will require in order to be able to work effectively with any particular piece of software;
- developing off-computer problems and activities to help develop and reinforce these skills, understanding and knowledge (e.g. gathering and selecting information, planning a sequence of moves, making and testing predictions, making and reading maps, note-taking, understanding directions and co-ordinates, knowing about the Victorians, etc.);
- encouraging discussion to make the problem-solving skills and strategies developed by the program explicit, and to require children to verbalise and justify their hypotheses, plans, understandings and decisions.

Given this kind of careful planning and support by their teachers, children can learn a great deal of importance by playing adventure games. I cannot express the significance of this venture for children's education better than Loveless:

> Our fast-changing, technological society requires individuals who can adopt this approach to learning through experience and investigation; who have a positive approach to problem solving, flexibility and transferability in new situations. 'Real' scientists, geographers, athletes, mathematicians, historians, artists, photographers, musicians and mountain climbers are able to be in control and participate in situations, make hypotheses about what is going on and test them, and explore new possibilities in order to extend their understanding of the new and unpredictable.
>
> (Loveless 1995: 71-2)

If we can help children to be in control of their learning and to deal more confidently and effectively with the unpredictable world they are entering, then we have performed a valuable service. Involving children in the engaging world of computer-based adventure games can, I believe, make an important contribution to developing positive attitudes to problem-solving and the skills needed to carry it out.

Chapter 3

Children's learning using control information technology

Philip Stephenson

Introduction

It is my intention that this chapter will go some way towards answering the question, 'What is control information technology and why does it merit a place in the primary classroom?' Advocates of control IT claim that it not only gives children an understanding of how an ever-expanding area of workplace technology is applied but also offers a context for the development of skills and attitudes, particularly those of investigation and problem-solving, which have positive implications for other curriculum areas (for a more detailed exploration of the nature of problem-solving, refer to Chapter 2). This chapter hopes to support these assertions by addressing three main areas:

- the progression of the particular skills and concepts that characterise control IT;
- how this progression maps on to a broader, constructivist view of cognitive development;
- how conceptual and procedural understanding transfers to other curriculum areas.

It is clear that control IT offers great benefit to learning yet, according to Ofsted inspection reports, it remains the least developed area of IT application in the primary school. The constraints that have limited the proliferation of control IT are also discussed.

What is control technology?

Control can be described as the issuing of instructions that result in a job being done. Telling a child 'Pick up the pen' is a control instruction, albeit in its simplest form. At a hierarchical level above this, control involves feedback, for example, 'Pick up the pen if it falls off the table.' The sequence can be further refined by adding an element of repetition: 'Always pick up the pen if it falls off the table.'

For the children as controllers to move through these levels of ever-increasing intellectual complexity in the context of control technology, they need to develop the problem-solving skills of trial and adjustment, prediction based on hypothesis and a willingness to engage concurrently in 'What will happen if?' dialogues.

Control technology is a means of carrying out control-using devices to effect one or more stages in the process. A simple example might be one child asking another child to switch a light on for ten seconds. The first child is giving the instructions while the second child operates the switch and counts. Only one aspect of this example, the switch, involves a technology application. Introducing IT into this kind of control activity replaces the role of the child as the manual operator of the switch or switches, as these actions are controlled by the computer, under the command of a program activated or written by the child. At the same time control IT demands greater intellectual involvement of the child, such as decision-making based on previous experience and prediction. Obviously learning experiences that can accelerate and enhance the development of these intellectual processes can be of great value, particularly when facilitated by a thoughtful teacher. Nevertheless, for children to be able to take on the role of accomplished controller, they need to engage in learning tasks appropriate to their stage of cognitive maturity. As I will discuss further below, engaging in such activites will not of itself break down the barrier between concrete and formal thinking.

The perceptive teacher will recognise the progression of both the skills and the concepts inherent in control IT and will match the learning experiences he or she offers to the particular level of development of the child. The progression of procedural understanding (i.e. skills) is essentially the development of the child's ability independently to plan structured investigations to solve problems. In doing so, the learner has to be able to identify problems, suggest solutions, design and carry out tests which are fair (i.e. variables are controlled) and reproducible, evaluate outcomes and, if necessary, to re-enter the cycle until a successful conclusion is reached. Each of these various stages or procedures have to be taught through particular learning experiences focusing on particular elements of the process. Progression comes through the increased complexity of learning tasks, the linking of the various procedures as a whole process and the gradual withdrawal of support, with a growing expectation of independence.

The progression of conceptual understanding focuses on encouraging the learner to be confident with the ideas of sequencing commands, repeating commands and responding to commands. There are clear stages to the construction of a complete and coherent understanding of these concepts and, as with the procedural elements, these should be taught with an understanding of the progression clear in the teacher's mind and reflected in their planning.

Developing progressive understanding

What kind of learning experiences in control technology are teachers able to offer children, which recognise these fundamental elements of progression?

Floor robots

In terms of progression, the first experience that children will have of control IT is likely to be that of operating a floor robot. There are two kinds: the self-contained robot, which carries its own software and panel (such as 'Roamer' and 'Pip'), and the floor 'turtle', which is a robot connected to a computer by wire or IR (Infra-Red) signal. In the case of 'turtles' (robots connected to the computer), all interaction is through the computer using software such as 'LOGO' and 'Dart'. It is likely that early experiences will be with the free-standing robots which are not encumbered by the more sophisticated command language used to control turtles. A further advantage of the free-standing robots as far as early years children are concerned is that the robots are communicated with directly and not via a disembodied computer interface.

In the simplest form the robots (whether self-contained or computer controlled) understand four basic commands: Forwards, Backwards, Right Turn, Left Turn. The commands are quantified using arbitrary values for distance and degrees for turn (for a more detailed analysis of these commands refer to Chapter 4). Obviously for children of 4 or 5, the use of degrees as measure of turn is inappropriate but children are happy to accept that the number '90' makes the robot make a quarter turn and will use this on the understanding that this is the robot's 'special way of speaking'. Young children need no more knowledge than this to begin exploring the robot's capabilities.

Most commercial floor robots have additional functions such as time counters (so that pauses can be built into sequences of instructions), musical notes, flashing lights, etc. It is also possible to modify the external design of the robot (such as converting it into a giant beetle or suchlike) making it fit a particular context that the children are working in (in the case of the beetle, the topic might be 'minibeasts') and, of course, making it more fun. In addition, the robots can be adapted so that their paths can be traced using a pen.

The progression of skills, or hierarchy of learning, using floor robots needs to be clearly identified when planning activities for children. As with all learning, it is vital that progression is underpinned by extensive pre-operational and concrete experiences so that a broad foundation of initial understanding underpins the construction of new understanding and modified ideas. Reinforcement of these early experiences is vital at each stage of progression to ensure that a stable pyramid of concepts and ideas is established. Children soon become adept at moving the robot around, giving the impression of sound understanding and tempting the teacher to 'move them on'. Succumbing to this temptation too early can lead to the construction of top-heavy structures of knowledge, which are prone to collapse as the higher-order concepts are introduced.

Teachers may choose to integrate the use of 'human robots' with the use of floor turtles, and encourage children to use random commands to effect isolated actions in either case. Children can be encouraged to perform actions by placing themselves in the role of robot, reacting to verbal instructions given by another child. Some teachers prefer to precede the use of floor robots with this type of human robot activity. In doing this the children become familiar with the language of control and also learn something about the range of robot actions.

With this foundation children can be encouraged to build more complex strings of instructions in the form of simple sequences. This requires the ability to foresee the outcome of a string of events. Often teachers will return to using gym or playground space to play 'human robots'. Children work in pairs, one issuing control commands to the other. This very self-oriented activity provides a concrete experience upon which to build the robot-oriented activity.

Both these approaches involve the children in exploratory play. As their ideas outgrow what can be achieved by simple button pressing on an independent robot and they become involved in more complex sequences, it is necessary for them to use a control language such as LOGO. For some children, it may be appropriate to return to the context of human robots to help ease the transition from simple to complex command sequences.

Learning to 'speak control'

A common introductory activity is to make the robot 'walk' or 'draw' a square, which requires only two commands (Forward and Turn 90) which are repeated four times. Children quickly realise that there is a pattern to the square-drawing sequence and the majority of robot control devices or software have a facility to exploit this understanding:

FORWARD 10
RIGHT 90
FORWARD 10
RIGHT 90
FORWARD 10
RIGHT 90
FORWARD 10
RIGHT 90
can be rewritten: REPEAT 4 [FORWARD 10 RIGHT 90]

For a more comprehensive discussion of this procedure and the development of the use of a variable within it, see Chapter 4.

This transition from simple sequence to identifying repeats is vital and can be effected by offering a wide variety of linked exercises. Typical of these would be to steer the robot through a maze or to undertake the drawing of more complicated regular geometrical shapes. In the case of floor robots linked to a computer, such as the LOGO-controlled turtle, the idea that a sequence to fulfil a specific task is particular to that task can be reinforced by teaching the learner how to save the sequence on disc and to re-use the program on later occasions, possibly on a different machine elsewhere in the school.

It is also at this stage that children can be introduced to the idea of calibrating the distances travelled by the floor robots, which are generally set in arbitrary units specific to the particular machine, into units more familiar to them. A typical starting point for this process would be: How far is 'Forward 10' in, say, hand-spans or human heel-to-toe steps?

In terms of progression, children move towards the notion of editing or changing a sequence. In the case of the square this might be 'What do we change to make a rectangle?' In some respects, the sequence retains the original order but with significant amendments. Adjustments to sequences can become more and more complex – 'What do we change to make a triangle?' – and demand highly developed spatial awareness and knowledge of angles as well as fluency in the language of control. (There is however some debate about how effective floor robots are as a means of *teaching* angle, and indications that knowledge of angles in the LOGO environment may not transfer to other contexts.) By this stage, children should be able to operate a screen turtle (in the case of 'LOGO' or 'Dart') without the need for the concrete experience of the 'real' turtle on the floor beside them.

Control sequences can be recursive, repeating themselves over and over again and variables can also be introduced to the recursive sequence so that not only does the pattern repeat, but it also grows. Recursive sequences require that the learner is visualising and writing sequences as complete programs. An example would be:

TO SHUTTLE [name of program made up by user.]
FORWARD 10
BACK 10
SHUTTLE [i.e. do the whole thing again.]

It will be seen that the forward–backward motion will be repeated an infinite number of times unless the machine is actually switched off!

These latter stages are the domain of early formal operators at the end of their primary school careers but are essentially a mere sophistication of the process introduced when drawing the square. The next significant *procedural* progression is the introduction of sensing devices and programs that allow robots to react to what they sense. Sensors are available that detect impact or pressure, magnetic fields, light, sound and temperature. Robots can be thus programmed to move in one mode until they detect, let us say, a wall or bright light source, after which they move in another mode. A simple example might be:

Move Forward until pressure sensor detects an obstruction.
Move Back 10 Turn Right 90.
Repeat the Program.

Using these kinds of feedback–response commands, robots can negotiate mazes unassisted, follow white lines on the floor or be led by magnets. The progression is summarised in Table 3.1.

Table 3.1 A summary of the progression of control IT sequences

Process	Typical questions to promote activity
Isolated commands	Make the robot go forward.
Sequencing isolated commands	Make the robot go around the chair.
Repeat commands	Make the robot draw a square using only one line of instructions.
Recursive programs	Make the robot flash its light on and off until you switch it off.
Sense and control	Make the robot able to find its own way around a maze.

Alongside these procedural elements, children can be encouraged to develop an investigative approach by introducing them to the idea of having problems to solve. In order to progress, it is obvious that the child must have the skills to solve the problem available to her (e.g. if the challenge is, 'Can you draw a square?', the child must know the commands Forward and Right 90). From there, problems can become more complex while at the same time the level of support the child receives in teacher input and imposed investigative structure in the form of worksheets can be reduced. The goal is for children to be able to solve real problems by identifying possible solutions, designing and effecting an appropriately controlled test, evaluating the outcome and then modifying an unsuccessful solution in an attempt to achieve success. For children at this stage, the world of sensing and controlling provides unlimited opportunities for this type of problem-solving activity.

Interface output/input boxes

Control technology experiences in the primary school are not limited to the applications of floor robots or floor or screen turtles. The use of interfaced switching boxes to control lights, buzzers, motors, electromagnets and so forth provides a vast range of opportunities for developing problem-solving and investigative process skills. The hardware generally consists of a computer linked to an interface or 'buffer' box. This interface box normally has four or five output switches (of variable voltage and reversible polarity (i.e. the direction of current can be altered), both of which can be controlled by the user) and one or two input ports (where sensors can be connected) which inform the computer of environmental changes such as obstructions, magnetic fields, changes in light intensity.

The instructions are given in a control language similar to that described when operating floor robots. In fact some packages (e.g. Lego Dacta Control) use LOGO as the control language, on the assumption that children will be happier working with a language with which they are already familiar from their early experiences with floor turtles (which would normally have been introduced before involving the children with interface boxes).

The essential elements of a control language for interface systems are:

TURN ON/OFF
WAIT [Time period]
IF ON [Response to a sensor]

Initial experiences with the interface box will involve the children simply using the device as a sophisticated switch: connecting various components such as light bulbs to the interface outputs, and turning them on and off through the computer. At this point children can also be shown the commands to alter the voltage and to reverse the polarity. Children can make predictions about how making these changes will affect such phenomena as bulb brightness, motor speed and direction of turn, or field strength of an electromagnet.

As with floor robots, the next step in the hierarchy of concepts is to begin sequencing simple instructions and qualifying them with time limits. An ideal starting point would be to write a program for a flashing lighthouse lamp. One flash can be generated with the instructions: Turn On, Wait 1 Second, Turn Off. To generate another pulse, the child will have to repeat the instruction, strung alongside the original instruction: Turn On, Wait, Turn Off, Wait, Turn On, Wait, Turn Off. Children soon realise the limitations of this and are aware that a very lengthy program would be needed (in the amount of typing!) to maintain a flashing light for any practical length of time.

At the stage of this realisation, they will also be able to recognise the repetitive nature of the sequence (comparable to the repeat evident in the program commanding a floor robot to draw a square) and will search for a 'repeat' function. In the case of most control languages this can be done in two ways. For a limited number of repeats (in this example, flashes) the controller could write: Repeat 6 times [Turn On, Wait 1 Second, Turn Off, Wait 1 Second]. This will make the light flash on and off 6 times. Children take a while to realise the importance of the final 'Wait' command in this sequence. To them, the 'turn off' element of the program is a negative or non-event and, as such, does not require a time value. Of course, the period of darkness is as important as the period of light in a flashing sequence.

The other method of repeating a sequence which, in this case, would be more appropriate is to build a recursive loop into the program. Quite simply this is done by writing: [Turn On, Wait 1 Second, Turn Off, Wait 1 Second] Do It Again. This causes the light to flash *ad infinitum* or until the power is switched off. There are many ways of reinforcing and extending understanding within this particular concept level. As with juggling, the introduction of two or more components to the system increases the level of challenge to the programmer. The classic way of introducing children to this is by asking them to write a program to control a set of traffic lights. Each light of the system (red, amber and green) will have its own switch. It is possible to have two or more switches on at the same time.

In this chapter, it is made clear that the application of recursive programs comes at a particular developmental stage and should be introduced at the appropriate time. Some pundits argue that it is possible for children to 'discover' recursion if allowed time at the computer unconstrained by over-structured learning tasks and, indeed, it is true that some children appear to instinctively apply recursive principles in some situations. However, in these cases such application may only be specific to the exercise and the child does not see the recursive process as an element that is transferable to other situations.

Control at this level often proves a remarkable challenge, mainly because children often feel that the computer is blessed with artificial intelligence and is in 'harmony' with the controller's intentions. For example the vital 'Turn Off' instruction is often omitted because it is assumed by the user that the computer will realise that it's time to switch off the green light because we've asked to light up amber. The children require a large amount of work at this level to ensure that the control language is internalised and for them fully to recognise the total logic of the control language. Support activities such as pre-writing programs before testing, being told a series of events and asking them to write the program, describing models made from maths cubes to a partner who must build a replica model based on the exact verbal instructions and similar exercises, will all help to construct a firm base upon which to build the next layer of procedural understanding.

Most control languages can be edited so that children can respond to 'What if?' questions by suggesting solutions with predictable outcomes, testing and evaluating. In other words, they can apply their knowledge to the investigative, problem-solving approach. In the case of the traffic light sequence program, the question could be, 'What if the traffic in one direction was heavier than in the other and needed more time to pass the junction?' The controller needs to consider what amendments are needed to the existing program to solve the problem, to predict what outcomes the various suggested solutions will have and to test those outcomes.

As with the floor robots the final developmental stage for most primary school children is building in a 'response to senses' element to the programs they design. Real-life examples can stimulate classroom work to move children on to this aspect of control technology. For example, looking at how movement sensors on motorway bridges detect traffic movement and activate speed limit controls accordingly can be reproduced by the learner using the appropriate sensor and an amendment to the existing traffic light sequence program. The opportunities for children to undertake meaningful (real-world context) and challenging problem-solving activity using such hardware and control language are vast. With the appropriate early experiences, reinforcing and extending learning tasks associated with simple sequencing, and with a structured intro-duction to the sensory element of control technology, there are few better ways to develop children's ability to deconstruct systems, work logically and to operate at a high level of procedural understanding.

Advocates of control IT believe that the 'real world, real outcome' nature of computer control provides a context for just these sort of experiences. This is, however, based on the assumption that the problem-solving skills that are developed through IT control are transferable to other domains of intellectual activity. This seems to be an area crying out for further investigation.

Control IT and a broader view of cognitive development

If it is the case that the problem-solving skills developed through IT control are transferable, how does the conceptual progression (hierarchies of learning) identified in control IT applications map on to a constructivist model of learning? The pre-operational child (in Piaget's terms) can only operate the computer control application (whether it be a floor robot or interface) as a simple switch, giving each command as it comes without recourse to what has gone before and what might happen if . . .

Proponents of introducing control technology as early as reception classes accept that young children will use the control panel of the floor robot (for example) as little more than an expensive on/off switch. But, they say, the robot's concrete response to pressure on the 'Forward 1 Step' button enables the child to engage in a process with real, successful outcomes, and at the same time, to begin to internalise the language of control. So they recommend applying control IT from the outset, rather than waiting for the child first to reach the state of cognitive maturity where the problem-solving and sequencing processes have been established through more conventional (but often more abstract) means. Experience of children working in reception classes with floor robots invalidates the ever-common first response to the idea of early primary children using control IT of 'It's too difficult for them!'

Children operating at the concrete operational level would be expected to form mental representations of the actions they observe, identifying certain patterns. While not yet able to extend such representations to the solving of problems or predicting answers to 'what if?' questions, the concrete-operational child will be able to string commands together that enable a simple traffic light sequence to run, or make a floor robot draw a square. Such IT activities are often preceded or run alongside PE activities that make simpler cognitive demands, where children command other children to move using simple instructions. When operating floor robots or walking predetermined paths, children at this stage should begin to recognise that patterns of movement involve repeated instructions in the sequence. In the case of drawing a square, the command 'Forward 1 Right ¼ Turn' is repeated four times. Most programmable floor robots such as LOGO turtles, Roamer and Pip will allow children to write repeats into their sequences. Children operating light sequences such as flashing disco lights should also begin to identify repetitive elements in their instructions although it is harder to recognise repetition in flashing lights than in the rigid, sequential movements of the floor robot. An example would be:

Turn on Red	Wait 1 Second
Turn off Red	
Turn on Yellow	Wait 1 Second
Turn off Yellow	
Turn on Green	Wait 1 Second
Turn off Green	
Turn on Yellow	Wait 1 Second
Turn off Yellow	

REPEAT the program

Here, the child should be able to identify and implement the repeat: Turn on, Wait, Turn off.

Children operating at the concrete stage can obviously engage in a wide variety of control IT applications, increasing their fluency with the hardware and software, with the language and with the process of control IT sequences. Their difficulty comes when challenged with new possibilities: 'You've drawn a square, what must you change to draw a rectangle or triangle?' or 'Real disco lights have moments when two or three lights are on at the same time, what must you change?' Equally, they will have difficulty in advancing to the next conceptual level in the control IT hierarchy, that is, sensing, where devices monitor their environment (the presence of obstructions, light levels, magnetic fields, etc.) and have programs that have a built-in reponse to changes in that environment. Their inability to identify possibilities means that children operating at a concrete level do not see how to integrate a flexible 'If' instruction into the rigid, sequenced world of the simple control program. Helping to develop an understanding of the concept of a 'variable' can be useful in progressing to the next stage (see Chapter 4).

Formal thinkers with the foundation of years of control IT experience will be ready to enter this world of 'anything is possible' problem-solving. The positive image that children have of using control IT applications, and their chances of tackling 'real' problems in which outcomes are clear and measurable means that, once at this stage, they can move quickly to extend their understanding of the problem-solving process to wider contexts. The move from concrete to formal operations is clearly demonstrated in the following example. It also raises the question as to whether innovations such as control IT can accelerate children's passage through the constructivist stages.

Children were challenged to construct a computer-controlled winch that could raise a deep sea diver a certain depth at a time, with a pause at each stage to prevent the diver getting the 'bends' by coming up too quickly. The motor driving the winch could only recognise on/off and a time, so the main challenge for the children was to ascertain how long the motor would have to turn in order to raise the diver a particular height. Clearly an ability to organise a simple trial and adjustment sequence upon which a prediction could be based would be the solution. However, those children operating at a concrete level had problems with this. Although fluent with the commands and language of the IT, they could not see the relationship between time and distance: 'How can we make the winch wind a certain distance when our machine can only measure time?'

Even with guidance, whereby the children were given a structured investigation, the problem remained unsolved. The children were asked to measure how much string was wound after 1 second, 2 seconds and so on. Even though a clear pattern emerged:

1 Second   5 cm
2 Seconds   10 cm
3 seconds   15 cm

children had great difficulty in predicting how much time was required to raise the diver 30 cm. As yet they were unable to extrapolate the data. The teacher had been convinced that while the children would have been unable to do a similar extrapolative exercise in a more formal, paper and pencil mathematics exercise the more concrete, 'hands-on' nature of the control IT would have led them more easily to the understanding. But even those who grasped the extrapolative technique within the control IT context failed to transfer the knowledge to other contexts, such as relating the distance walked, say across the school field, to the time taken.

Older children set a similar challenge had little difficulty in recognising the relationship between time and distance, and were able to solve the timing problem without the aid of a structured investigation; this process was already internalised. That prediction skills were clearly established was evidenced by the cry, 'It's wound up 3 cm in one second, I bet it'll be 6 cm in two!'

The trial proved the prediction correct and no more data were required to extrapolate the fact that the winch would need to wind for 10 seconds in order to raise the diver 30 cm. More confident, and more experienced, children proffered other solutions to meet the need, such as using gear meshes on the winch to alter the rate of winding and so forth. These children were also much more able to deal with extrapolating data in different contexts, such as temperature change over time and currency conversion problems.

There seems little doubt that while the use of control IT applications does not enable children to bypass the accepted stages of conceptual development, it provides not only an enrichment at each level that has benefits across the curriculum, but can accelerate conceptual development and process skills such as predicting, hypothesising, testing, problem-solving and so forth in a way that more traditional methods fail to do.

Transfer of knowledge: a cross-curricular view

There are three ways that experience and understanding of control technology can enhance other areas of learning as part of an integrated and coherent curriculum. The fundamental element is the context it provides for developing an understanding of investigative, problem-solving approaches. The procedural cycle that children work towards is shown in Figure 3.1.

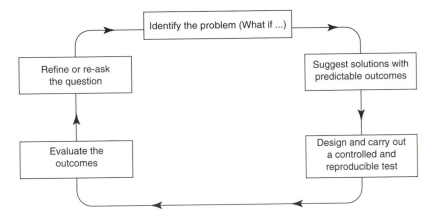

Figure 3.1 The procedural cycle of problem-solving

It is, in essence, the same cycle that they work towards when developing an understanding of the procedural aspects of experimental and investigative science or when undertaking a real maths investigation. The cycle of events that characterise the analysis of primary history sources such as artefacts is similarly akin to the problem-solving process that, this chapter argues, can be promoted by control IT experiences. The essential debate is whether children identify such links and if understanding developed in one context is transferred to another. For example, do children who show proficiency at problem-solving when working with a sensing floor robot work equally adeptly when solving a non-IT-related design technology problem?

The fragmentation of the primary curriculum, particularly towards the end of Key Stage 2, as a result of government initiative and schools' response to this policy pressure makes this a hard question to answer. I have seen that the structures used to encourage children to develop good investigative skills in, for example science, are often repeated again in design technology and in maths, as if the process were exclusive to the individual subjects. In reality, of course, this is not the case. The ability to investigate analytically is very similar whether you are addressing the problem of a leaking tap or undertaking genetics research. As with all these things, the point at which children realise the common procedural link between subjects is not only a reflection of their experience and conceptual maturity but also of their awareness that such knowledge is important and the degree to which the teacher makes these links explicit.

For this reason it is important that children are given a structure for the way they undertake investigative and problem-solving activity, and that structures such as framework sheets that help children plan and organise their ideas are comparable across the curriculum. Too often, the development of procedural understanding has been part of the 'hidden curriculum', with the assumption that by doing it, children will inevitably understand and cross apply it. Sadly, for many children the procedural elements are too hidden. The structured approach to teaching investigative processes that the application of control IT offers (which is also consistent across the curriculum) can go a long way to overcoming this problem while at the same time allowing the child to be involved in independent, challenging, meaningful and experiential learning, which offers both the opportunity of intellectual enrichment and the development of life skills.

The second cross-curricular element associated with control IT is the development of attitudes that all disciplines demand. Control language requires precision and logic yet at the same time, imagination and spatial awareness. The process of undertaking control IT activities encourages curiosity and a willingness to test ideas and to modify these ideas accordingly. The problem-solving context is inevitably a social one and children will generally work together, learning how to operate as a team (working as a group, not in a group!).

The third cross-curricular element is the specific relationship between control language and maths. Many schools identified the application of floor robots as being principally a part of the maths teacher's armoury and believed that the control IT element was a fortuitous 'add on' to this experience. Some schools were concerned that when the IT National Curriculum orders identified control technology as an integral part of the child's curriculum entitlement they would be unable to meet the challenge, this despite using floor robots from Reception onwards as a maths activity!

It is clear that fundamental numeracy skills such as estimation, measurement of time and distance, angle, etc. can be either taught or applied through control IT experiences. But a cautious view should be taken of the assumption that a child's perception of angle when commanding a floor robot around the room is the same, or as abstract, as would be needed to analyse geometrical shapes and principles.

Constraints

Despite the obvious benefits that control IT offers the primary school learner along with IT measurement (data logging) it is still less widely applied than might be expected. The review of inspection evidence of specific subjects for 1995 (Ofsted 1996) acknowledged that while many schools had broadened approaches by introducing such control elements as programmable toys, over one third of schools failed to meet the requirements of the National Curriculum in this area. As ever the constraints are three-fold: resources, capability and a lack of awareness of precisely what control IT can offer the learner.

Control technology can be, and often is, viewed as an expensive luxury, despite the status of legal requirement and proven benefits to learning. A simple self-contained floor robot costs just under £100 (in 1996) and with sensing accessories gets up towards £200. A basic interface package with sensing probes can be anything up to £300. However, while I agree that the products are not cheap, I found that the children working in my four-class school all had ample opportunity to use our floor robot and the Key Stage 2 children enjoyed regular access to the interface unit. Teachers were able to plan coherent schemes of work reflecting continuity and progression safe in the knowledge that the hardware was timetabled so that the work could take place. In other words, it is not necessary to install control IT in every classroom to enable all children to have meaningful and planned access.

More challenging is the constraint of capability: the lack of teachers who are knowledgeable, confident and can organise teaching which recognises not only the skills element of the IT but also the conceptual progression and how it maps onto the child's level of intellectual maturity. Teachers must be able to set appropriate tasks so as to elicit the best possible learning outcomes. Initial teacher training and continuing professional development must address this issue despite the challenge of an apparently ever expanding curriculum. A generation of teachers is required who can confidently organise control IT experiences in the classroom and so enable children to benefit from all that this way of working can offer. This generation of teachers may have to take advantage of the large, unpaid workforce of parent and volunteer assistants to support the application of control IT in the same way they have assisted reading and art in the past.

The third constraint relates to the statement made earlier regarding the proven benefits that control IT confers on the primary school learner. There is still a majority who view control IT applications as exclusive and specific, failing to recognise the breadth of opportunity that it offers in assisting and enhancing the intellectual development of the learner as a whole.

Summary

In this chapter I have argued that control IT offers not only a specific intellectual experience, and not only introduces an ever-expanding modern technology that operates in the outside world, but also provides children with a procedural way of working that mirrors and complements similar processes across the curriculum. Children engaging in these kind of activities generally show a very positive attitude and are often more willing to take on the challenge of independent problem-solving using control IT than they would be in more 'traditional' contexts.

I hope to have shown how the progression of concepts and skills associated with control IT maps clearly on to the constructivist view of learning. Finally, I have touched on the constraints that can and do limit the application of control IT in primary schools, but argue that they are worth the cost, of both resources and training, so as to ensure that this vital and valuable element of the curriculum assumes the high profile its merits justify.

Chapter 4

Understanding and using variables in a variety of mathematical contexts

Anne Thwaites and Libby Jared

Introduction

We would like to begin by asking anyone for whom mathematics is not a favourite subject not to be put off by the title. Before going any further, it may be useful to discuss the place of variables in the primary curriculum. We are using the term 'variable' here to describe something whose value can change (i.e. vary). It may well be a rare occasion when one hears the word 'variable' spoken to a primary school child but nevertheless there will be many ideas developed, and activities going on, in the classroom which are implicitly laying the foundations for the explicit understanding of this term. In writing this chapter for a readership of primary practitioners, we firmly believe that the idea of a variable, and activities which use this idea, have been taking place within the primary curriculum for some time and are important in their own right. Indeed other contexts where variables are fundamentally important are discussed elsewhere in this book in relation to control technology, problem-solving and science. The fact that an understanding of the importance of the concept of a variable can enhance the development of algebra *per se* and do much to lay the foundations of secondary school work is both a bonus and a reason why practitioners need to be aware of the potential of such activities.

Our intention has been to provide a chapter accessible to any reader interested in laying the foundations of more abstract mathematics while using the computer within the primary classroom. We should perhaps call abstract mathematics algebra, but mention the word algebra and many people will quake in their shoes. However we seek to reassure them that there are no terrors here, as it is clear to us that there are a lot of experiences that children can benefit from before they ever need to use the formal notation of letters: ideas which can be nurtured in young people's minds from almost their first day at school. The key notion of algebra which this chapter embraces is indeed 'the variable'. It is with this in mind that this chapter looks at three approaches using IT – though some activities may start away from the computer – which can help to develop this concept. These approaches are: the turtle graphics elements within LOGO, spreadsheets and calculators.

We choose these three areas for their different presentations of incorporating variables in an indirect and easy manner. Turtle graphics (defined here as a method of drawing on a computer screen using the travelling commands to go forward and back through a chosen distance and the turning commands to turn left and right through a chosen angle) encourages the writing of instructions. This process is discussed at length in Chapter 3. Initially these instructions may have numerical values incorporated in them; however the need for, and advantages of, using differing values (i.e. variables) in these instructions becomes apparent. A spreadsheet is a grid of boxes arranged in rows and columns, where each box can have a number or a formula allocated to it. The contents of these boxes can be varied following an input of instructions and hence again make use of variables in a powerful way. Calculators are now on the market which give the facility for trial and improvement for basic arithmetic. Such calculators may be used to present opportunities, at an early age, for children to meet variables in a context that is much closer to the way in which they are thinking about number.

Variables and algebra

For many years it has been recognised that algebra has marked the point at which a number of children have begun to lose their hold on mathematics. Paragraph 201 from *Mathematics Counts*, commonly known as the Cockcroft Report, includes the comments that 'formal algebra seems to have been the topic within mathematics which attracted most comment' and 'algebra is a source of confusion and negative attitudes among pupils' (Cockcroft Report 1982: 60). Yet in the first two versions of the National Curriculum, algebra had a place of its own throughout the Key Stages. Within the post-Dearing version, there is still a clear place for aspects of algebra within the Programmes of Study; for example, in Key Stage 1 (Number): 'explore, record, explain and predict basic number patterns' and in Key Stage 2 (Number): 'progress to interpreting, generalising . . . expressed initially in words and then using letters as symbols' (DfE 1995c: 3, 7).

The inclusion of these key fundamentals of algebra has been the source of concern with some teachers who hold vivid memories of manipulating formulae (invariably presented as mystical x and y) with no clear understanding of what or why they were doing it. The SESM (Strategies and Errors in Secondary Mathematics) project findings show how pupils find difficulty with formalisation of algebraic method (Booth 1984). The use of letters for numbers seems to be key to these difficulties. Little seems to have changed, as Mann and Tall report 'all too often . . . pupils have been required to use and manipulate symbols in ways which have little meaning to them' (Mathematical Association 1992: 67). At the time of those studies formal algebra was restricted to the secondary curriculum. There have as yet been no widespread reports on the teaching and learning of algebra in the primary classroom, but it seems reasonable to assume that the problems will remain at least as bad, if not worse, when working with younger children. If teachers within the primary classroom can use strategies to overcome such obvious deficiencies, an important contribution can be made to the mathematical understanding of algebra.

It could be argued that many of the ideas we are writing about in this chapter give rise to dynamic situations, that is, situations where something is capable of changing. For example, the number of units the turtle moves, or the price of chocolate in a 'tuck shop' spreadsheet may change. An appreciation that such dynamic situations can be described as a number of interacting variables is an essential precursor to modelling, a major feature in the Information Technology National Curriculum. Ogborn makes the bold suggestion that 'we need to begin modelling without, or with the absolute minimum of, mathematics' (Ogborn 1992). He goes on to state, 'there is good evidence, supported by commonsense observation, that young students see the world as built of objects and events, not as variables'. However in order to begin to use models to describe even the simplest system, it is necessary to be able to view that system as a series of interacting variables. For example, in order to model a traffic light system which controls the flow of traffic it is necessary to consider the variables flow of traffic, timing of lights and so on. (For further discussion of this topic see Mellar *et al.* 1994.) The activities we describe, whilst embedded in the Mathematics Curriculum and concerned with variables, could be thought of as introducing the concept of the world seen as a series of interacting variables, through the back door.

Working away from the computer

The importance of introducing work which does not involve touching the keys of a computer cannot be overestimated. On many occasions the rate of progress at the computer will be in proportion to preparatory work away from it. We have made this point in a previous work, which discusses the way that children will initially work, from the concrete to the abstract (Jared and Thwaites 1995). In this way of working the starting point is an object from which characterisation leads to the construction and interpretation of data representations; hence the physical ideas given here, in the following paragraph. There is then a later developmental stage where the return process, in which the child works (back) from the abstract to the concrete, can be expected; characteristics can be identified which in turn lead to defining objects and consequential relationships. An example of this is a child viewing another person's LOGO instructions or picture screen and interpreting (or indeed visualising) it back as a real-world object.

There are numerous classrooms where the opportunity to introduce the idea of variables is present but where teachers may be unaware of the possibilities. For example, most classrooms have noticeboards which display the day of the week, the date, the weather, who is taking the register to the office, who is feeding the gerbil and so on. These are actually all using the notion of a variable. If the notice is prepared as a series of labelled boxes, or envelopes, into which the changing day, date, description of the weather or name can be put, then the fundamental idea of a variable is in place. Here is an object, state or job which has a name (for example day of the week) and a value (such as Monday, Tuesday). The name remains constant but the value can change. Such practice can reduce the need for comments such as 'examples . . . have set out to present algebra as a notation to express generalised arithmetic without first establishing the fundamental idea of a variable' (Mathematical Association 1992: 67). By drawing on such a common visual aid, the idea of the variable can be made explicit.

We have used the box idea extensively with children and adults to either introduce or present an alternative approach to variables. Individual portion cereal packets are a suitable size and shape. Placing Post-it notes on the outside of the box makes the name of the variable visible. Strips of card with the value of the variable can be placed inside the box enabling changes to the value to be made easily. We find that the dynamics of this set-up helps understanding. The notion of using a box to represent a variable is one described by Metz in relation to work with LOGO (Metz 1988).

To conclude this section we draw attention to the power of discussion and questioning. Whilst children's thinking is undoubtedly developed through physical activities and working at computer-based tasks, without discussion and questioning this development cannot be taken to its limit. Of course every teacher will appreciate the importance of both techniques in all areas of the curriculum and will be involved in practising a variety of situations, be it on a one-to-one basis (either teacher–pupil or pupil–pupil), in small groups or with a whole class. Within a busy classroom, there may be a tendency to feel that the computer can take on the teacher's role, but whilst the computer can give feedback it will never replace personal communication. Pupils will not feel the full benefits and enjoyment which the computer can bring if the teacher is not fully involved in all aspects of the work. With computer-based work it is vitally important that the teacher does not relinquish the responsibility for discussion.

LOGO

In this section we will be discussing the role of turtle graphics. Whilst acknowledging that the full commands of LOGO includes work that is not turtle graphics, we will call all the turtle graphics work here LOGO.

In Metz's work, children in a Year 2 class were attempting to draw chairs for the three bears in the story of Goldilocks. Having produced a procedure (a named set of instructions) to draw one chair, the children wanted to go on and alter it for the other two sizes. She grasped this opportunity to introduce a group within the class to variables; fortuitously, they had drawn the chair using only one value within the forward (FD) commands. 'I used an empty box to represent the name of the variable LENGTH and the children put multilink cubes in the box, to the length of the line they wanted drawn' (Metz 1988: 18). So here the name of the variable and its value can be clearly distinguished. Metz comments 'the concept of variable is not usually part of an infant's experience of mathematical ideas. And yet some of these young children demonstrated convincingly that they were able to understand and use this concept in graphical and non-graphical work' (p. 20). Blythe reports a similar introduction to variables with LOGO with 7-year-olds. She says, 'the various ways in which this group of eight children reacted to a new concept clearly demonstrates that if children are ready for a more complex idea they will use it and value it' (Blythe 1990: 84).

Consider the instructions needed to draw a square: it is necessary to go forward a set distance, say 200, and turn through 90 degrees four times, i.e. repeat 4 times forward 200 right 90. In LOGO language this becomes REPEAT 4 [FD 200 RT 90]. Rather than having to type this in time and time again to get more squares, one can create a procedure that will automatically draw the square when the name allocated to the procedure is given. Take the following example of a procedure, named SQ, for drawing a square of specified size, 200 in this case:

```
TO SQ
REPEAT 4 [ FD 200 RT 90 ]
END
```

Whenever SQ is typed a square of size 200 will be drawn.

After only a brief introduction to LOGO, the idea of wanting to change the size of a shape comes to the fore in many pupils' minds. Initially this may be achieved by starting afresh and simply replacing the old value with the new. How much more convenient it would be to use variables within the procedure. Within the procedure SQ above, the 200 is the only part that would need to be changed in order to make a square of size, say 100 (i.e. replacing the old value with the new as described above). The introduction of the variable labelled SIDE makes this procedure capable of drawing any size of square. The changed procedure would be:

```
TO SQUARE :SIDE
REPEAT 4 [ FD :SIDE RT 90 ]
END
```

In running the procedure the computer will expect a specific value. Supplying this is akin to the pre-computer activity of using a box for a variable and writing the value of the length of the side on a strip of card in a box labelled SIDE. Each time the procedure SQUARE is typed, the computer will expect a number to accompany SQUARE which is the value for the side of the square which is to be drawn. For example, the instruction SQUARE 40 would result in a square of side 40 being drawn.

If a child can write a procedure for a specific task, such as drawing a square, then the ability to decide which parts of that procedure need to be changed, in order to make it of any size, is a clear indication of generalising about the nature and properties of a square. Leron suggests that 'the use of variables enables the procedure's definition to capture neatly and concisely both the invariance . . . and the variability within it' (Leron 1988: 186).

The next stage in considering variables within LOGO is to introduce the MAKE command. This enables a variable to be changed in size while retaining the same name. The syntax of the quote and colon in front of the word used to name the variable, in this case MOVE, indicate the name and the value of the variable respectively. The following procedure draws a spiral on the command SPIRAL.

```
TO SPIRAL
MAKE "MOVE 5
REPEAT 10 [FORWARD :MOVE LEFT 90 MAKE "MOVE :MOVE + 5]
END
```

In all the work we have described within LOGO, the variable is acting as a place-holder for a number whose value will be known at the time at which the procedure is carried out. If children have met the analogy of the variable as a labelled box, then the syntax appears to be readily accepted by them. As Mann and Tall suggest, 'once they [the children] have gained some experience of working with LOGO . . . the use of symbols becomes both accessible and relevant' (Mathematical Association 1992: 67). It is important that there is no need to be able to manipulate any algebraic type of expression. Although LOGO has the reputation for being pedantic and, at times idiosyncratic, the very immediate response on the screen of the result of instructions allows the learner to deal with these abstract concepts in a concrete situation. Hence the learning of these concepts takes place almost by osmosis as a by-product of achieving the expected picture on the screen.

Spreadsheets

We have so far shown that LOGO can be a low-key approach to introducing variables. We would now like to go on to consider another area where the use of a variable is made more explicit and children are introduced to algebraic expressions with more traditional notation.

In brief, a spreadsheet can be thought of as a large area of cells or boxes which can be filled in a variety of ways. Each cell has an address according to where it is positioned within the array. Labels and numbers can be put into the cells; however, the great sophistication of a spreadsheet arises through the facility to put a formula into a cell that calls upon the contents of other cells.

Initially the size of the spreadsheet need not be vast, in comparison with those used in the business world. Some primary programs have about seven columns and twenty rows, which is more than adequate for a starter. Indeed to begin with only three or four columns and rows may be needed and it is possible to customise some spreadsheets so that a limited area appears.

Healy and Sutherland describe a range of tasks that can be used to introduce children to spreadsheets (Healy and Sutherland 1991: 8–11). Early on they encourage one pupil of a pair to set up a formula in one cell, B3 (its address being column B and row 3), which is dependent upon the value of another cell, A3 (see Figure 4.1a). For example the pupil could chose the formula in cell B3 as the number in cell A3 times 2, which in spreadsheet notation would be = A3 * 2.

By trying a series of numbers in cell A3, the second of the pair has to attempt to work out the formula chosen by the other person (see Figure 4.1b). There are occasions when the two have in essence the same formula but are describing it in two different ways. For example, = A3 * 2 could be expressed as = A3 + A3. The variable in this work has been the number placed in cell A3. This can open up a

	A	B	C	D	E
1					
2					
3	4	=A3*2			
4					
5					
6					
7					
8					
9					
10					

Figure 4.1a A simple spreadsheet showing the number 4 as data in cell A3 and a formula in cell B3 related to the number in cell A3

	A	B	C	D	E
1					
2					
3	4	=A3*2			
4					
5					
6					
7					
8					
9					
10					

Figure 4.1b The 'answer' in cell B3, calculated from the formula entered in that cell, arrived at by multiplying the number entered in cell A3 by 2

wealth of discussion as to whether the two formulae are 'equal'. Healy and Sutherland point out that when the two formulae chosen have not been identical, 'the spreadsheet task had provoked them into reflecting on the equivalence of two algebraic/arithmetic expressions' (Healy and Sutherland 1991: 10).

It will not take very long before the pupils attempt to make their formulae involve more than one operation in order to 'stump' their partner. This gives an immediate and useful introduction to more formal algebra without necessarily the realisation that it has achieved precisely that. For example, a pupil who chooses to double a number and then add three will set up a formula in a spread-sheet cell of the form = A1 * 2 + 3. This is using a symbolic representation and we believe the pupil will make the transition at Key Stage 3 to y = x * 2 + 3 all the more readily. Indeed the spreadsheet can then be used to show the equivalence of this expression to 2 * x + 3 or 3 + x * 2 and so on. Cavendish and Walters affirm this by saying 'using spreadsheets . . . helps the child to build up their understanding of algebraic formulae before they meet algebra in conventional teaching' (Cavendish and Walters 1994: 112-13).

Earlier, in illustrating algebraic ideas within Key Stage 2 of the National Curriculum, we included in the examples from the Programmes of Study the word 'generalising'. We firmly believe that algebra builds from ideas of general-isation and that certainly simple spreadsheet work can be the ideal thinking ground for developing such generalisation. For example, if children have been building patterns with counters or by drawing dots to form a sequence of triangular numbers, they can count the number of counters or dots needed to make each triangle. These are called the triangular numbers. For example, the fourth triangular number is 10 (see Figure 4.2a).

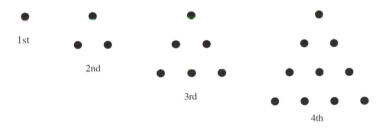

1st

2nd

3rd

4th

Figure 4.2a The first four triangular numbers

It is then possible to enter two columns into a spreadsheet, one showing the term 'number' (1, 2, 3, 4 . . .) and the other the value of the associated triangular number (1, 3, 6, 10 . . .). The next relatively easy step is to set up a third column which gives the difference between two consecutive numbers in the second column (see Figure 4.2b).

Pupils may then see different ideas and patterns relating to these different sets of numbers. For example, some may see how one triangular number can be

fig 4

	A	B	C	D
1	term	triangular	difference	
2	number	number		
3				
4	1	1		
5	2	3	2	
6	3	6	3	
7	4	10	4	
8	5	15	5	
9	6	21	6	
10	7	28	7	
11	8	36	8	
12	9	45	9	
13	10	55	10	
14				
15				
16				

Figure 4.2b Spreadsheet showing the first ten triangular numbers in column B and the difference between consecutive triangular numbers in column C

established from the previous one – which in mathematical terms would be termed a recurrence relationship. Others may see possible connections with the square numbers (two consecutive triangular numbers added together always form a square number). Such patterns can be generated by setting up appropriate instructions in further columns of the spreadsheet. An additional strength of this type of work is the natural occurrence of opportunities to experiment. Even if patterns such as those described above are not immediately seen, pupils can investigate possible links by setting up trial columns alongside the column of triangular numbers and making improvements to the relationship.

There is further scope for trial and improvement methods using the spreadsheet, easily accessible to the primary pupil. Long before the widespread use of computers or indeed calculators, the Cockcroft Report in its chapter entitled 'Mathematics in the primary years', paragraph 318, was advocating 'Questions such as "if 2 × [ ] + _ = 17 what numbers can we write in the [ ] and _ ?" can be used to introduce algebraic ideas' (Cockcroft Report 1982: 93) and thus recommending their place within the curriculum. However these days it is just such a question that can lend itself to investigation with a spreadsheet as an alternative method of solution. With one cell to represent the [ ] and a second to represent the _ , a formula can be set up for 2 × [ ] + _ in a third cell. There is then room for lots of trial and improvement which possibly leads to the employment of higher strategies than hitherto. Indeed it can lead to the powerful notion of two (different) variables. With two variables, the strategy of holding one constant while varying the other may need to be suggested after some initial attempts, although some children are very ready to use that type of systematic approach themselves.

All the investigational work described in this section is structured so that the pupil can change parts of a formula very readily. We can only agree with Healy and Sutherland when they say,

> the most exciting part of the spreadsheet environment is that it allows pupils to express general mathematical relationships which are far more sophisticated than those which they can normally express in their paper and pencil work. This potential for expressing generalities is linked to the value of a spreadsheet environment from the point of view of developing algebraic understanding.
>
> (Healy and Sutherland 1991: 3)

Calculators

We conclude this chapter with a brief excursion into using the calculator, firmly believing that calculators are part and parcel of IT resources within the classroom. In the primary school, there is obviously more scope for each one in an entire class to have access to a relatively cheap calculator than to extensive time on the computer. This allows the computer to be freed for other activities. Access to calculators can alleviate the pressure of thirty or more pupils all trying to share the one computer with the teacher being forced to decide priorities between the conflicting demands of its use across all curriculum areas.

Calculators can assist the introduction of variables in similar ways to those already described with LOGO and spreadsheets and thus provide further experience in developing the roots of algebra.

As part of the Primary Initiatives in Mathematics Project (PrIME) the role of calculators in mathematics learning was investigated, in 1986–90. Within this major project there was also the Calculator Aware Number (CAN) project. Rowland describes an activity he observed in a CAN primary school where the children were choosing a number less than 40, keying it into their calculators and then adding 10. Having recorded a series of such numbers, Carl (in Year 2) came up with the observation 'the second number [digit] is the same and the first [one] is one more' (Rowland 1994: 11). Here the calculator (or it could have been a spreadsheet) has removed the possible errors of doing a large number of such calculations and has allowed this child to see a generalisation. This can lead on to problems of the type [ ] + 10 = 36 where the unknown is in the first position. These type of questions have long been considered by many teachers as being more problematic for children than ones of the type 10 + [ ] = 36.

The advent of calculators such as the Texas 9X, which can display expression and result (for example in the form ? + 10 = 36 or indeed ? + ? = 27), consequently allow trial answers. Such calculators are using the notion of a variable in order to allow different possibilities to be keyed in. Indeed the calculator gives feedback if the trial is incorrect by indicating that it is too small or too big. This allows for increased investigational work of the type described above for spreadsheets. (One word of warning is needed here; on the Texas calculator each of the two possible unknowns are entered as ?, although each variable indicated by ? can have different values.)

Another feature of these primary years calculators allows a function to be defined. Any basic four-function calculator can be set up to carry out an operation repeatedly, for example, pressing the keys 3 + 10 = = = ... results in the calculator turning into a '10 adder' as 10 is added the same number of times as the equals key is pressed. Some of the newer calculators, such as the Texas 9X, carries out the same repeat facility via an operation key, but its power lies in the fact that it displays the number of times 10 is added as well as the result of the operation.

Summary

We hope that some of the possibilities that IT creates within the mathematics curriculum have been made explicit in this chapter, having addressed three different approaches in some detail, namely: the turtle graphics elements within LOGO, spreadsheets and calculators. However the underlying theme throughout is that such work can be made accessible to pupils at Key Stages 1 and 2 in order to bring about improvements in understanding of more complex mathematical ideas at later Key Stages; hence the fundamentals of algebra can be initiated implicitly from an early stage within the primary school curriculum. Discussion has centred on the notion of a 'variable' with a description of a range of activities that will enhance a child's understanding and development of such a concept. Comment has also been made on the movement in a child's development from the concrete object through to the abstract, with the possibility of later moving from the abstract back to the real world; the importance of working away from the computer when appropriate; and the necessity for teacher intervention and support on computer-based tasks. The concepts involved have a wider significance than solely within mathematics. Many of the activities described are clearly related to the control, modelling, science and problem-solving aspects of the curriculum and rightly reflect the important role IT plays in helping children to develop an understanding of the related concepts of a variable.

Chapter 5

IT and thinking skills in humanities

Peter Cunningham

General issues

Computer support for the learning of humanities in the classroom might in practice play quite a modest role. Information technology does not provide an appropriate solution for all learning situations, and thinking skills in the humanities will often be better developed by other means. But by reflecting on the nature of those thinking skills, and on the potentialities as well as the limitations of information technology, we can make better decisions about where and when to introduce the computer in teaching humanities in the primary classroom. IT will be most helpful where its use is sparing, selective and reflective.

In any case, the experienced classroom teacher is acutely aware of the practical constraints of working with one computer (or less!) to a classroom. Whilst keeping one eye on the future in a rapidly developing world, we need to consider the very uneven reality of school provision. The promised future of laptops and palmtops will of course extend the kinds of activities suggested below, but much of the software described below requires a good quality colour screen for best effect, and will only be applicable to the desktop machine shared by the whole class for the next few years at least. Sharing the hardware fairly will, as ever, be a significant organisational issue. It is an aspect of management, at the whole-school and classroom levels, in which the maximising of access through small group work, and the needs and attitudes of gender and ability groups must be considered.

We will be considering below some general software applicable to projects and tasks across the humanities. Word processing and desktop publishing programs, data-handling, and encyclopaedias on CD ROM will all have their place, and an important strategy is to use just one or two examples of each across the curriculum, so that children (and teacher!) have a chance to gain experience and become steadily more competent with familiar packages. There is also available in the market-place a huge range of dedicated software focusing on particular humanities topics, and the best advice here is to restrict the class to just a few items, with which everyone can become thoroughly familiar. However, the classroom computer is not the only site of IT. Intelligent and creative use of teletext can be made for information retrieval relevant to geography and religious education, and some excellent projects have exploited the fax machine as a means of communication with children and schools in distant lands.

It is positively valuable, as well as more realistic, to choose a single piece of software and study it closely, in order to become clear about the particular skills which it supports. For that reason, this chapter is as much about the thinking skills as about the programs available. Knowing exactly what a computer can and cannot do to support pupils' understanding and intellectual development starts with the fairly simple process of isolating a concept or skill within a humanities topic where the use, and *critical discussion* of a computer program will be positively beneficial.

Thinking skills in the humanities

Humanities as a curriculum area normally embraces geography, history and religious education. Both geography and history are identified as distinct subjects within the National Curriculum, and religious studies as a statutory requirement although outside the National Curriculum. All three seek to understand aspects of the society and environment in which children live, from the immediate family and local neighbourhood to the international and global context of human and physical geography. All are characterised by questions of value as well as of fact (Kimber *et al.* 1995). As a means to exploring these questions a range of skills needs to be harnessed. Least amenable to support from IT are perhaps the personal, moral and spiritual dimensions of religious studies. History and geography have overlapping concerns with time and place which computers can vividly support, but the relativities of time and place are also essential to many aspects of religious education.

Many of the issues about information technology are common to the teaching of all the humanities subjects. To avoid too superficial a treatment of all three, this chapter will draw its main examples from history, making cross-reference to the other humanities where appropriate. In its early form as a school subject, history entailed the memorising and regurgitation of quantities of data. Its essence lay in learning lists of kings and queens, acts and facts, that were considered essential to reinforcing children's sense of their national identity. Geography was alike in the emphasis on knowledge to be acquired and facts to be stored but here the data were countries and commodities, capes and bays. RE too could come debilitatingly close to the memorising of sacred texts and religious events.

It is less the development of information technology itself, than the changing nature of these three subjects, at all levels but especially in the education of young children, that makes computer skills so essential now to children's learning in the humanities. Developments in the nature of history and geography predate the invention of the microcomputer. This is a key point to remember, as we are arguing not for exploiting humanities in the extension of IT skills (which might be a different set of arguments), so much as identifying the areas where IT specifically enhances acquisition of thinking skills essential to history, geography and RE (Bastide 1992, Blyth 1994, Cooper 1995, Copley 1994, Marsden and Hughes 1994, Wiegand 1993). On the other hand, it has to be recognised that electronic storage and rapid retrieval of information has contributed significantly to the redundancy of memorising procedures. Of course memory still needs to be trained, but the fact that so much detail is instantly accessible through printed and electronic media helps also to re-order our priorities in learning.

Thinking processes in both history and geography entail a combination of 'science' and 'art', and in this respect the ways in which information technology can support them are very diverse. For example, social and economic history can entail the collection and manipulation of statistical data, as can human geography or the study of weather. But social history and human geography, like religious studies, also require the handling of qualitative data, personal experiences and subjective judgements. In the recording and understanding of these IT will play a very different and perhaps a more limited role. Geography skills to be supported by IT were authoritatively classified some years back on the eve of the National Curriculum orders as 'data-handling and analysis', 'decision-making and problem-solving' and 'discussion and presentation of information' (Geographical Association and NCET 1989). More recently Kent and Phillips have specified additionally 'modelling', 'measurement and control' and 'evaluating geographical effects of IT' (Kent and Phillips 1994). We will concentrate, for the purposes of this chapter, on the concepts and skills specified in National Curriculum requirements for history, bearing in mind that these relate in many respects to the intellectual demands of geography and RE.

Attention to learning objectives and thinking skills in the humanities predated the National Curriculum by twenty years (Bruner 1966) but the statutory orders have given statutory endorsement to a conviction that the critical processes of understanding are what is important. In the geography and history orders, however, the relationship of content to skills is presented in contrasting ways, and it will assist our thinking in depth about history, to compare formats of the Key Stage 1 and Key Stage 2 requirements of the two subjects at the outset.

In the geography programmes of study at Key Stage 1 and Key Stage 2 development of skills is listed first, with the emphasis that these skills are acquired through investigating places and themes. The general skills are observing, questioning, recording and communicating, and in the course of these pupils should be taught specifically to use geographical terms, to use instruments for measurement, follow directions and use plans and maps (including the making of their own), as well as using secondary sources of information. In these contexts, various IT applications will immediately spring to mind, but the geography programmes of study are more emphatic and more specific than those in history when it comes to IT. At Key Stage 1 CD ROM is given as one *example* (and therefore not statutory) of secondary sources that children might use to develop their geographical skills, whilst at Key Stage 2 IT enters the statutory part of the text as an information source and a means of 'handling, classifying and presenting evidence'.

In history, by contrast, though the 'Common Requirements' of the programmes of study refer, as for other National Curriculum subjects, to 'opportunities, where appropriate, to develop and apply . . . IT capability', the specific reference to IT sources at Key Stage 1 which had earlier appeared in the 1991 history order was dropped in 1995. Even at Key Stage 2 the kinds of historical evidence listed no longer include specific mention of IT as a medium by which historical evidence may be accessible.

In the published form of the 1995 revision of National Curriculum history requirements, the relative priorities of skills and knowledge were implicitly reversed to counter what conservative critics had seen as an undue emphasis on skills, potentially divorced from the context of historical information. So the programmes of study at both Key Stage 1 and Key Stage 2 are now set out in print with Areas of Study (Key Stage 1) or Study Units (Key Stage 2), preceding Key Elements, which define the skills entailed in learning history. The history order insists that content and Key Elements 'should be taught together', and that the Key Elements are closely related to, and should be developed through the Areas of Study or Study Units'. However it is these 'Key Elements', including historical *knowledge*, which form the basis of assessment criteria offered in the Level Descriptions of the 1995 order.

In the course of teaching about various periods and aspects of the past we have to encourage in children the development of skills and concepts listed within the Key Elements at both Key Stage 1 and Key Stage 2. These are designated as:

1 chronology
2a historical knowledge
2b cause and effect

3 interpretation
4 evidence
5 historical communication

More simply put, and in a more logical order, these Key Elements answer the questions: 'What happened?' (KE 2a historical knowledge), 'When did it happen?' (KE 1), 'Why did it happen?' (KE 2b cause and effect), 'How do we know?' (KE 4 evidence) 'Can we rely on historians' accounts?' (KE 3 interpretation) and 'How do we set about giving our own historical account?' (KE 5 historical communication). The thinking skills entailed will be dealt with below in that order. In some of these areas IT might significantly contribute to the extension of particular thinking skills and in others it might at best only tangentially support pupils' learning.

Historical knowledge

The most obvious application of recent developments in information technology is the provision of extensive secondary sources through the medium of CD

ROM. Several examples of the increasingly abundant titles available are listed in the Appendix of Software, some of these being specifically historical and others more general works of reference. In the not-too-distant future these sources will also be available on-line in many primary schools through the Internet. Encyclopaedic compilations of information can be searched more extensively and more rapidly than in any conventionally printed work through the use of key words, and the data can include pictures and statistics as well as text, which can be selected, downloaded into a pupil's own file, edited and printed out. Some criticisms of poor humanities teaching used to focus on the mindless copying out of chunks of text; a disadvantage of the new technology is that in bypassing the manual copy, even a mindless reading of the text may be curtailed!

Teachers need to remember and pupils need frequently to be reminded that, like any published book, information gained through IT will be the product of selection and interpretation, and in the manner of electronic media, authorship may be even less immediately apparent than has traditionally been the case with printed books. Learning to question and to be sceptical of information from any source is an essential skill in the study of history, and we shall revisit it below under the heading of 'interpretation'. (See also Chapter 11 for a discussion of the appropriate use of electronic sources.)

There are, however, more interactive ways in which knowledge may be acquired through the medium of the computer. Historical information, along with chronology, can be well supported by the versatile device of the concept keyboard. This is a flat board in A3 or A4 format which contains a grid of keys; a drawn overlay can be laid over the board and the keys programmed to relay information to the computer. In the case of one piece of software, a ready-made street plan is drawn and touching the numbered houses will convey the function of the building found there as it changed across three periods of time. Here is an ideal opportunity, in the context of a local study, for children to explore the changes that have occurred in a local street or local area, over a period of time. The software is sufficiently accessible and user-friendly to allow the teacher to set up the necessary overlays and information for children to examine the history of one of their own local streets through the medium of the keyboard. As a more advanced exercise, in Years 5 or 6, the children themselves can make use of the program to record and communicate their own research on such a theme. Important here, in developing historical thinking, is that the work on computer *follows* work 'in the field'; computerised information has to be understood as a diagrammatic representation of historical evidence that the children have examined and conceptualised at first hand, both in the form of the landscape itself, and of old maps or street directories, which will give some indication of how the landscape or street has changed over time. These printed sources are generally easy to locate in local libraries and record offices, and can be photocopied for use in the classroom.

This kind of task on the overlay keyboard may focus effectively on change over time, and the pace of change can be explored according to the number of dates at which the streetscape or landscape is explored. For a street plan, the software and accompanying documentation provides a model overlay, and adapting this to a local street plan prepared by the teacher is an easy task. At a more sophisticated level of mapping, ordnance survey maps on various scales can be used as overlays to be programmed by teacher or by pupils. Touching any detail on the map would produce on the screen information about the origins, development and perhaps disappearance over time of features such as buildings, canals, railways and roads.

The outcomes in terms of 'thinking skills' will include attitudes such as confidence and motivation in information retrieval. These attitudes can be developed through the use of books and printed materials, too, but undoubtedly the computer will motivate some children and the sense of empowerment which can be gained through accessing quantities of information can be sensitively developed so that teachers should observe a growing confidence even among children initially intimidated by IT.

Understanding chronology

Chronology involves an understanding of time on a historical scale, the use of dates and technical terms to describe the passing of historical time, and the ability to place objects and events in historical sequence. Understanding history requires developing a sense of past time. This may seem obvious but is nonetheless complicated. For most adults looking back, the horror of school history lay in memorising dates, and certainly this exercise was of dubious value. We use many chronological concepts in everyday conversation: 'ancient' and 'modern' are loose terms in most adults' vocabulary, yet many of us would be hard put to sequence correctly the Roman, Viking and Norman settlements of Britain.

In the teaching of history, children's understanding of chronology has frequently been taken for granted as a concept which might be expected to emerge as the children accumulated knowledge of different eras. It is now a matter of general consensus, reflected in National Curriculum requirements, that children can be helped to acquire a more structured view of the past. Research on children's historical understanding has shown a clear developmental sequence in the understanding of historical time, and some of this research has identified the use of the timeline in developing their understanding (Cooper 1995).

Timelines can be of the 'low-tech' variety, and indeed there is a strong case that they should be so in the earliest stages. The living timeline is great fun: children, each bearing a picture of some historic object, or large card with a date or time-phrase (such as 'last century', 'medieval' or 'prehistoric') can sort themselves out to stand in a properly sequenced line. The co-operation and dialogue involved in this exercise is demanding and constructive. 'Intermediate technology' is introduced with the string or washing-line and pictures or cards suspended with safety pins or clothes-pegs. The essence of all this is that pictures of objects, dates or chronological terms can be continually arranged and rearranged, in a straight sequence or according to a given scale, with new items introduced and inserted as the timeline develops.

For the 'high-tech' timeline, computer technology is ideally suited, and software has been developed which assists the task at various levels of sophistication. Two notable examples are listed in the Appendix of Software. In each of these there is the opportunity for individual children or classes to create a timeline on the computer. This consists of a central line of dates either side of which may be assorted symbols and titles to represent different kinds of event, with more detailed pockets of information and pictures which can be accessed by a click of the mouse. The kinds of event may be put into various categories such as 'social', 'economic', 'political'. A ready-made timeline of events for a given period will be available, to which individual children or groups of children may add entries with text and possibly with pictures.

The timeline can be progressively built up as relevant information is acquired and sorted, and the timeline then shown in a variety of scales and detail. One limitation of the computer is the impossibility of getting a clear overview on screen of the whole sequence; small sections of the timeline can be inspected, but an overview requires making a print-out. On the other hand, the possibilities of building up a large database, of editing and extending at will and of having thirty or so personalised versions easily stored and re-used, are all distinct advantages offered by the computer.

At Key Stage 1, topics relating to 'ourselves' offer a golden opportunity to begin exploring historical time and sequence in a structured way. A simple timeline of the five or six years of individuals' lives can be prepared, with details such as the ages at which playgroup, nursery or school were begun, sisters or brothers born, pets acquired or deceased (or, in developmental terms, skills acquired such as walking and learning to tie shoelaces). Simple dates in family history over one generation can provide an extension of this, with some appropriate data researched by the child herself, such as the birthdates of parents and older siblings, and family events such as house moves (though sensitive handling here is required on the part of the teacher). Using a chronological database, this personal information can be stored and printed out in the format of a continuous timeline.

Progressing to the study units of Key Stage 2, this personal family timeline can be developed by linking to public events in 'Britain since 1930' (Study Unit 3b). The format will allow for parallel sequences of, say, public and personal events, or events classified according to type: pupils might be asked to research parents' recollections of both personal events (weddings, house moves, holidays) and public events such as cultural phenomena (pop groups, sports events), technological advance (major achievements in space exploration, the development of microelectronics) or political crises (wars, changes of government). The public events can be further researched in works of reference and incorporated into their timelines. Timelines for other study units can cover a long time-scale, for example going back from the present to prehistoric times, or can cover a discrete period like the century of the Tudors or of the Victorians in a much more detailed way.

Such activity helps to establish in a visual, graphic and flexible way, concepts of decades and centuries, and the sequence and pace of change in different fields. Pupils can move from 'decades' to 'centuries' and on to incorporating 'millennia' on their timelines. In particular, the initially confusing way in which we label centuries can be graphically illustrated by a timeline. So too can the relationship of year dates AD (anno domini) or CE (common era), which simply increase as time moves on, to those BC (before Christ) or BCE (before the common era) which, confusingly, decrease as time progresses. In scanning through the time-line on screen, and printing out on paper, children will reinforce and internalise their understanding of this difficult concept.

Individuals or small groups can be directed to construct their own timelines based on continuous research about the era being studied. Specific issues will then arise which may need discussion. Some historical events such as the first successful powered flight or the discovery of penicillin, are easy to identify by a single date. But historically more significant dates, and less easy to identify precisely, might be the commercial development of air transport and the impact of the general use of antibiotics on public health. Published timelines in the software packages do not always make it easy to read this distinction between single historical events and longer-term processes. Some dates are contested – such as the creation of the first teddy bear. Other historical events, such as wars or reigns, are continuous, and have a beginning and end, while significant dates in the lives of notable people of humble or obscure origin might be a matter for conjecture, as in the case of Mary Seacole, the 'Caribbean Florence Nightingale'. In these instances children will have to make decisions about where to locate events on their timeline. The great value of computers is the ease with which a timeline can be edited, changed and corrected; print-outs of a timeline as it develops should be frequently made, discussed and compared.

Some historical adventure games incidentally incorporate use of timelines as a way of reinforcing this skill. These timelines cannot usually be edited or added to, but their repeated use reinforces familiarity with the sequence of dates. However the groundwork for a firm understanding of timelines as a representation of historical chronology will need to have been laid by more dedicated tasks of the kind described above. We need to be clear about the interrelated skills for children of reading timelines and of constructing their own. Both activities are necessary.

Outcomes are measured in children's accurate use and understanding of time phrases and dates, in their ability to order events over an increasing timescale, and in their increasing confidence with chronological problems of the kind referred to above. From a practical point of view children are more likely to demonstrate these outcomes through other media than IT, but computers remain one means amongst others to develop the skill.

Handling evidence

Historical enquiry involves learning to look closely at, and ask questions of, different kinds of historical source material, such as buildings, oral reminiscence, pictures and music, and documents. 'History is on your doorstep.' 'History is all around you.' Good history teaches children to be aware of, and how to recognise, the evidence of the past in their own environment. This process securely grounded, precedes the more sophisticated critical handling of evidence, including documentary sources, though relatively little hard research is available on this aspect of learning (Davis 1986, Hodgkinson 1986, Shawyer *et al.* 1988). Dealing at first hand with evidence, using historical sources, is arguably the most crucial of all the intellectual skills that are developed through history, and certainly the most enjoyable for children. And it is here that the computer is perhaps at its least adequate.

Understanding of historical evidence should begin with realia or artefacts, which children can examine with all their senses. At the simplest level, an old tin sandwich box can be compared with Tupperware or cling-film, a mechanical meat mincer contrasted with an electric food processor, a quill or fountain pen with a ball-point pen, a chalkboard with a whiteboard. Such contrasts initially test the children's powers of observation and accurate description through the spoken word or through drawing. We then proceed to engage their powers of deduction: what do the observed differences tell us about change over time, change in technology and in the effects of technology on people's lives?

We can progress from objects in the home or in the classroom environment to objects in museums. And we can apply the same skills of observation and deduction to larger-scale evidence such as street-furniture and buildings. Information technology simply cannot substitute for this process. The scale of objects, three-dimensionality and colour, the 'feel' and even the smell of objects, can provide important clues to the past, and are highly stimulating features for children to investigate. None of this direct experience is available through a monitor screen. The magic of seeing and even touching a solid object which was handled and used by real people in the past literally 'puts you in touch' with history in an awesome way – equivalent to the 'aesthetic shock' of viewing a Monet original which no reproduction could ever evoke.

Through well-planned and consistent work with artefacts, motivation and curiosity will be established, and more important, a knowledge of what questions to ask of objects, and how to deduce answers. However, growing familiarity with three-dimensional evidence at first hand allows the application of those skills to two-dimensional representations. This is a necessary progression as the artefactual evidence for, say, ancient Egypt or the Aztecs may not be readily available even in a local museum. Postcards and illustrated books are useful sources, but the problem for teachers often lies in identifying these with speed and efficiency. There is also sometimes the problem of providing them in sufficient quantity.

At this point, the accessing of images through IT becomes a valuable resource for the teacher. These may be still images in enormous quantity, or video clips and audio sources relating to more recent times. Computer graphics at classroom level have until recently provided very poor pictures of objects, and this is a valid criticism of many otherwise quite good programs. But VGA is now greatly improving the quality of images available. The problem of quantity is solved by CD ROM discs, which can carry vast numbers of images. Moreover the three-dimensionality of objects can be represented on CD ROM through video clips.

The use of CD ROM as a reference tool for historical images also becomes a useful and a realistic context for introducing children to information storage and retrieval systems. The best of the CDs will have good indexing systems which assist children in the task of searching for and selecting appropriate, relevant historical sources, as well as supporting explanatory text. These are specially prepared multimedia databases which juxtapose images, text, video and sound to give a sense of the evidence in historical context. Others are simply large databases from photographic archives which require far more support and information from the teacher, since the captions do not provide very full or consistent documentation to put the evidence in a historical context. These are less likely to be useful for direct use by children, except for the most able, at Key Stage 2, but may well provide a useful resource for the teacher in preparing teaching materials.

With documentary evidence, similar considerations apply as those discussed in relation to visual evidence. Nothing on the computer screen can replace the sensual delight of looking at old books for example. Documentary evidence is a surprisingly neglected source at Key Stage 1, and infant teachers could be encouraged to ransack jumble sales, charity shops and even perhaps the school stock cupboard for children's books that may be thirty, forty or fifty years old. How are these different from new books, and what does that tell us about changes in technology of paper-making, printing and binding? Why do they smell differently? What do the signs of wear and tear tell us about how the books have been used, and is there any evidence of who their owners were? And what do the differences and similarities in types and style of story and illustrations tell us about continuity and change in the tastes of their readers? Developed reading skills are not needed for this task, whilst books are a very familiar medium for most young children. At Key Stage 2, reading an original old newspaper that was once handled by a reader long dead, or a census return as written up by the tireless enumerator who plodded from house to house, is an important dimension to the historical experience.

Once a specific historical context for the document is established, when it comes simply to reading documents for historical information, the reproduction in photocopy, microfiche – or on disk, may be equally useful. The quantity and convenience of documentation stored in this way is clear, and again CD ROM is now making this form far more accessible. Large databases of, say, census material covering an entire locality over several decades would be one example. Some of the information may be input photographically to disk and appear on the screen in its original format, in copperplate handwriting for example; or else the data may have been transcribed and input from the keyboard. In original form, children may be faced with the challenge of deciphering earlier forms of handwriting or printing.

The skills in reading the historical content will apply to documents in reproduction as much as to the originals. Who was the author, and how was the information collected? Who was the intended audience? How reliable is the information – is it likely to be inaccurate or biased for any reason? And how relevant is the information for pursuing the sort of investigation in which we are interested? What the computer can offer is readier and more convenient access for a large class of children.

The outcomes in respect of children's ability to understand pictorial and documentary evidence can be assessed by inviting them to write 'picture captions' and 'museum labels'. Such captions can be interactive, asking questions to promote reflection in the spectator, or speculative, suggesting ideas about the object which may not be easily verifiable. This is an assessment not only of information acquired, but of the ability to evaluate the significance of a particular object, to select appropriately from the supplementary information available and to ask relevant questions or put forward reasonable hypotheses. Needless to say, these tasks can be done on disk. The likelihood is that shortage of hardware and other classroom constraints will dictate a more traditional medium, but computer print-outs may be useful, providing documents for the task.

Statistical data are a more abstract form of historical evidence than artefacts, pictures and documents, but statistics represent hundreds and thousands of real-life situations of individuals who lived in the past. Size of families, rates of mortality and school attendance figures, for example, represent the real-life circumstances of people. For this reason, the computer is an unsatisfactory means of *introduction* to historical statistics. Children should begin by collecting their own historical data, for example from gravestones in a local churchyard or from reproductions of original documents such as census enumerators' returns, which are available for the decennial census of the later nineteenth century from local record offices or local history collections. The obvious benefits of IT lie in storing and handling this data, but for their historical understanding children need first to understand the relationship between the data and what it represents. The analytical tasks of representing correlations in the form of bar charts, histograms or pie charts can be well performed by the computer, and will reinforce concepts developed in mathematics, but the tasks set for children to do must have a real historical purpose and not be sorting and calculating for its own sake.

It is therefore critical to think carefully about the kinds of question pupils are set to answer from statistical data. From a practical as well as an educational point of view, we have to be cautious about the amount of time spent gathering and recording statistical data in history. Though it is important for children to discover some of the problems which may arise, with perhaps incomplete or inconsistent sources (house numbering in Victorian census data is a notorious example), the time required to input large amounts of data is often not cost-effective in terms of children's learning. Some excellent ready-made databases have been published, and examples are given in the Appendix of Software. Obviously, some important historical explanations can be investigated through the correlation of statistics, such as the decline in infant mortality and reduction in size of families, or figures for school attendance and growth of literacy. As an outcome of children's understanding of historical statistics, tasks can be set in the manipulation of data, the presentation of histograms or pie charts, which computer technology is aptly fitted to assist. But as we shall see in the next section, the contribution to considering cause and effect comes from the nature and quality of the questions raised, and the discussion which is stimulated by the manipulation and presentation of statistical evidence.

Cause and effect, and interpretation

At a popular level, much of the interest in history lies in a kind of collective nostalgia about our relatively recent past, and a delight in exotic aspects of the past that were so different from present society. A popular fascination with the circumstances of life in the Second World War, such as the experience of aerial bombardment or evacuation, or with the new prosperity and cultural trends of the 1950s and 1960s offers the possibility of contextualising 'folk memory' handed down in the family: validating and putting flesh on the anecdotes of what children's own parents or grandparents were doing at the time. Equally children can be excited by more distant and exotic ideas of rampant and fatal disease, as in the Plague or the Black Death, that are so starkly contrasted to their own personal experiences of late twentieth century life (though by no means absent from the late twentieth-century world), or by rituals such as per-forming naked in the Olympic Games of Ancient Greece, and mummification of the dead in ancient Egypt that appear such strange customs to modern British sensibilities.

For serious historians this fascination with the dimly familiar or the quaintly different may frequently be a starting point, but it is the question 'why?' – the puzzle of causation and the need for explanation – that motivates their curiosity. The intellectual challenge of history is continually trying to explain *why* things happened as they did. And this is often at the root of differences of interpretation. Achieving accurate reconstructions from past evidence may be one aspect of interpretation – deciding, for example, what an Anglo-Saxon hut or a Greek trireme really looked like. But the most contentious differences of interpretation arise from arguments about the causes of events: *Why* did the Aztecs engage in human sacrifice? *Why* did Britain acquire an empire in the nineteenth century?

As young children acquire historical knowledge, we want them to appreciate relevance, to see that some facts may be more significant than others, to look for patterns in the development of human affairs. Here, at first sight, IT may be less helpful, and this is a point at which we confront the limitations of the computer in the classroom. An understanding of causality is acquired above all through engagement in live discourse, argument, the sharing and opposition of ideas. Much of this argument is bound to involve both rational and emotional responses to the phenomena that we are trying to explain. It is not beyond the competence of the computer, any more than other communication devices such as books or radio, to present us with alternative explanations and to invite speculation, even to engage in dialogue. But the application of artificial intelligence at the classroom level does not yet provide a substitute for the sensitive and well-informed teacher thrashing out ideas with her pupils.

One trap lies in the apparent authority of computer-based resources in an age dominated by information technology. Where, in the past, uncritical deference may have been accorded, say, to academic authorship or to the 'quality' press, we may now be inclined to trust uncritically in the information presented by computers. There is evidence to show that pupils' judgements were coloured by the assumption that CD ROM, and even more the Internet, must be so comprehensive as to present all there was to be known on a given topic. It is this mentality that the inclusion of 'interpretation' as a thinking skill in history is designed to challenge.

Interpretation of history entails developing children's understanding that the past may be represented in a variety of ways. Some stimulus to thinking about problems of interpretation can be gained through a critical use of simulation programs, the most widely available genre and the most variable in quality. Simulations are obviously designed to reinforce other key elements such as historical knowledge – the key features of historical periods – at the same time as motivating children in their enquiry. But by discussing these programs after children have worked with them, and by making comparisons and contrasts with the information found in books, this type of software can also serve another purpose. Towards the end of Key Stage 2 we can begin to encourage children to look critically at computer simulations as one form of representation or *interpretation* of past societies, alongside other 'secondary sources' such as books written in modern times and films or videos made about earlier civilisations.

When discussing computer simulations, as we should, with the whole class or with small groups, we should bombard children with questions such as 'How authentic?' and 'What's missing?', and comparisons can be encouraged with other representations such as books and films. Of course children, and teachers too, may lack sufficient evidence to reach authoritative conclusions, but it is the readiness to question, the state of mind, that is important. Computer simulations can be a good stimulus to this sort of questioning precisely because they can so readily appear convincing to children.

Outcomes will be measured not in children's ability to manipulate the simulations, but in the additional information that they have derived, and in their readiness to discuss the programs critically. As teachers we can monitor and record the selectivity and scepticism which pupils apply to knowledge acquired and interpretations received. Their oral and written accounts will habitually be prefaced with qualifications like 'as far as I can tell from what I have seen', or 'according to the accounts or interpretations we have been given'.

Communication

Another vital skill for the humanities is organising and communicating information, using appropriate modes of language and technical vocabulary. The skill of 'communication' in geography, history and RE clearly has much in common with communication across the curriculum, but there are aspects of the skill particular to historical study. Official recognition of this fact has wavered during the short career of National Curriculum history. It was originally one of the proposed attainment targets, but dropped from the statutory order of 1991 only to reappear in the post-Dearing settlement of 1995 as Key Element 5: 'Organisation and Communication'. This Key Element has three subsections, of which one has much in common with the general principle of language across the curriculum, and with the range of writing modes that are specifically required within the English order. It is that pupils should be taught 'to communicate their knowledge and understanding of history in a variety of ways, including structured narratives and descriptions'.

A useful and motivating pretext for 'structured narratives and descriptions' is provided by the task of writing a historical newspaper, containing accounts of events. This provides the ideal platform for collaborative group-work in which individual children can contribute pieces of writing, maps, illustrations and so on, produced according to their own level of ability, and contribute to a finished product of which the whole group can be proud. Imaginary eyewitness views of events and critical comment in the form of editorials can be produced, while the making of drawings, or the selection and editing of images chosen to illustrate an account, and the captions written to accompany the illustrations, will all require the application of another aspect of this key element: to recall, select and organise historical information, including dates and terms.

At Key Stage 2, newspapers as a context for writing have particular value in Study Unit 3a 'Victorian Britain', or Study Unit 3b 'Britain since 1930', where contemporary newspapers from the period can be studied (in reproduction) as primary sources, and children can imitate the stylistic features of these originals. For earlier periods, so long as we make it very clear that the newspaper is an anachronism, that people in Tudor times or in ancient Greece did not use this form of communication, we can still produce a newspaper or magazine in modern form as the medium for reporting our historical discoveries.

It is here that the computer provides a valuable tool for desktop publishing. The quality of the finished product is important for children's pride in their work, the possibilities for drafting and subsequent correction and amendment of text and layout gives flexibility, and of course the ability to produce multiple copies for each of the contributors, and for their parents and friends outside the class is a further attraction of the medium. The program 'Front Page Extra', in what now appears as a very primitive form of DTP has for more than a decade given thousands of children the experience of making a historical newspaper, but software now available offers the opportunity to produce a very satisfying and sophisticated looking end product using quite user-friendly techniques. Some examples are listed in the Appendix of Software. Moreover the introduction of CD ROM enables the child historian to draw on a lot of historical information, text and images and to exercise choice and judgement in the selection of these.

This task can be carried out using scissors and paste (with generous help from the photocopier), but the possibilities of reviewing and editing are central to refining the process of historical interpretation. In addition, the quality of the finished product is highly motivating. It is of course crucial that, in learning to manipulate the technology, children are using this as a means to an end: the development of the historical concepts discussed above in the juxtaposition and manipulation of text and images to convey a historical account and interpretation. Multimedia technology holds exciting possibilities, already realised in some schools, for inclusion of moving images and sound in children's own compilations. (Also see Chapters 8 and 11.)

Conclusion

The foregoing survey may well feel exhausting – it is by no means exhaustive! There is much available software, some dedicated to history and some not, which will genuinely assist children in the development of thinking skills essential to the understanding of history. Its use must be *sparing*; force of circumstances and shortage of equipment may ensure this, but the proper rationale is that there are so many rich first-hand experiences to be provided away from the computer screen, for children learning history. *Selectivity* is the second criterion; from all the software available, some of it quite cheap, choose just one or two programs and seek to exploit their potential in a variety of ways, rather than playing the whole field. Finally, be *reflective*. The vital element, both for reinforcement of the learning objectives and for assessment of educational outcomes, is discussion: discussion of the historical concepts and discussion of the ways in which the technology has helped or hindered us. Turn the computer off and talk!

Chapter 6

Investigating science

Linda Webb

Introduction

When I asked a primary teacher recently how she felt about using spreadsheets in her science work, she responded with the comment, 'Well, it's just natural, isn't it?' As a science graduate and science co-ordinator she felt that using spreadsheets was very similar to the way results are usually tabulated, manipulated and displayed in a science experiment. In the same week I asked a group of primary teachers attending an in-service science course if any had used spreadsheets in their normal classroom work. Of the twenty teachers on the course only one (the teacher referred to at the beginning) said 'Yes'! This corroborates informal data collected from trainee primary teachers, who report that little IT, let alone spreadsheets, is being used in primary science.

So why is this apparently 'natural' means of handling data so little used? In this chapter I shall outline some arguments in support of the use of spreadsheets, and discuss why they may not be being used, referring in doing so to relevant literature; finally I will describe two case-studies of classroom practice.

Reasons why spreadsheets are a useful tool

Some pointers to the advantages of using spreadsheets in primary science emerge from this paragraph by Southall (1992: 10):

> From the point of view of data handling in schools, the availability of a cheap, small computer means that pupils can use it to collect their data directly on location; this eliminates the usual intermediate stage of recording observations on paper. Direct entry can cut down errors; it can also let pupils interrogate the data on the spot. This may result in them making an early discovery and prompt them to collect further or different data and to test out a hypothesis.

Although this was not written specifically about science many readers will immediately recognise this as the practice that we aim for in primary science, thus showing how IT can support investigational work. In this section I shall consider the development of investigational work in primary science, the growth of interest in using spreadsheet software in science, and then how these two come together within the National Curriculum. Finally I shall consider support materials for the use of spreadsheets in primary science.

Practical and investigative work in science

As Paul Black (1993) argues, one of the main purposes of science education is 'learning about science'; one of the functions of schools is to be the guardians and transmitters of a society's culture, science being a very important part of that culture. He goes on to say, 'It involves learning about the concepts and methods which are combined in scientific enquiry' and 'A first essential is that students should come to understand science and to understand how science is made by being engaged in doing it', also arguing that the experience of science that school learning gives should be authentic. Not surprisingly, then, this notion of 'doing science' is now enshrined in the National Curriculum under 'Experimental and investigative science' and that performance in this area counts for 50 per cent of the assessment at Key Stages 1 and 2

Since Armstrong introduced his 'heuristic' method in the late nineteenth-century, practical science has waxed and waned in popularity. (See Layton (1973) for a fuller description.) The introduction of Nuffield science in the 1960s as a reaction to the recipe-style experiments of previous decades was a breath of fresh air, but not without its problems. Its underlying principle of 'I do and I learn' obtained by the pupil experiencing 'being a scientist for a day' owed more to gut feelings than to a study of cognitive psychology or philosophy of science. Indeed as Ros Driver (1981) pointed out, it was more often a case of 'I do and I am even more confused'. So although the Nuffield initiatives introduced a great deal of innovative practical work into the science curriculum its 'discovery' methods, which were to guide the student to pre-determined conclusions, became largely discredited (Woolnough and Allsop 1985).

In primary schools there was a move away from the 'nature table' approach to a broader agenda of interesting topics, but the 1980s saw a change to an emphasis on the processes and skills of science, particularly through the work of the APU (Assessment of Performance Unit). Some teaching schemes appeared that concentrated solely on process skills, with the severe reduction of specific topic knowledge. Despite all the initiatives, however, science remained a minority subject in primary schools until the Education Reform Act of 1988.

The move to more genuine investigation had its origins in an HMI report in 1960, which advocated that pupils should carry out personal investigations as part of their laboratory work. In this report, *Science 5–16: A Statement of Policy*, published in 1985, this notion was further supported by the statement, 'The balance in practical work should be more towards solving problems and less towards illustrating previously taught theory.' Some four years later the importance of investigational work in science was recognised by its incorporation into the National Curriculum for science, where it has remained, with some modifications, throughout the various revisions. Although this assumed model of scientific method is open to debate (Jenkins 1995) it is, nevertheless, a genuine attempt to make 'doing science' as real and relevant as possible. In addition, whatever psychological theory of learning is in vogue, there is no doubt that young children do learn a great deal from 'concrete' experiences, and that well-thought-out and structured investigational science does aid learning about science.

Developments in IT and spreadsheet usage

Alongside these curriculum changes in science there have been dramatic changes in Information Technology. The introduction of IT into the primary schools is described elsewhere in this book (see Chapter 1), so I shall confine my comments to data-handling within primary science.

From the early 1980s a number of books have been published about the use of IT in primary schools, but the reference to data-handling is extremely patchy, and references to science and, in particular, spreadsheet use is almost non-existent. In 1984 Terry said about computers in general,

> The computer is a machine which excels at rapid, accurate calculation and information handling, and is a very suitable means of reducing the inauthentic labour in the learning process, supporting the pupil by providing him with facilities for calculation, information retrieval and so on.
>
> (Terry 1984: 35)

In Crompton's (1989) book there is very little reference to data-handling or science, whereas Anita Straker (1989) does pay more attention to data-handling. She describes how content-free software provides a flexible tool for children and teachers: 'It can be a fast retriever and sorter of information allowing children to carry out research, to pose and to test hypotheses, using a far greater collection of data than they would otherwise have been able to manage.' Certainly the skills she refers to here are essential for the study of science.

From 1987 articles about spreadsheets began to appear (Beare 1992, Brosnan 1989, Elliott 1988, Goodfellow 1990, Osborn 1987, and Webb 1993) but these were generally aimed at the enthusiast (mainly in secondary education) and involved detailed descriptions about how to enter the data and what formulae to set up to do the calculations, with less emphasis on the specific learning gains such exercises might facilitate. Despite the introduction of data-handling software specifically aimed at the primary school (Keeling 1987) the potential for the use of spreadsheets was still not widely appreciated. In a chapter about data-handling Southall outlines all the educational benefits of using a computer for data-handling. Whilst he does not specifically refer to spreadsheets, all of his perceived benefits apply to this means of data-handling. Briefly, the benefits of data-handling software that he outlines are:

- It provides an environment for the development of problem-solving skills.
- It provides opportunities for children to develop communication skills and information handling skills.
- It broadens learning styles.
- It encourages the development of higher level competencies.

> The speed and flexibility of the computer makes certain tedious tasks easier to perform. Data can be selected, ordered and transformed into histograms, bar charts, and pie charts quickly and easily. This frees children to concentrate their attention on the higher level skills of analysis, interpretation, synthesis and prediction.
>
> (Southall 1992: 10)

Yet in his book Southall makes no reference to spreadsheets and very little reference to science.

Even more recently a book by Jerry Wellington (Scaife and Wellington 1993), an expert and well-known writer about IT in science, could only manage to write a chapter of one and a half pages about spreadsheets! Harris (1994), in a very informative article in *School Science Review* describes how IT could be used in primary science. Until this article appeared little attention had been paid to the potential for using spreadsheets within primary science.

Nevertheless the role of IT in science had been recognised and in the original version of the National Curriculum (DES 1989) Attainment Target 12 was solely devoted to IT, although many of the statements of attainment related to the *study* of microelectronics and computer technologies, rather than the use of IT. This profile was not so high in subsequent versions, but has always appeared in some guise or other. In the next section I shall go on to consider how spreadsheets can be used to support and enhance work in experimental and investigative science.

Experimental and investigative science in the National Curriculum

At both Key Stages 1 and 2 in the National Curriculum (1995) the Programme of study states that pupils should be given opportunities to:

- use focused exploration and investigation to acquire scientific knowledge, understanding and skills;
- use IT to collect, store, retrieve and present scientific information;
- present scientific information in a number of ways, through drawings, diagrams, tables and charts, and in speech and writing (Key Stage 1), or use a wide range of methods, including diagrams, drawings, graphs, tables and charts, to record and present information in an appropriate and systematic manner (Key Stage 2).

Table 6.1 shows the teaching objectives required by the National Curriculum listed under 'Experimental and investigative science'.

Table 6.1 The teaching objectives for National Curriculum 'Experimental and investigative science'

Key Stage 1	Key Stage 2
to make a record of observations and measurement	
to use drawings, tables and bar charts to present results	to use tables, bar charts and line graphs to present results
to make simple comparisons	to make comparisons and to identify trends or patterns in results
	to use results to draw conclusions
to indicate whether the evidence collected supports any prediction made	
to try to explain what they found out, drawing on their knowledge and understanding	to try to explain conclusions in terms of scientific knowledge and understanding

The spreadsheet, with its array of cells arranged in rows and columns, allows the pupils to collect and present their data in tables in exactly the same way as they would do in their own notebooks. Once the data have been entered into the spreadsheet they can be presented in a variety of graphical forms e.g. bar chart, pie chart, line and scatter-graphs. These can be used to identify any trends or relationships, and any further mathematical work can be done by building formulae into the worksheet (see Chapters 4 and 7).

You could argue that a database has the same graphing facilities as a spreadsheet and has many more sorting and retrieving facilities. However, for practical and investigative work in science I would recommend the spreadsheet in that the means of entering and tabulating the data is very close to the way in which scientists have traditionally collated their data, and that the wealth of mathematical operations that it is able to perform is invaluable.

The reader can now, I hope, begin to see that spreadsheets are a powerful tool that can enable children to:

• Record observations and measurements

   This will be in a clear tabulated scientific form. Averages, highest and lowest values, means and totals can be quickly calculated in the spreadsheet.

• Create bar charts, pie charts and line graphs

   Once the data have been highlighted these charts or graphs can be created in seconds, thus releasing the child from the drudgery of plotting graphs on graph paper. Any errors in data can be seen quickly and new data collected and inserted. If the graph is not in a useful form, a different one can be substituted from a chart gallery at the click of the mouse button.

- Use the data to make comparisons, identify trends and patterns
  Time freed by the instant graph plotting can be used more profitably to interpret the data. Furthermore, more calculations can be performed instantly to verify the trends and patterns identified.

So far in this discussion I have concentrated on the study of the subject 'science' rather than the pupils as individuals. Many children will quickly learn how to use a spreadsheet and be able to enter and manipulate their own data. For the slower learner, the spreadsheet can also be highly useful; the teacher could set up a template making it quite clear where the data should be entered. Formulae can be written into some cells so that arithmetic operations are performed automatically, and graphs can be set up so that a suitable graph is plotted as the data is entered into the computer. Thus the learner can concentrate on the more important aspects of data interpretation, rather than getting immersed in the laborious business of the arithmetic.

Support materials

Despite the lack of academic literature supporting the use of spreadsheets in science, there is an increasing amount of curriculum support material available. The National Council for Educational Technology regularly produces information sheets about all aspects of IT use in school. Its information sheet on spreadsheets (NCET 1995) explains clearly what a spreadsheet is and what it is good at, and reviews currently available packages. It also recommends the reading of further texts such as those by Flavell and Tebbutt (1994), Frost (1995) and NCET (1994b and 1994c).

Nevertheless, there is little evidence that spreadsheets are being used at all to support learning in primary science. I shall explore possible reasons for their lack of use in the next section.

Reasons why spreadsheets are not being used

In the introductory chapter to their book about computers in classrooms Beynon and Mackay (1993) consider the issues surrounding the introduction of computers into the classroom. They report on a study undertaken by Hall and Rhodes (1988) in six primary schools in inner London. They reported that 'several factors were identified that inhibited micro usage, amongst these being lack of appropriate training, access problems, dissatisfaction with software, and lack of convincing evidence that there are, in fact, educational benefits'. I shall consider those reasons and others that have been cited elsewhere. Although the reasons given by Beynon and Mackay refer to the general use of IT I think they are also relevant to spreadsheets. Some reasons overlap with others but I shall try to identify them all individually. Whatever the reason, I shall try to relate it to the specific use of spreadsheets.

1   Hardware

(a) *Number of machines*

In the primary school there is typically a computer in each classroom, small group work is the norm, thus one computer for a group would be a usual model to adopt.

(b) *Type of machine*

There is no question that the modern 32-bit machines enable spreadsheets to run much faster, and support much more sophisticated spreadsheet packages. These sophisticated packages bring their own problems, which I shall discuss later, but the simpler software that is available on the older machines can provide a useful introduction to graphing and other data-handling. They have sufficient power to handle the size of data set that young learners might collect, and perform all the mathematical functions they are likely to need.

2   Software

Certainly, putting data into the early spreadsheets was very time-consuming, for example in having to tell the computer what was text and what was data. When you eventually came to working with the data or plotting a graph you may have forgotten what was the original point of the experiment. As I said above, modern computers support very fast, sophisticated spreadsheet software, which overcome the deficiencies of the older machines but bring their own problems. Richard Beare (1992) explains that the most common spreadsheet programs were written for business use and have two main disadvantages:

(a) The sheer power of the software and the multitude of different things that can be done with it mean that much time must be spent in gaining familiarity with it before its true potential in the science classroom can be realised.

(b) The types of graph most commonly required in science are not as easily produced as those most commonly used in business.

His criticisms were with a secondary school science class in mind, so imagine just how more valid these criticisms would be in a primary context.

The major educational software developers have either designed their own software packages, or have produced scaled-down versions of the 'office' software for use in the primary classroom. For the real spreadsheet enthusiasts some of the loss of functionality might be irritating, but once they have learned the functions that the package does support they should be able to work comfortably within them. With these customised 'office' packages it is often possible to reveal different levels of functionality as the sophistication of the child's data-handling increases.

3 **Lack of confidence**
There are many reasons for teachers' lack of confidence in using IT; some are considered below:

(a) *Using the hardware and software, which may be unreliable*
This can only be improved by familiarity. The evidence of the portables project (Stradling *et al.* 1994) was that where teachers were allowed to take computers home and play with them in their own time and make their mistakes in the privacy of their own home then their overall confidence increased and they were more ready to use IT in the classroom.

(b) *In mathematical and scientific skills*
All teachers at some time in their training and academic career have had to demonstrate their proficiency in linguistic skills. So arguably, in using a word-processing or desktop publishing package, it is only the software itself that has to be grappled with. With a spreadsheet package the user must have a degree of understanding of mathematical and graphing processes that may be beyond those they normally teach in the primary school. Also, as evidenced by Ofsted reports, many teachers have little confidence in their ability to teach certain physical concepts in the National Curriculum. They are also unlikely to have much, if any, experience of the investigative approach to science as learners themselves.

The many teacher development courses funded by government initiatives in recent years have sought to redress this lack of subject knowledge, as have in-service courses provide by local education authorities. Certainly there is more time devoted to maths, science and IT in initial teacher training courses, which does something towards decreasing this lack of confidence.

4 **Support**
(a) *Teacher support*
As mentioned above there has been a lot of in-service support for various aspects of IT and science delivery. However, this is targeted at only a small minority of primary teachers and it is assumed that this 'expertise' will either cascade or trickle down to the other teachers in the school. Since primary teachers do not normally have non-teaching periods, and it is expensive to buy release time, this cascading inevitably has to take place outside normal teaching hours. Given the many competing demands for 'training' time it is not surprising that IT does not always come very high up on the list of priorities.

(b) *Curriculum support*
Teachers may use the excuse of lack of curriculum materials as a reason for not using spreadsheets in the classroom. The imaginative enthusiast would see any practical activity as an excuse for using spreadsheets, but might be accused of putting the IT before the science! For those not so enthusiastic or imaginative there are a variety of materials available. As mentioned in an earlier section, the NCET is always a good point of reference, and its materials in

'Enhancing science with IT' are well researched and linked to the curriculum (Frost *et al.* 1994). Roger Frost's (1995) book is a source of some interesting ideas, and some local education authorities, such as Suffolk (1995), have produced curriculum materials as an outcome of centrally funded projects. *Primary Science Review* (1991, 1995) also has examples of spreadsheets used in the primary classroom.

5 Time

Any teacher will tell you that she barely has time to complete the absolutely essential tasks associated with teaching, never mind learning new skills, such as IT! I have two propositions here:

(a) If you really want to do something you will find the time to do it!

(b) Success breeds confidence (conversely there is nothing more off-putting than a lack of success).

Time is a real problem, and later on I will describe a strategy for sensible use of time that has enabled professional development to take place in a primary school.

6 Teachers remain unconvinced of the educational benefits of using IT in science

Whether this statement is true, or is merely an excuse to cover up a lack of confidence or a real lack of interest in using IT is a real point for discussion. At present there is little empirical evidence to justify the use of spreadsheets but the previous section does present a powerful educational argument to support their use.

7 Disappointment with the outcomes

Some teachers may try to use spreadsheets but are disappointed with the outcomes of this use. This may be because they are not sufficiently familiar with the software and are thus unable to take advantage of its many facilities, or they may be aware of some of its deficiencies but nevertheless expect the software to perform functions of which it is in fact not capable. Equally they may not be clear about the outcomes they want, i.e. have not set clear objectives, and are thus disappointed with the outcomes obtained. Such disappointment may produce a disinclination to use IT again, as they fail to identify the problem as one of poor understanding of the task and view the use of the computer as the root of the problem.

In *The ImpacT Report* Watson (1993) presented a dismal picture of the use of IT in primary and secondary schools. The three-year study, which began in 1989, focused on children's learning in the school subject areas of mathematics, science, geography and English, but difficulty in recruiting enough science classes resulted in the science field-study covering only one year! Of the general issues that emerged it is interesting to read that some of the IT activities were inhibited by factors such as the teacher's lack of understanding of the philosophy underpinning a particular piece of software or of the pedagogical implications for the effective use of the software. Furthermore, some teachers using IT had difficulties in managing pupils' access to computing facilities consistent with the plan of the topic or lessons. All of these reasons point to a lack of support for teachers who are trying to use IT in the classroom.

Case-study 1

I recently visited a medium-sized rural primary school in Essex with some 220 pupils from Reception to Year 6. The class teacher, who was also the science co-ordinator, was aware that, in order to fulfil the requirements of IT in the National Curriculum her pupils should have some experience of spreadsheet work. The problem being investigated was what material would make the best canopy for a parachute. To investigate this problem the children were going to make parachutes of different material and test them to see which one worked best. The children discussed what variables should be kept the same to make the experiment a fair test. They also discussed how they could ensure 'accuracy' in their results, and agreed that if each person in the group took a turn to time how long it took the parachute to fall from the same height, and they dropped each one four times, the average or mean of the results would be a 'better' value than just one reading. They then proceeded to make and test their parachutes.

In order to carry out their investigation on the flights of the different parachutes the Year 5 class had been split up into eight groups of four pupils, the groups being mixed up in terms of gender and ability. Each group did the experiment in turn and then entered its results into a simple spreadsheet. Prior to the classroom activities the IT and science co-ordinators planned how they would do this. The school had a system whereby curriculum co-ordinators were released from normal teaching for an hour each week to support a colleague in the classroom. When the first group did its experiment, the IT co-ordinator spent time showing the children (and the class teacher) how to use the spreadsheet. The children entered all the data themselves and built up the formula to calculate the mean, which was [= (B3 + B4 + B5 + B6) / 4]. They also plotted a bar chart of their results. Examples of Group 1's work is given in Figures 6.1a and 6.1b. These children could then have been used as 'class experts' to teach other members of the class how to perform these operations, releasing the teacher from the need to demonstrate the technical aspects of the IT use, and giving her more time to concentrate on guiding the development of children's understanding of the science.

I met some of the pupils and their teachers a couple of months after they had done the investigation and asked them various questions. I was pleasantly surprised at just how well many of the children remembered the processes of using the spreadsheet. I asked the children if they had enjoyed using it. They said they had because it had saved them lots of time calculating the means. Their teacher would have made them do it the long way, not even using a calculator.

	A	B	C	D
1				
2		Sugar	Foil	Cling Fi
3	First	2.58	3.28	2.31
4	Second	1.36	2.84	1.68
5	Third	1.5	2.32	1.21
6	Fourth	2.02	1.53	1
7	Mean	1.865	2.4925	1.55
8				

Figure 6.1a Case-study 1: table of four sets of readings of drop times (in seconds) of parachutes made of various materials: sugar paper, foil and cling film

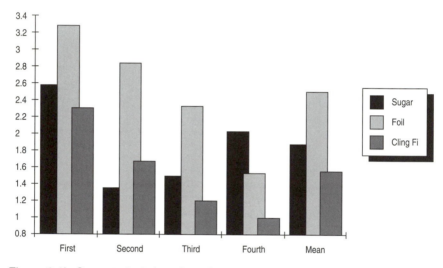

Figure 6.1b Case-study 1: bar chart derived from table of readings of parachute drop times

When asked about the graph one girl said that if she had done it herself it would have taken her 'two thousand hours!' (and pulled a face!)

Issues arising

Skill development

Does using the spreadsheet to do the calculations de-skill the pupils? All the pupils I talked to could explain to me exactly how to calculate the average (and were quite relieved that they had not had to do the laborious task themselves). It may even be that removing the hard grind enabled the pupils to appreciate the process rather than getting bogged down in the algorithm.

Time

The teachers said that they had invested a lot of time in planning and carrying out the investigation, but would expect a pay-off in Year 6 . They hoped that the children might ask to use spreadsheets in the future to analyse data.

Decimal points

The original figures the spreadsheet calculated gave 3 decimal places. The children found this confusing although the teacher managed to explain it away. I later showed her how to use the number menu to pre-set the number of decimal places that are displayed. She said she had not been aware of this feature but would certainly use it the next time.

Legend

The way the spreadsheet was originally set up was to have the names of the materials in a row at the bottom of the columns of numbers. Thus when the graph was plotted a label (or legend) did not appear at the bottom of each bar to tell them which column of data it represented. The children appreciated the need for a legend and so created their own. This seeded a discussion on how best to present the data. (In fact the legend automatically appears when the headings are at the top of the columns.)

Willingness to learn

The two teachers realised that some aspects of the investigation could have been done a little better, but they were happy to learn from their mistakes. They thus showed an admirably flexible approach to developing and extending the range of learning experiences they could expose the children to, and a willingness to learn with their pupils.

Data presentation

Because of the way the data were presented the children found the graph confusing (see Figure 6.1a). The graph shows five clusters of three bars, one bar for each material, one cluster for each of the four timed drops and a fifth for the mean. The cluster of the mean alone would have illustrated more clearly which material made the best parachute. The other clusters could have been used to start a discussion on how variable the readings were for each material, and whether the way the measurements were made could have been made more reliable.

As it was the children could not really talk to me about trends or patterns in the five-cluster bar chart and were not even aware of any results that did not fit the pattern. The graph obtained was probably more complicated than those they normally drew but more important, was not necessarily the most sensible one to draw. The children, however, were pleased with the presentation of their results, perhaps providing motivation for further work with spreadsheets! However, they were no better informed about the original question which was, 'Which material makes the best parachute?'

Case-study 2

In this second case-study some Year 6 children performed a similar sort of experiment to the previous case-study, but with paper helicopters. This group of children were investigating how the wing length of a paper helicopter affected its efficiency. Again they timed how long the helicopter took to fall a certain distance. In Figure 6.2 you will find one child's account of his experiment. As before, the method was achieved through debate and discussion, and the children had a firm grasp of the notion of 'fair testing'. They also set up their own spreadsheet after discussion with the teacher. This school, on the outskirts of Cambridge, is well equipped with portable computers, having taken part in the NCET-managed portable computers evaluation (see Stradling *et al.* 1994). On this occasion they were trying out the spreadsheet facility on some palmtop computers. The results table is self-explanatory, and the graph shows average flight time plotted against wing length (see Figure 6.2).

Issues arising

Calculation

As before, the spreadsheet was used to carry out the repetitive calculation, but the children had built the formula and so showed a solid understanding of what they were doing. Here the children used stop watches that timed to the thousandth of a second, and the children enjoyed the use of the complex numbers they generated as a result.

Data presentation

In this investigation the children were gradually increasing the length of the wings of the helicopter every time they ran a series of flights. They used an average of three drops to give a mean time for each wing length. They knew at the outset that they were looking for a pattern, a relationship between the wing length and the time to drop. The children discussed this before they began to collect data, and were encouraged to make a prediction. Their prediction was that the longer the wing length, the longer it would take to drop. They also predicted what a graph which showed this might look like. However, the teacher guided them to a line graph rather than a bar chart, and had to show them how

Helicopter experiment

Method

We decided to drop each helicopter three times from the top of the wall bars for our first drop the helicopter didn't have any wings, we changed the wing length by 3cm every three drops until we got to 15cm. We did 45 drops altogether. I dropped Charlie's helicopter and Matthew timed it, Charlie dropped Matthew's helicopter and I timed it, Matthew dropped my helicopter and Charlie timed it. We did it like that so we could each record our own results.

Results

These are my results

Charlie 1	Charlie 2	Charlie 3	Average time	Length of wing cm
85	91	68	81	0
87	66	88	80	3
88	103	94	95	6
103	97	118	106	9
128	146	131	135	12
121	138	113	124	15

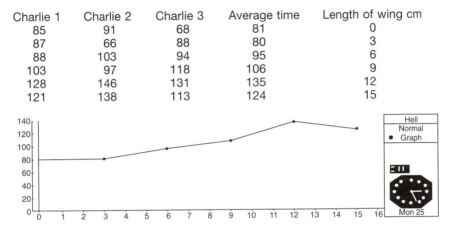

Conclusion

The length of the wing made a difference but not that much. We had the biggest average at 12cm and the smallest average at 3cm. Apart from 3cm and 12cm the averages got higher as the wing length got bigger. We found that our hypotheses wasn't right.

We could of made it a fairer test by having a different helicopter for each time we cut it. We also found that they didn't spin very well. I think that if they spun all the time our hypotheses would of been right. I think this because if they spun quite quickly they would stay in the air longer like a real helicopter.

Figure 6.2 Case-study 2: A child's account of the helicopter investigation

to use the spreadsheet to make a line graph, which in the case of the palmtop software was very complicated.

The graph they got did not show the result they expected (after a certain wing length the helicopter becomes unstable and drops more quickly). The first children to finish the graph assumed they had made a mistake, and wanted to see other people's graphs. Since the majority showed the same pattern, they became intrigued and were easily persuaded that maybe it was not as simple as longer wings mean a slower drop. The question could be investigated further, perhaps by making smaller changes to the wing length and finding the absolute best length.

Discussion of the two case-studies

What is immediately evident when comparing the two case studies is that the results are presented differently and in fact the structure of the whole investigation is different in the second case-study. The teacher there had had much greater experience in setting up scientific investigations, and thus had a much clearer idea of the data that the children should collect and how it should be presented. This was in fact the key difference between the two outcomes, although to those involved it may have felt that the main difference was that the first teachers appeared to be less experienced with the use of IT. These two examples illustrate that using IT can in fact reveal the teachers' unfamiliarity with the data-handling task, or in some cases the science. (This issue is addressed at length in Chapter 7.) Moreover, in the first case-study the teachers began with the need to 'do some IT', in the second a science investigation was designed where the data-handling and display was more easily done using IT.

Data collection

In both case-studies the helicopter or parachute was dropped a number of times and the average time of fall calculated by the spreadsheet. In the first case each child in the group had a turn at dropping the parachute, and a different child timed the fall, thus involving all members of the group in each part of the experiment. In the second case each child dropped the helicopter three times with the same pupil timing the fall for the three drops, thus ensuring greater reliability of the results. (In fact each child in the group had a turn at doing the experiment and each reported independently.) It is important to distinguish between fair testing as an activity which is fair because everyone has a go, and a scientifically fair test where the conditions are identical each time you collect a repeat of the data!

Presentation of results

In the second case-study the results were plotted as a line graph of the average drop time only; the graph itself meant it was easier to interpret the relationship between wing length and drop time, which was the phenomenon under investigation. In the first case-study the graph was undoubtedly confusing for the pupils. They were highly delighted with their presentation of the results, especially as it was in colour, but the graph used did little to help them see a pattern or form a conclusion. A simpler graph with only the mean readings would have made the overall relationship more obvious.

Within each group of results there was a fairly inconsistent pattern of fall times, which is not surprising given the age of the experimenters. The children deduced their conclusions from looking at the mean values, but these masked some very unreliable results. More time could have been spent examining the raw data, to help the children evaluate their method. They might have recognised a few highly unreliable readings and repeated at least these, or recognised that taking more than three or four readings each time might be a better way to get a more reliable mean value. These considerations could have been elicited by viewing the data in the spreadsheet, or in a table drawn on paper, but the ease with which the averages were generated, and the graph was produced by the spreadsheet, perhaps masked this important part of the process. There is however no guarantee that the various possibilities would have been considered in the absence of the spreadsheet. As ever, the key here is effective teacher intervention to ask the pertinent questions at the right time. In order to do that, the teacher must have a firm grasp of what those questions might be.

Classroom management

In UK primary schools, there is a tradition of approaching work across the whole curriculum by splitting the class into small groups, and each group may or may not work on a different activity. In this scenario the class teacher may find it easier to work with only one computer, and each group would work on its science investigation at a different time and analyse and present its own set of results. The primary teacher is thus less inclined to consider doing whole class investigational work, especially where using the computer is involved. However, in the two case-studies described it would have been equally possible to have all the class working on their investigations at the same time, then each group could have entered its data into one large spreadsheet. Any averages calculated would have been from a much larger set of data and thus a more reliable set of means would have been calculated. These results could have been plotted on a graph, possibly by each group in turn, and individual copies given to groups. Finally the results could have been discussed by the whole class together. This would have given all the children an opportunity to contribute their ideas, and they might have gained a great deal from listening to the views of the other children and their teacher. This might have been a rich discussion from the data-handling point of view, particularly if the type or detail of graph chosen by each group had varied.

Summary

A brief history of the investigative approach to science precedes a discussion of the way in which using spreadsheets can make some aspects of this process more accessible to children. A number of the factors which may limit teachers' use of spreadsheets in primary science are given, and some solutions to these are offered. Finally two case studies are outlined. Each offers a different approach to an investigation of falling objects, but both use a spreadsheet to collect, manipulate and present their data. These examples serve to illustrate many of the general points raised in the chapter, and in particular that a poor understanding of the objectives and desired outcomes of an investigation can cause disappointment and confusion. This is not a function of the use of IT, although this may be the focus of the dissatisfaction. In fact the use of IT may serve to highlight inadequacies in the approach to the task, and the understanding of the basic nature of the underlying process and its outcomes. This theme is developed further in Chapter 7.

Chapter 7

Developing graphing skills

Angela McFarlane

Introduction

Children begin drawing graphs in infant school and will continue to do so at least until they leave formal education. The teaching of graphing skills is usually confined to the mathematics areas of the curriculum, with the assumption that the conventions learned there can then be applied in many contexts, including the humanities and science. This particular convention for communicating information is ubiquitous both in school and beyond. It has become embedded in popular culture; advertisers, politicians and the popular media frequently use graphs to convey information or opinion. They are all well aware that the graph offers a powerful method of expressing trends and patterns in the relationship between two or more varying factors, with a high degree of visual impact. Used well, graphs help the reader to understand these relationships better; used badly they can confuse and mislead (accidentally or otherwise!).

The widespread use of graphs might lead us to assume that graphs represent a method of communication that is widely shared. However, research evidence shows that in fact the conventions of graphing are poorly understood (Assessment of Performance Unit (APU), Science Reports 1988 and 1989, Swatton and Taylor 1994, Taylor and Swatton 1990). By the age of 11 the majority of children can make a good job of plotting a line graph, but only if they are told what range of values to use on each axis, which variable to plot up the side and which across the bottom. In other words they can work out co-ordinates all right, but the fundamental knowledge of how a graph is supposed to work is missing. When it comes to interpreting graphs drawn by others, the situation is also worrying. The majority of 11-year-olds are unable to describe and use patterns in graphs or to make predictions based on the data shown (Taylor and Swatton 1990). This skill deficit might not be too worrying if we could be confident that it was addressed in secondary education, but in fact the situation is little improved among 15-year-olds.

It's a pretty picture but what does it mean?

The sad fact is that graphing represents a classic case of inauthentic learning for the majority of children (see Bonnett, in this volume, for a comment on authentic learning). They can go through the motions of plotting a graph by hand, but there is little personal understanding or relevance associated with the exercise. For most children it seems graphs are not seen as a natural or effective method of communicating ideas, rather drawing a graph is analogous to chanting a phrase in a foreign tongue with no comprehension of what you are saying. Anita Straker commented in 1989,

> In the past children frequently spent so much time drawing graphs and colouring them in that little time was left for looking at the graphs to see what they revealed. Where comments were made they often simply repeated the details which were shown on the graph. Being able to interpret information from a graphical display, to interpret what it means, and to offer some explanation for it, are skills which are becoming increasingly important across the whole curriculum.

> (Straker 1989: 38)

Unfortunately the intervening years have seen little improvement. Ofsted reports show that most graphing in primary schools uses bar charts, often quite inappropriately (Ofsted 1996).

Interviews with children in Year 9, carried out by myself and colleagues during a research project, exposed some worrying tendencies to use bar charts unquestioningly unless directed otherwise. These charts were seen as easier to draw and read, and children revealed no knowledge of strategies for working out whether they were appropriate. Conversely, line graphs were frequently described as 'more accurate' with no evidence of understanding what this phrase might mean. Any evidence of understanding the *concepts* of interpolation or extrapolation (we did not expect these terms to be used by children, nor did we use them ourselves) was extremely rare (Friedler and McFarlane 1997). Few children showed any awareness of the ideas that they could use a line graph to estimate values between, or beyond the actual points they had plotted. These findings are particularly worrying when viewed in the light of the frequency with which this method of communication is likely to have been used during their school life, in a wide variety of curriculum contexts, and the extent to which it is likely to be used to influence the child's opinion on a whole range of important issues in the world she inhabits beyond school.

The 'hierarchy' of graphing

There is evidence that the judicial use of IT can help to remedy the obvious skill deficit which exists in children's understanding of graphing, beginning early in the child's experience. To better understand the development of children's graphing I want to examine in some detail the early experiences children may have as part of the school curriculum, and the assumed hierarchy of ideas implicit in the progressive development of the graphing process. I will also look at the nature of data briefly, as this too is a key concept which underpins successful data interpretation. These ideas are crucial to an intelligent use of the related IT tools for teaching graphing. I will then go on to suggest ways in which the use of IT can help to make these concepts explicit to the learner.

As early as infant school, children may begin using pictograms. An example might be a chart reflecting pet ownership. A picture of a dog, cat or any other animal represents each animal owned, and these pictures are assembled in columns to show how many people own each type of pet. The completed chart, provided the pictures are all roughly the same size, shows at a glance which type of pet is most common, which least popular, how many pets are owned in total, etc. This form of chart is so popular in primary schools that a number of database and charting programs have been developed for schools that will allow the user to build pictograms easily and quickly, using pictures provided with the software or drawn by the teacher or children. Figure 7.1 shows such a computer-generated pictogram of the types of dwelling members of the class live in.

Once the basic experience of building a pictogram has been established, it can be reinforced by using the computer to carry out the labour-intensive activity of drawing and gluing. As elsewhere in this book (see, for example, Chapter 2 on problem-solving and Chapter 4 on variables), this is not in any way to suggest that the drawing and gluing activities away from the computer are of lesser value, or should be omitted. Indeed these more concrete stages are likely to be essential precursors for at least some children. But when the objective is to teach about the protocols associated with building pictograms, or interpreting the data collected, the time-consuming manual operations can be distractions. Time spent in drawing a picture of the family pet may well cause a young child to forget entirely about the pictogram task. Moreover, if errors in execution of the task creep in, for example the dogs are all drawn at widely different sizes, the resulting chart can be very misleading and it is very demotivating and time-consuming to have to do it again.

It is easy to see how the abstraction of the bar chart is developed from the pictogram when each pet in the above example is replaced with a square of equal size. The line graph is then commonly introduced by drawing a line running through the top of each bar on a bar chart. This seems like an obvious and simple way of linking a more concrete representation – the bar chart – to an otherwise somewhat abstract one – the line graph. However, discussions I have had with students in initial teacher training, and with some classroom teachers, confirm that there is often confusion about the type of data that it is legitimate to display in a bar chart and the type of data that require a scatter plot or line graph (both types of *xy* graphs) to display it meaningfully. Indeed, teachers may be unaware of the importance of any distinction between bar charts and *xy* graphs and treat both in the same way. Worse still, the *xy* graph may simply be

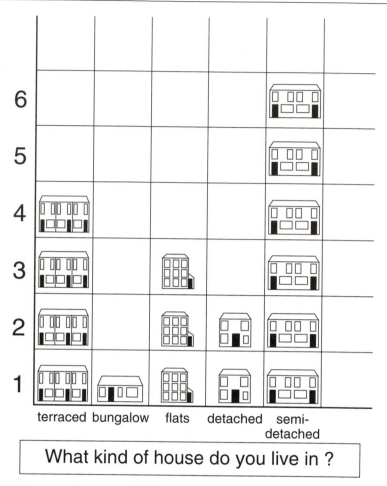

terraced bungalow   flats   detached   semi-
detached

What kind of house do you live in ?

Figure 7.1 A computer-generated pictogram showing the number of children living in each type of dwelling

regarded as a 'harder' or 'more accurate' kind of graph, reinforcing the confusions which can develop in the minds of children referred to earlier.

Children may then remain unaware that bar charts are best used to display discrete data, and *xy* plots are better used for continuous data.

Not all data are the same

For teachers of young children the distinction between discrete and continuous data may seem unnecessarily pedantic. However it is important that teachers, in the process of structuring learning opportunities, understand the difference because otherwise the progression from bar charts to *xy* graphs can be very misleading for children. As mentioned above, in order to progress to *xy* graphs, teachers often get children to join the tops of the bars in a bar chart. This may seem like a good way to move from the more concrete to the more abstract representation, and for certain data types that may be true. But consider for a moment what that line drawn between the tops of the bars means. The line between two points on a line graph is not simply a way of making the peaks and troughs more obvious, it is saying that you can reasonably expect any co-ordinate on that line to be valid. It represents a way to work out what happens in between the points you plotted. In the case of the pet chart, where five children own dogs and ten own cats, a reading from a line drawn between these suggests, for example, that 7.5 people own an animal which is half way between being a dog and a cat. The pet data are discrete, each pet can only belong in one category, so a line graph of the pet data is not valid.

This language, 'discrete' and 'continuous' is unlikely to be appropriate for many primary age children but the concepts it represents can be made accessible. For example, take a data-gathering exercise which looks at the size of children's feet. If this is measured as shoe size, you must fit into one size or another: shoes are only available in discrete sizes, and you cannot buy a 5.67, or a 36.89 for example. These data therefore fit very well into a bar chart where each bar represents a particular shoe size, and its height is proportional to the number of people who take that shoe size. However if the data collection is approached rather differently, and the actual length of each child's right foot is measured, the data will no longer fit into discrete categories. A human foot can actually have any available length (within a rather large range) so this data is continuous, and can be more meaningfully plotted on an *xy* graph. The final tricky question is, should this be a line graph or a scatter plot, in other words is it legitimate to join the points up? If you join up the points this is saying that it is reasonable to assume that any point drawn anywhere on that line is likely to be valid. However the class data only represents the members of a class, and since it cannot be true that there will be someone in the *class* with every available length of right foot, it is not fair to suggest this is true by joining up the points. Unfortunately once the line is drawn, it is very difficult to rub out!

Consider the two graphs, bar chart and scatter plot. The bar chart is useful for looking at the distribution of shoe size in the class. You can see at a glance which is the biggest and smallest size in the class, which the most common and which the rarest. The scatter plot may appear to provide more detail, but the features that stand out clearly on the bar chart will be harder to see. So in this case the bar chart of shoe size has more to recommend it than the scatter plot of foot length. This is not because it is easier to draw or read, but because it reveals information on frequency, i.e. how many times each size occurs in the class, more clearly than a scatter plot. If frequency data are what you want, the bar chart is the tool to use, and the discrete data were the best kind to collect.

Other cases of inappropriate representations of data may be harder to detect; for example, suppose that children measure the temperature in the classroom every day at the same time. Temperature is clearly an example of continuous data. It can have any value in a given range (even if the school thermometer can only measure to the nearest degree!). Also, there is a second variable here, namely time. So it seems reasonable for the children to record the temperature and time as co-ordinates on an *xy* plot. So far so good, but they may then join up the points to make a line graph, since this looks like a good way of seeing if the temperature is generally rising, falling or staying the same as the weeks go by. However, the result may not fit what you know to be the actual events, which is not surprising when you consider what the line graph is implying about temperature changes.

If the temperature at 10 a.m. yesterday was 12 °C, and today at the same time it is 14 °C, a line drawn between these two points implies that the temperature has risen by 2 °C, steadily over the intervening 24 hours, which is unlikely to be true! Joining up these two points is therefore not a valid graphing action; the line does not allow you to work out the temperature at any time in between your two measurements. This practice of interpolation is not one you might expect children in primary school to name, but it is a simple enough idea and can be posed to quite young children successfully. It allows them to make the choice between joining the points into a line graph, or leaving them as a scatter plot, which in this example is the valid way of displaying the data.

Admittedly this dot-joining convention is one that is openly broken in advertising, mass media and so on, even in reference books. Sometimes this is valid, where overall trends are more important than local 'blips'. For example, the annual unemployment figures over a decade may show a trend that is more politically significant than the daily, weekly or monthly variations, so a line is drawn to emphasise the annual pattern at the expense of the monthly one. This is fine so long as everyone understands what is happening, and the generalisation is valid. However, to know if the generalisation is valid, you have to understand the basic rule in order to know when to apply it rigorously and when it is acceptable to bend it.

So to summarise, there are three types of graphs commonly used in schools: bar charts, line graphs and scatter plots. These are usually arranged hierarchically in the school syllabus, with bar charts coming before line graphs, and scatter plots given scant attention or ignored since line graphs are used instead. (Pie charts are also commonly used to display data, and are good for representing proportions. They are usually a special type of bar chart, where the fraction of a group falling into a given category is proportional to the size of the slice of pie. Given the difficulty with assigning the proportion of the pie a value as a fraction of 360° it is difficult to see how these have become so popular in primary schools.)

The perceived conceptual progression from bar chart to line graph has as much to do with the difficulty associated with drawing them as with the concepts and conventions behind the patterns and relationships they reveal or disguise. Because bar charts are easier to draw and a short step on from the highly accessible pictogram, it is assumed they are easier to understand. Moreover it is implied that they are a less sophisticated kind of graph, rather than a graph that does a different kind of job. As so often happens, there is also an assumption, rarely articulated, that a child's cognitive development mirrors entirely her motor development. Research at Homerton College and elsewhere has shown that in the area of graphing this is not necessarily the case. The use of IT in the form of computer-based graphing packages can liberate children from the limitations of their motor skills, and free them to engage with the ideas behind graphs at an early age.

How can IT help?

The variety of opportunities presented by the examples in the previous section, and the many other possibilities for data-handling, can stimulate the teacher to consider the importance of having clear objectives in terms of outcomes before even beginning to collect data. If the children are not yet experienced enough to set their own objectives, and plan a route to achieve them, the teacher must be clear about the possible outcomes of a data-handling exercise. Why are the data being collected, what questions do you want to address? Many teachers I meet have had very demotivating experiences with IT-based data-handling activities. Because they are using the computer to handle the information they encourage children to collect and key in much larger volumes of data than they would consider using with paper-based recording and display methods. All too often they then find that they cannot perform the kinds of manipulation they had in mind, because they have inappropriate data sets. The need to set clear objectives at the outset of a large-scale data manipulation exercise is all too obvious. Whereas this element may be fudged when small amounts of data are collected and little time is devoted to a task, the bigger projects the availability of IT tools may inspire mean that this crucial stage of the teacher's planning cannot be overlooked. The success or failure of a data collection and interpretation exercise will depend on the questions you wish to ask of the data. The data must then be gathered and displayed in formats which can inform the answers to those questions. The range of possible formats available in a good data-handling package can stimulate the teacher to consider all the options, try out a few ideas prior to the onset of the task, and be more confident in her approach to the activity as a whole.

Computer graphing

So how can the discussions and demonstrations of the features of different kinds of graphs, which I have outlined above, be made explicit to young learners? Clearly, getting children to draw many graphs of different forms using the same set of data would be very time-consuming. Requiring a child to go through a long and involved procedure simply to illustrate how inappropriate the end result is, is also clearly counter-productive. However, there are many software tools available to schools which will generate a number of types of graph: spreadsheets, databases and dedicated graphing packages are common. They will all allow children to plot their data in a wide variety of formats, some of which are valid and some not, some which are simply better at revealing the relationships between the variables recorded.

In an ideal package it is possible to configure the number and type of choices children make about the way they display their data. Unfortunately, many packages designed for primary use will use a bar chart unless something else is selected, irrespective of the appropriateness of this format. This helps to reinforce the idea that bar charts are 'easier' or somehow more 'natural'. There can also be a problem associated with commercial spreadsheet packages, which were originally designed as accountancy packages. These assume data are most likely to be in discrete categories and therefore produce meaningless bar charts of any data that are not discrete. Even where xy plots can be generated, the procedure can be very convoluted compared to the simple route to a bar chart. The selection of an appropriate graphing package for use in school is therefore very important, and those designed for primary schools are usually to be preferred. The way in which graphs are formatted is a good indication of how workable the package will prove to be in the classroom. Some databases even offer support with the design of a template for collecting data, which helps to make explicit the type of data to be collected, and therefore which kind of graphs are appropriate. This makes it particularly easy for the teacher to try out a few ideas and see, with a small set of data, if the things she wants the children to try are valid.

The advantage of these software packages is not simply that they are quicker and neater at graphs than children are; indeed by the time the data are painstakingly keyed in, they may not be quicker at all at producing the first graph. Their virtue lies in the flexibility they allow. Once a child has drawn a graph manually, even if she has made some serious errors, it is unlikely that she will re-draw the whole thing, and if she does she is unlikely to do this joyfully. As a result she may see only one graphical representation of her data. Because of the effort involved, serious errors may be pre-empted by the teacher giving instructions, for example on what type of graph to use, what to write along the bottom and up the side, and what scale to use on each axis. Even if these decisions are made through discussion, they may not have much reality for the child before she has seen a graph of her data. The outcomes of Swatton and Taylor's research suggest that this part of the learning process using traditional methodologies may be extremely unsuccessful, since the majority of children remain unable to make these choices for themselves (Swatton and Taylor 1994). How much better, then, to produce a variety of graphs of a data set, quickly and easily in the graphing package, and then spend time discussing which one is the best to use and why. The inappropriate plots can often provide the richest source of discussion. Even the quirks of some graphing packages are useful in this way;

the automatic reduction of the full range of the y-axis to the highest value in the data set can provide a very useful entry to the importance of scales, and the need to compare like with like. This feature, often corrected in later versions of software, makes any small variation in a data set look highly significant; for example, a change of one degree in air temperature over a 24-hour period creates a line which shoots diagonally across the whole page.

Using manually plotted graphs children rarely get an opportunity to compare the appropriate and the inappropriate in a positive way, and miss out on a rich set of learning opportunities as a result.

Data logging

Some research that I and colleagues undertook in primary schools produced results suggesting that using computer-based data-logging systems with children as young as 7 and 8 can be very effective at helping to develop a more authentic understanding of line graphs. These data-logging systems produce graphs on the computer screen as sensors connected to the computer detect changes in their environment. The use of this type of equipment with children aged 8 to 16 has been part of the National Curriculum for Science in England and Wales since its inception in the late 1980s, but very rarely used in the primary school.

In our research, after an assessment of their skills in interpretation and construction of bar charts and line graphs, groups of Year 3 and 4 pupils conducted a science investigation into the relationship between temperature and time when hot water was left in bottles wrapped in a variety of materials. Half the children used thermometers and worksheets to record their results, the others used temperature probes and live line graphs drawn on the computer screen as they watched. Prior to this each group had had experience of using the relevant apparatus to measure temperatures in the classroom and around the school, including iced water and very hot water. An important feature of these preliminary activities is that they involved the children in investigating changes in temperature, from very hot to cold to warm etc., and enabled them to measure the effects of moving between them.

This early experience was very important because it familiarised the children with the whole idea that temperature was something that could be measured. It also introduced the data-logging group to the ideas that the line on a line graph went up and down more or less steeply depending on how fast something changed, and hardest of all, that it went along flat when nothing was changing. This helped them better to interpret the graphs they generated during the subsequent investigation.

When the children were reassessed after these experiences, the group using the probes and live graphs, i.e. data logging, showed significant development in their understanding of line graphs, and their ability to represent relationships between variables using this convention. This applied to questions related to the context they had met, extrapolations from it and contexts which were very different. The children who had used conventional methods, and had in fact spent much longer on the topic in most cases, showed no significant improvement in any of these skills. All children were taught by their class teachers and none had worked on line graphs before this investigation (McFarlane *et al.* 1995).

In this project the children who used data logging were introduced to line graphs not as a Cartesian plot, where the ability to identify positions correctly on a grid was the first objective; rather they were introduced to line graphs as a representation of the relationship between two variables, namely temperature and time. They saw a system they had direct sensory experience of, and the power to influence directly, depicted as a line graph. Their ability to read and interpret temperature/time graphs was greatly enhanced as a result, and it is particularly significant that their ability to sketch temperature/time curves that predict the behaviour of a novel system also improved.

The children using thermometers showed no significant gains in the same skill set, despite being taught by more experienced, highly skilled teachers using exemplary methodology, but restricted to traditional resources. Even though these children plotted points manually on to a grid as they took measurements, a process which might be thought to mimic the real time data logging very closely, there was no evidence of any improvement in their understanding of graphs as a representation of changes in the variables they were studying, according to the test instruments used in our research. They had also had to spend a long time mastering the thermometer before the investigation could begin.

The children who had used data logging were better able to read, sketch and predict the shape of temperature/time graphs some weeks after the investigation. They were also able to use the knowledge they had gained to work with graphs on paper, not just in the context of the original investigation. Indeed similar work with older children used graphs of totally unrelated data in the tests, and the ability to understand these also improved after the data-logging experience (Friedler and McFarlane 1997).

Although these experiences of data logging all took place in the context of a science investigation, there is evidence that the children showed an ability to apply the knowledge of graphing they gained in alternative contexts. This alone argues for the value of the experience, since the carry-over of skills from one context to another is notoriously difficult to achieve. Moreover they were often post-tested some weeks after the investigation, so there is evidence of persistence of knowledge. This was further supported by informal visits to the children up to a year later, when they were still able to talk intelligently about the investigation and the graphs they produced (Cole 1993). Finally, although the equipment needed to carry out this work is expensive, unlike much other computer-based work it can be managed with a small number of sets in a school. It is not necessary for all the class to work on an investigation at the same time, indeed it is often easier to manage when this is not the case.

In our research project, unusually for a primary school, computers and the data-logging equipment were made freely available. However the teachers chose, after some initial experimentation, to use no more than four computers in the class at the same time. One teacher only ever had one pair working on the data-logging activity with a single computer at one time, with the rest of the class often engaged in entirely different work. Also unusually in the light of other findings (Eraut and Hoyles 1988) the teachers adopted these strategies so that they could devote the time required to the groups who were using the computer, without abandoning the rest of the class. They were thus able to pose the necessary timely questions the data-logging groups needed to help them get the most from their experiences. It was also possible for the children who had experience of the equipment to act as mentors to later groups, freeing the teacher from the need to provide purely technical support.

With appropriate timetabling one or two sets of this equipment can address the needs of an entire primary school. Given the enormous potential of the resulting learning experience this has to be a good investment of scarce resources.

Implications for the curriculum

In traditional curricula children are taught to draw graphs before they spend time interpreting them. Furthermore they have little experience of discussions about why graphs are useful, and what different types of graph have to offer when looking for patterns and relationships in data. In many curricula, even in science in the secondary school where you might reasonably expect to find it, the skills of interpretation – linking the events depicted and the symbolic representation of those events – are rarely explicitly taught. Rather, this appreciation is expected to develop by osmosis. The National Curricula for Science and Mathematics in England and Wales do little to encourage changes to this approach.

Traditional teaching methods are quite effective at teaching pupils the skills required to handle graphs manually by the time they are 11 years of age (APU 1988 and 1989, Swatton and Taylor 1994, Taylor and Swatton 1991). However the same sources show that even by the age of 13 the vast majority of children are not able to appreciate the graph's power as a model of underlying relationships presented in this symbolic way.

The data collected by the project at Homerton College suggest not only that the use of data logging with children at the age of 8 is manageable within the average primary classroom, given a degree of external support to help teachers become familiar with the equipment and its effective use, but that to do so has very positive learning outcomes, which are not achievable in other ways. Furthermore it suggests that to introduce the children to the line graph holistically, as a model of the relationship between changing variables, before introducing the manual skills of plotting, might be a way to bridge the conceptual gulf which otherwise develops. In related research by the authors (Friedler and McFarlane 1997) with older children at 13 to 14 and 15 to 16, we have found that even quite able pupils go through the motions of manual plotting of graphs in science automatically. They cannot articulate why they use a bar or line graph, or indeed why they use a graph at all, to represent data. 'Because we always do in science' was a common response. Perhaps shifting the emphasis away from the manual plotting skills towards the higher-order interpretative skills, and reversing the order in which these skills are introduced in the curriculum by using real-time plotting by computer to remove the need for the manual plotting skills initially, would go a long way to bridge this conceptual gulf. Removing the need for manual plotting permits the introduction of line graphs at a very much earlier stage of intellectual development. Furthermore, it means the pupils first meet line graphs as a representation of the relationship between changing variables, not as an exercise in Cartesian co-ordinate mapping.

The use of computerised spreadsheets and databases to give pupils rapid access to many different representations of the same data set is a useful strategy in improving the understanding of the complexities of the graph symbol system. It seems that the contiguous manipulation of physical variables and dynamic plotting which data logging offers may be an even more powerful way to introduce quite young children to the links between line graphs and variables, and their interactions.

If these gains are to be achieved widely in primary education there will be a need for external support for schools. Not only is there the financial issue of equipment provision, but also the issues of staff and curriculum development. Primary school teachers will be required to manage the use of computers in the context of investigative science, two areas currently presenting considerable challenges. The research project at Homerton College assisted the teachers in both the control and experimental classes, with the support of the school management and the researchers, to introduce a style of investigative science which they would not otherwise have used at that time. As a result of the project the teachers using the data-logging equipment achieved remarkable results within a very restricted time-scale. The resulting learning gains made by children in the data-logging groups repaid the investment in time and resource handsomely.

Summary

The use of graphs is widespread throughout the school curriculum and beyond. However the fundamental principles of graphing, which type of graph to use, how to construct it and the interpretation of patterns and relationships in data which a graph can reveal, are poorly understood by children in primary and secondary school.

Using computer-based graphing applications such as spreadsheets, databases and graphing utilities can allow data-handling exercises to focus on presentation and interpretation rather than simple construction. A progression of ideas associated with the understanding of bar charts, line graphs and scatter plots has been offered in this chapter, and ways that these ideas can be made explicit using IT have been suggested.

Finally the unique power of data-logging systems to help even young children develop an understanding of line graphs as a way of revealing the relationship between two variables has been discussed. The results of a research project co-ordinated by the author, which used data logging in a science investigation with 8- and 9-year-olds, support the view that the traditional hierarchy of graphing skills should be questioned. With suitable resourcing and staff development, the effective use of IT could help to overcome a major skills gap in the ability to use graphs effectively.

Chapter 8

Thinking about writing

Angela McFarlane

Introduction

The issue of literacy, along with numeracy, is something of a political football in the 1990s. There is a commonly expressed view that levels of literacy among primary school children have fallen. If true, this is clearly a matter of deep concern for parents, teachers and ultimately society as a whole. A subliterate population is surely the hallmark of a culture in decline. This is a massive issue, which cannot be dealt with fully in this volume. What I do want to focus on is the importance of writing and the role that IT can play in developing this aspect of literacy. I then want to raise some questions about the changing nature of literacy and the 'new literacy' which the information age is said to herald.

The role of the word processor

The potential of the word processor to enhance learning in schools, particularly in the context of the English curriculum, has been widely praised for many years. The *Kingman Report* indicated that the word processor can have widespread implications for the way children write:

> The word processor, with its ability to shape, delete and move text around provides the means by which pupils can achieve a satisfactory product. . . . Through the use of word processors pupils are drawn into explicit discussion of the nature and likely impact of what they write. They will begin to talk about appropriate structure, correct punctuation and spelling and the vocabulary appropriate for their audience.
>
> (DES 1988a: 37, 4.13)

However, at the time that report was written this potential was largely a matter for speculation rather than the result of consideration of evidence (Adams 1990). On the basis of a perception of value rather than the fact, word processing was embedded in the three National Curricula for the United Kingdom, along with desktop publishing, from its first iteration in 1988 (see, for example, DES 1988b). However it should be noted that the descriptions of the use of computers in the National Curricula have always been couched in terms that are permissive rather than mandatory, and this remains so to a large extent in the current version where the use of computers 'where appropriate' is the recurrent urging, but alternatives are always offered. (A cynical interpretation might be that government cannot commit itself to a statutory requirement for all children to have use of computers without also committing itself to provide the resources for adequate computers and software, not to mention staff development.)

Possibly as a result of curriculum legislation, although there is evidence that its popularity pre-dates the statutory requirements, many teachers do include word processing as part of children's school experience. Approximately every two years since the mid-1980s the ministry responsible for education, which seems to have changed its name almost as often, has conducted a survey of IT in schools in England and Wales. No other source has such a strong historical perspective, or the same volume of data from hundreds of schools. Despite any reservations concerning political spin which may be put on the presentation and interpretation of data in these reports, these surveys do provide a valuable insight into what might actually be going on in terms of IT use in classrooms. The reports show consistently that the most common use of computers in the classroom, as reported by the schools themselves, is for word processing. It accounts for up to 50 per cent of the computer use in each year group, only beaten by the use of puzzles and practice exercises in Year 1, and way ahead of the nearest rivals, which struggle to make double figures in most cases (DfE 1995e).

This fact is interesting in itself. It seems safe to assume that the common use of a scarce and expensive resource, the computer, for this one activity means that teachers regard the experience as valuable, possibly more important than the many other potential uses of the computer. Or is it simply that this is the use of the computer teachers themselves are most familiar with, so they feel more comfortable with this activity in the classroom? Or worse still, is this something the children get on with on their own with little need for supervision from the teacher? In a review of research into group-work at the computer Eraut and Hoyles (1988), quoted in McMahon (1990) commented that 'assigning pupils to work on computers allows the teacher to attend to the rest of the class in peace'. McMahon further commented that the choice of items of educational software might depend 'more on its capacity to keep pupils busily occupied than on the learning gains it might promote' (pp. 157–8).

The popularity of the word processor in school might then owe much to the wishful thinking of senior educationalists and politicians, and the degree to which the activity of writing at the word processor keeps children absorbed. This interpretation, however, ignores the experience of committed teachers who have found that word processing is a valuable tool in the classroom, and the work of all the educationalists, including teachers, who have documented this. The use of word processors has been common in primary classrooms since the early 1980s, so there is a prolific literature on the subject. Kuhn and Stannard have recently conducted a very useful review of the literature related to the use of IT in the English Curriculum, which gives a comprehensive account of the role of word processors in the development of writing (Kuhn and Stannard 1996). This will provide a useful starting point for anyone who wishes to pursue further the related issues that I will raise here.

Since the computer is still rare in the primary school, with an average of one for every eighteen pupils (DfE 1995e), children do not usually get to use one each. Writing with a word processor therefore becomes a pair or group activity for most of the time. Perhaps as a result of this there have been a number of studies of the development of collaborative writing using the computer. Crook, in his book published in 1994, provides a comprehensive account of the whole issue of collaboration surrounding the use of the computer. Until recently there was a comparative lack of information on the development of the individual young writer who has free access to a word processor. In the evaluation of portables managed by the National Council for Educational Technology (NCET) which reported in 1994 (Stradling *et al.* 1994), a large number of children were given free access to individual machines over a period of time. I shall return to some of the findings on individual and pair or group work at the word processor, reported in these two sources and elsewhere, in the following sections.

The ergonomics of using the word processor

It is difficult to see how the restricted access any one child will have to a computer in the average classroom, especially for hands-on experience, is likely to be enough for significant amounts of writing to take place using a word processor. This is particularly likely in the case of girls and other less physically dominant members of a class. Lipinski *et al.* (1986) showed that when there is competition for the computer, because it is a scarce resource, boys tend to win out, owing to their more aggressive social behaviour. As with any kind of computer use, teachers need to be aware of this problem and operate a conscious equal opportunities policy, with perhaps a rota of access. This needs to extend beyond the formal class time, as a great deal of significant computer access takes place in breaks and after school where a school can facilitate open access to the computer.

It seems likely then, that the most common scenario for word processing in a primary classroom will involve a pair or group of children around a computer. This will probably be a desktop computer with a vertical screen which makes the text visible to all the group members, a large keyboard most easily accessed by the person in front of it, and probably with a mouse, which can be passed around if the flex is long enough and there is enough room on the surrounding table top to operate it. This dynamic changes where portable computers are available. With a good quality notebook computer it is still possible for up to four children to see the screen easily, and it can be easier for the actual keying-in to be shared as the whole computer can be moved across from one group member to another. Moreover the smaller size of the machine means it does not totally dominate the children's working space. It can sit among other items related to the current task, such as books, equipment needed for a maths, science or technology activity, historical artefacts, a globe, etc., without overshadowing them.

The task

And what of the nature of the task? At one end of a spectrum the group might be simply keying in a text already written by one member or the whole group, primarily to improve the presentation and possibly to include some spelling and punctuation corrections. At the other end they might be involved in creating an entirely novel composition, fact or fiction, which could incorporate media other than text. Unfortunately the bulk of activity may lie too far towards the copy-typing end of the spectrum. Adams (1990) claimed that too often the word processor is used in the classroom as an intelligent typewriter. 'There is still too little opportunity given to pupils to learn to compose on screen rather than to transfer their hand written drafts to the screen for final "tidying up"' (p. 237).

In order to decide what different types of word processing activity can offer to the development of children's writing, it is necessary to begin with an examination of the process of writing. In 1988 Hunter published a subsequently widely quoted analysis of the writing process in terms which helped to see how word processing can be used to support the development of the particular skills involved. He described a hierarchy which begins with the pencil stroke to form a letter, proceeds through the creation of words, sentences and paragraphs, to chapters and an overall structure, intention and plot of a book. Interestingly these were placed on a continuum. (Where would works such as Swift's *Gulliver's Travels* and Roddy Doyle's 1993 Booker prize-winning *Paddy Clarke Ha Ha Ha* fit, or be judged, if such a continuum were to form the assessment framework? Certainly, if punctuation were to be included as an assessment criterion, the outlook would be bleak indeed.) How valid the continuum is in a wider context is rich ground for a book in itself, but Hunter does use the framework idea to make a point that is surely far less controversial. Whatever the precise nature of the wider task as a whole, children in school, especially the very young or those with special needs, are in danger of experiencing writing largely as the first two of these tasks. They may spend an inordinate amount of time trying to form letters on the page and create words, with little if any vision of the process as a whole.

This dilemma takes on a wider perspective when the view of the importance of writing as expressed by Jessel is considered:

Being able to capture and represent our thoughts in the form of written text and have them available for further scrutiny is an important ingredient in thinking and learning. Text can convey ideas and the recording of text allows ideas to be re-read and reflected upon . . . If we wish children to work in this way it is important to encourage them to view writing as a mutable entity, something to be experimented with in the process of their learning.

(Jessel 1992: 23)

So the importance of developing the habits of viewing text as something to be considered, evaluated and revisited is not an issue restricted to the composition of stories, but rather a fundamental facet of the learning process. Indeed this view can be integral to the development of thinking itself, as text is believed to be at the heart of the development of rationality. Before the existence of text in the development of humankind, or before the individual learns to access it in his or her own development, the mind has only current experience and what can be remembered as the raw material of thought. The development of text, in the history of human evolution, facilitated reflective abstract thought. This realisation has clear implications for the attitude a teacher has to the importance of both reading and writing (Bonnett 1994). The teacher should no longer regard these processes as simply encoding and decoding nature, which is how 'conventional literacy' is commonly viewed; rather the objective must surely be to develop the skills and attitudes valued by Jessel (1992), and which Egan includes under the notion of 'comprehensive literacy' (Egan 1990).

Clearly the advent of the word processor has not brought about the processes associated with 'comprehensive literacy', which have been at the heart of intellectual activity since such activity first took place. The difference is that the use of electronic text makes the otherwise intensely laborious process of experimenting with text more accessible to even the youngest scholar.

Developing writing

It seems that there can be no guarantee that the use of the word processor in itself will result in the hoped-for developments in children's writing (see Peacock and Breese 1990). Indeed there is a body of evidence which suggests that the key to releasing the potential promise of the word processor, as with any other learning scenario, is effective teacher intervention. It is the already effective teacher who uses software effectively (Katterns and Haigh 1986). I therefore wish to look now at the process of creating, reviewing and developing texts, and the kinds of task teachers can design and the intervention they can offer to assist the development of 'comprehensive literacy'.

Making a mark

Clearly the computer can alleviate some of the difficulties children have with controlling a pencil in the early stages of physical writing. Before they progress to using the QWERTY keyboard and generating free text, this can be via a concept keyboard or other writing support software, which provides words or pictures that children can use to build a narrative of their own. The use of the QWERTY keyboard is in itself controversial, with some teachers concerned by the time it takes to locate the letters in the unfamiliar array, and whether early writers, familiar with the lower case alphabet will be able to decode the capitals on the keyboard and link them to the lower case letters appearing on the screen. The National Curriculum advises that children should eventually develop keyboarding skills beyond 'peek and poke' (where individual letters are located and poked with a single finger). However, the typing speed of a copy typist is not required. Children only need to be able to type at a speed which does not inhibit their thinking as they compose text. When the objective is to use the word processor as a tool to assist comprehensive literacy, children will rarely be copying pre-written text into the computer as a copy typist would be doing. As to the lower versus upper case debate, it is equally possible to find teachers determined that it is essential to stick labels on keys showing the lower case letters, and teachers sure that children have no problems with the transition. Clearly this is a problem easily solved where it occurs, and which may need to be addressed for some children at a certain stage of their development.

So it seems the computer can be used to assist children in forming letters, and subsequently words on the screen. This may not be any quicker than manual writing however, although children may write more words because they spend longer on the task (Peacock 1993). No one familiar with young writers can be unaware of the sheer physical demand of forming letters on a page. The comment of Maria, aged between 9 and 10, that 'The keyboard doesn't ache your hand', will surely resonate with the views of many young and not-so-young writers (Jessel 1992: 26). It is unlikely at this level that any one child will be typing for long enough stretches to be bothered by repetitive strain injury!

It is worth noting that the age at which children meet word processing may be important. A teacher involved in a very brief study of 5- and 6-year-olds using word processing found that 'Children who find hand writing easy are not motivated to use the computer on a day-to-day basis because it actually requires more effort to produce the same work. Children who have not mastered handwriting have not mastered keyboard skills either' (in Stradling *et al.* 1994: 18). Unfortunately this study, made over a few months, was unable to investigate this phenomenon further. Clearly children at that age would for the most part have been writing very short pieces of text. Also, the keyboard demands that you spell each word letter by letter, and if children are used to viewing words as a whole this may be more difficult than manual writing, where the task is to recreate a shape you know. Consider the way many of us who do not become instinctive spellers need to write a word to be sure how it should look. This is an area in which unfortunately there are more questions than answers, but what we can perhaps infer safely is that after Year 2 there is convincing evidence that the word processor facilitates most children in 'making the mark' through the keyboard, but before that age this cannot be assumed and needs careful monitoring.

Spell checkers can also help to improve children's spelling, both at the computer and beyond (Lynch 1991). But as with other support features, even for the simple actions of editing such as cutting and pasting or even just moving around the text to make changes, children need to be taught how to use the facility. The advantages and limitations of spell checkers need to be made explicit, for example a spell checker will not identify a mistake which is in itself a correctly spelt word. Children who have severe problems with letter order, for example, may not be assisted by the current generation of spell checkers, which requires them to choose between what they offer and a number of similar alternatives. If recognising these often small differences is the problem that the child is struggling with, clearly the spell checker cannot help. Furthermore, if the child's original offering is highly phonetic in nature, as is often the case, the spell checker is unlikely to be able to offer a suitable alternative.

Composition

Where the word processor is used purely as an amanuensis to help produce a more presentable end product, the true power of the technology is clearly severely under-exploited. The real power of a word processor for the writer is the flexibility it offers. When working on paper children are usually left with an end product which is essentially a first draft, perhaps with some comments from the teacher taken into account, and some spelling corrections made when the 'best' copy was written out. A narrative in electronic format is infinitely flexible. It can be revisited, changed, expanded or cut as needed to produce an end result the writer is happy with, and which perhaps better reflects the ideas the child had in her head. 'The mere fact that once a correction has been made the evidence of the mistake is gone, has been a great source of pleasure to many!' was the comment of one teacher reported in Stradling *et al.* (1994: 20). Copying out a story, especially more than once, is rarely pleasurable. Indeed the knowledge that any copying out is required can be a brake on children's creativity. As the 8-year-old quoted by Loveless stated, 'I write less. Then I have less to copy' (1995: 27). The facility for changing text with a word processor need not obliterate the stages of development the text has undergone, however. Print-outs of each iteration of a piece of writing can be made to provide a unique record of development, which can be used for assessment and profiling purposes. Reviewing previous versions of a piece of writing can make explicit to both the teacher and the pupil how the writer is progressing.

It is unlikely that children will begin the process of drafting and redrafting spontaneously. When Crook observed pairs of children working together to write stories using a word processor, it was evident that the story grew sentence by sentence. The children discussed the composition of each sentence, and the narrative content within it. However they rarely reread more than the last sentence of the story, although previous events were mentioned in discussions relating to what could happen next (Crook 1994). Similarly Jessel (1992) reports that pairs of children given a writing task where the final sentence of a story was agreed at the beginning, as an encouragement to plan a narrative, still composed sentence by sentence. Any spontaneous redrafting at the end was restricted to correcting spelling and punctuation. Changes to the narrative were only evoked by questions from the observer. Crook's and Jessel's observations confirm that the opportunity to compose must consist of more than simply time at the screen. Children do not appear to progress naturally to taking a broader view of the whole piece before they begin, or as they write. Nor do they spontaneously go back and redraft what they write without prompting.

These developments must be prompted by the teacher, who might choose to seed this progression by careful questioning and guided discussion, or by structuring writing tasks so that they involve explicit planning, editing and redrafting stages. Suitable strategies can include getting pupils to comment on each others' work, questioning children on details of the story such as why certain actions took place, or how they made the characters feel, or redrafting the same paragraph for different purposes (e.g. turning a story into a short play, or writing it in the style of a newspaper article). Where access to word processors is restricted, as it is in most classrooms, a group can write a short story, which individuals then continue to develop or adapt separately. This also has the advantage of assisting the teacher to assess each individual's achievement as the different outcomes are compared and contrasted.

In order to help develop the view of a piece of work as something to reflect on and revisit, it is important to make explicit to the child at the outset that this will be a part of the task. Especially where children have developed the habit of writing a story in a single sitting, with any later changes being made only to correct mistakes rather than to develop ideas, they may initially view 'having to do it again' as a failure or censure rather than an exciting opportunity to expand their ideas. Making the overall task, and its objectives, explicit to the learner both at the outset and as a task unfolds, is perhaps something we do not pay enough attention to generally. As a result children may not develop a sense of the process as a whole, even if they do have experience of all the constituent stages.

It is important to point out at this stage that a significant aspect of becoming a developed and experienced writer is the ability to make informed choices regarding the medium used for a particular purpose. The word processor may well be the first choice of many adult writers for most of the time, but some forms of writing, especially poetry or writing of a personalised nature, may demand other more traditional media to create the effect the author wants. Additionally the child as 'author' may wish to use media other than straight text to communicate ideas, a topic which I will return to in the discussion of 'new literacy' later in this chapter. In order to make choices about the most appropriate method of communicating their knowledge, ideas and thoughts, children must have had an opportunity to use a range of methods, both on and off the computer, such as is available to authors in our IT-rich culture.

Writing for a purpose

There are many types of writing in which children, and adults, engage which do not obviously fit the model proposed by Hunter (1988) and outlined above. Much of the writing that children do in school is not story writing. Examples include the results of children's research about the Victorians, the findings of a field-study trip, or an account of a science investigation. The purpose may be to make an accurate record of factual information collected from various sources, to put down personal observations or to describe a plan of action. The last of these is a vital component of any investigative task, and it is essential to successful problem-solving (see also Chapter 2 and Chapter 3 in this volume). Using a word processor for this kind of writing can be particularly successful in helping children to order their thoughts and agree a plan of action before they begin. Again, the way that the writing is made clear to the group as a whole, through display on the screen, seems to be a factor in engendering a sense of common ownership of the end product in a way that paper, where it is more difficult for more than the current writer to see the text as it forms, does not. Moreover the ease with which the text can be changed and developed as the group accepts suggestions from each member, without leaving the evidence of crossing or rubbing out, facilitates the refining of the final plan. My own observations in classrooms where children have been planning a science investigation and using a word processor to record their ideas also suggest that it is easier for a teacher to join in a group discussion and ask a pertinent question about the plan in progress very easily. She has no need to disturb the group dynamic to see the writing they have done, and any changes resulting from her questioning can be incorporated, as with those of the group members, without leaving a 'red mark' (Frost *et al.* 1994).

Who is the author?

The issue of changes and incorporations from other sources in children's writing, which do not leave a physical trace, is one which never ceases to arise in discussions about the use of electronic text I have had with groups of teachers and other parties interested in education. As mentioned above, in a longer piece of writing keeping more than one print-out as the work progresses can be a useful way of keeping track of developments. But another set of considerations arise when the subject of access to information sources in electronic format is under consideration. Here the issue of 'copying' other people's work seems to cause great consternation.

I can see the problem a lecturer in Higher Education might have in recognising whether an individual student, with whom she has had little personal contact, has actually written an assignment or downloaded it more or less wholesale from the Internet, or has acquired a disk from a student in the year above. I can also see how the Internet facilitates communication between students in different parts of the country, so that such assignment-sharing might be easier now than previously. However it is more difficult to believe that a school teacher, with knowledge of a child built on daily contact over months or even years, could fail to tell when a child has written something or when she has lifted large chunks, unacknowledged, from another source. No one would suggest that access to books is problematic because children might simply copy out sections into a piece of work and the teacher will be fooled as to the true author. The same skills that teachers have always used to detect plagiarism will surely apply equally well to the electronic version. Here as elsewhere, it is important we do not suspend our tried and tested critical faculties simply because we are faced with computerised technology. The whole issue of developing children's information-handling skills to address appropriate use of sources is addressed in Chapter 11.

What is 'new literacy'?

There is much talk of the so-called 'new literacy' in relation to the information age and the availability of rich information sources in electronic forms. Clearly, the ability to handle text to absorb and communicate information, ideas and emotions is, and will remain, an important skill set in our culture for the foreseeable future. However the criteria we use to judge an individual's competence in this medium might change. For an interesting discourse on why we venerate correct spelling, for example, see Spender (1995: 12–15). One aspect of IT that has enormous potential to influence what we write and how we write it, and how we judge the way text is written, is electronic mail (E-mail). This subject is dealt with in more detail in Chapter 11, but I would like to comment here that the availability to pupils of external audiences, from pupils in other schools to international experts in a range of fields, is a rich stimulus for the consideration of both purpose and audience in relation to what you write. The world of E-mail also has its own culture of language and symbol, largely a result of primitive text editors and the absence of graphics in the early days of this technology. For example, correcting typographical errors was impossible with early on-line editors, so spelling errors ceased to be a mark of ignorance and were assumed to be a glitch imposed by a technology that required perfect keyboarding skills. Also all kinds of abbreviations, now commonly understood by veteran E-mailers, have developed to save typing and therefore reduce on-line costs. One of the best known is probably the smiling face symbol, :-). The language of E-mail is widely regarded as having the characteristics of speech, which brings the audience closer to the writer (Potter 1987).

Developments in technology mean we are likely to be forced to deal with information in very different forms, both as 'readers' and as 'authors'. So far in this chapter I have only addressed the use of written text to convey information, be it a fictional narrative or an account of a museum visit. But the use of text has never been the sole means of recording thoughts in human culture, and the number of methods available to individual members of society has grown very rapidly in the last hundred years. Moreover, since the mid-1970s most of these media have been made available to children. Consider photography as an example. At the turn of the century the majority of the population might have had a photograph taken by a professional photographer to mark a family wedding; today there are cameras made and sold in quantity that are designed, and cheap enough, for use by the under-5s. In the mid-1960s television was a spectator sport. There was one set in the household of better-off families (perhaps rather like the multimedia computer today) and broadcasts were received during the afternoon and evening. Now even the poorest families have access to broadcast television, which is available 24 hours a day. Widespread ownership of video cameras means we can now make our own television, and these are so easy to operate that children may have access to such cameras at home or in school.

A 5-year-old coming to school will have had experience of decoding messages from a wide variety of sources and in a wide variety of formats. The narrative of a cartoon on television or at the cinema; the picture book which may have preceded or sprung from it; the cuddly toy of the main character – all convey aspects of a story to her. But her decoding abilities go much further; she recognises the logo of the burger bar and knows what it means, which button means play on her cassette player, which symbol means quit on the computer screen. The modern myth that if you want to program the video ask a 5-year-old is only partly mythical. In his opening address to the World Conference on Computers in Education in 1990, Alan Kay, who is credited with the original concept of the mouse-driven personal computer, said that technology was the stuff that was invented since you were born. The implication is that anything which pre-dates you is wallpaper – a natural and unremarked part of your world. And so not only computerised technologies, but all the languages they evoke, rely on and present, are an established and natural part of the 5-year-old's world. It should not be surprising, then, if reading and writing text is not the most natural method of communication for a child. Just as we expect art work to precede writing, so we might now need to consider where the use of images, video and audio come in children's developing literacy, as they are given more access to different media as authors, not just as 'readers'.

Perhaps even more challenging than the mixture of media children are now exposed to will be the implications for literacy that the advent of computer-based multimedia has. Multimedia, as discussed at greater length in Chapter 11, not only combines pictures with text, sound and video, but it breaks away from a linear narrative. In this environment there is no requirement to access the information available in a given order. The National Council for Educational Technology (NCET) runs an annual competition to find the best examples of multimedia authored by children. It includes categories for lower and upper primary schools as well as upper and lower secondary. The upper primary has always been one of the most competitive categories, in both the terms of quantity and quality of entries. The winning entries are published on CD ROM. The skill and sheer creative imagination that children bring to this new medium are remarkable. But perhaps the most revealing aspect of this competition is that the category for student teachers has been dropped, as it attracted so few entries each year. It seems that the chances of children meeting a newly qualified teacher literate in this medium are likely to be small, and not going to grow in the near future if their experiences in initial training are anything to go by. This is disappointing from another perspective too. At Homerton College we have found that introducing students in initial training to multimedia authoring leads to the production of novel and exciting teaching resources, but it is perhaps more significant that this approach provides a way of increasing student confidence with IT and therefore the likelihood that students will use IT in their subsequent teaching (McFarlane and Jared 1994).

Access to multimedia in schools is growing. In 1996, after a number of dedicated funding initiatives, an estimated 35 per cent of primary schools had a multimedia-capable computer and some multimedia titles published on CD ROM. In 1996–7 twenty-three projects throughout the UK, involving hundreds of schools and colleges, are evaluating the impact of access to multi-media over highspeed telephone lines – the Information Superhighway (DfEE 1995). Trials of provision of these vast information sources to the home, accessed through the domestic television via something as simple as the remote channel changer, are well advanced. In this culture, the fact that the teacher can spell better than her class is little comfort compared to her probable non-literacy in multimedia. The implications of these developments, and the potential reversal of skill balance between teacher and pupil, are likely to have a far-reaching impact on the dynamic of the classroom. As a primary school teacher I recently interviewed in relation to attitudes to information super-highways commented, 'The children who have computers at home have better ones than we do, and we are simply boring them!' This is a challenge which I shall revisit in Chapters 11 and 12.

Summary

Literacy is something which extends beyond simple manual encoding and decoding of text. It involves the habit of viewing writing as a way of developing and communicating a child's thoughts. The use of word processors helps to present text as something to be experimented with, redrafted and developed as ideas develop, or the demands of purpose or audience change. It liberates the writer from the heavy burden of manual editing and presentation. This chapter develops these ideas and suggests ways in which the teacher can provide classroom activites that make the process of crafting text more explicit, so that children come to see writing as an holistic act, each stage of which is vital to the whole.

Written text is not, and never has been, the sole means of recording and communicating ideas. However the mixture of media now available to a child both as 'reader' and 'author' is unprecedented. The issue of the 'new literacy' this multimedia culture has spawned is considered, and some of the related concerns it presents for teachers and teacher educators are raised.

Chapter 9

Working with images, developing ideas

Avril Loveless

Introduction

Stephanie and Fiona are 9 years old. They are sitting together in front of a computer screen, discussing an idea that has just occurred to them. On the chair next to them lies a plastic folder containing a photograph of them with their arms in the air, a crayon picture of a cereal bowl, some painted bananas and pears, some small cereal packets and some rather ripe slices of fruit. Yesterday they placed each of these items on to a scanner – including the fruit, saving and storing a visual image of each in the computer's memory. They are now discussing how they can use the computer to put together all these items in a poster that will convey the message 'Eat a Healthy Breakfast!' They have decided to enlarge the photographs, make the fruit look more green, reduce the cereal packet and choose some bright colours for the background. They are not yet sure how to position the text that will accompany the picture. When their work is finished they will print it out on paper, copy it on to a disk to pass on to their friends, use it as an animated presentation of their class work on a CD ROM and send it, via the Internet, all over the world. (See Figure 9.1.)

The experiences they have had and the decisions they have had to make during this activity have enriched their visual education. They have addressed issues of meaning, media, technique, display, audience and ownership. The use of information technology (IT) in this process has added to, and contrasted with, more familiar and traditional ways of working with images. It has also provided the opportunity to develop their ideas through transformation, multiplicity and transmission. Artists acknowledge that IT offers a unique medium in which to work and poses challenges to the ways in which visual ideas are expressed, communicated, shared and developed.

Matheison has described visual education as requiring three elements:

1 Perception through observation, memory and imagination, visualising ideas and drawing upon a wide range of resources from the environment.
2 The use of materials as media, developing the ability to select and control materials, tools and techniques to express ideas in a visual language, using colour, line, shape and pattern in two and three dimensions.

3 Knowledge and understanding of the language of art as expressed by themselves and by others.

(Matheison 1993)

These elements are reflected in the National Curriculum orders for art, and are highlighted in the sections 'Investigating and making' and 'Knowledge and understanding' (DfE 1995a) as being central to visual development. Visual

Figure 9.1 'The big breakfast: eat healthy yummy food': poster produced by 9-year-old girls working with Adobe Photoshop on a Macintosh, using scanned pictures and objects, at Glebe Middle School, Southwick

elements and techniques and media are explored through a variety of learning processes: expressing ideas and feelings; recording experience, observation and imagination; designing and making images; modifying and refining work; and looking at the art, craft and design of practitioners in other places and times.

IT in the classroom, library and home can support and extend children's visual learning both in practice and knowledge. It provides practical experiences of creating and working with digital images and also exploits the nature of digital imagery to give access to a wealth of information about artists' work. Children can use drawing and paint packages to produce their own work and then look at how visual ideas have been expressed by others – whether it be on a disk containing clip art, a CD ROM of the works in the National Gallery or the Louvre, a virtual gallery on the World Wide Web or the home page of a particular artist making his or her work available to anyone who wishes to use it.

Teachers must recognise the opportunities and challenges that IT brings to children's learning and incorporate it into their pedagogy. They need to understand the nature of the medium and processes that IT offers; the unique characteristics of electronic communication; the practical implications for planning and preparation in the classroom and the cultural context in which artists, crafts people, designers, photographers and film-makers are using IT to express their ideas. This chapter will attempt to address some of the issues raised in this fast-moving, stimulating and exciting field, which affect the medium, the culture and the classrooms in which we work.

How can IT support learning in the visual arts?

Artists work with various media, tools, techniques and processes in order to express their ideas and create a distinctive 'signature' in their work. Media such as paint, clay, cane, metal, fabric and photographic paper have particular properties which can be explored and exploited using a variety of tools – from brushes and knives to filters and fingers. Interacting with and manipulating the physical medium is an important part of the process by which the artist learns to make decisions about controlling the medium and understanding its potential and constraints.

Information technology can be considered to present a range of tools and techniques with which to work on a new medium: digital data. Computer graphics packages have been designed not only to simulate more traditional physical processes, such as painting, drawing and photography, but also to construct and communicate visual representations in new ways. IT provides the opportunity for children to explore not only mimicry and manipulation of visual images, but also the potential for accurate multiplicity and transmission. That is, the image can be copied and sent to an audience anywhere else in the world, not only to be viewed by that audience, but made available for further work and development.

In using IT in art education, teachers and pupils need to consider a number of questions that are raised by working with digital images:

- What contribution does IT bring to the visual arts in terms of medium, techniques and processes? What is the significance of the 'digital' nature of the images? What kinds of skills and understandings are required and how are they acquired? What kinds of decisions do artists make when working with digital images? What are the constraints of working with a digital medium?
- How does IT enable the production of visual images? How does it contrast with other techniques and processes? How can it support new forms of visual representation?
- How can digital images be displayed and communicated? How does its digital nature influence the structure or appearance of an image? What implications are there for the purpose, ownership and audience of those images?
- How do we become visually literate in our ability to construct and read digital images in the way we have become able to read paintings or photographs?
- What role does the teacher play in supporting children's visual literacy with IT?
- What practical implications do these questions have for art education in the classroom and the ways in which teachers plan and practise their ideas with the children?

The digitial medium

The nature of the data

In considering the particular nature and contribution of IT in the visual arts, it is useful to focus on the ways in which it mimics and contrasts with more traditional media and techniques. Mitchell (1994) gives a detailed and fascinating discussion of the similarities and differences between painting, photography and digital images and the ways in which the effects of each have been used to convey or challenge the notion of 'visual truth'.

Most computer graphics packages used in primary schools are designed to model a blank canvas on which a variety of 'tools' can be used to 'paint' or 'draw' an image on the screen. The user can select the tools and effects required by communicating with the program by moving a mouse device – pointing, clicking and dragging a cursor across the screen – or a pen and digitising tablet (electronic drawing pad), which is more responsive to the speed and pressure applied by the artist. The medium that is being worked with, however, is not paint, light sensitive paper or ink, but digital data.

The two-dimensional picture projected on the screen is subdivided into a Cartesian grid, the cells of which are called *pixels*: an abbreviation of 'picture elements'. Each one of these pixels has a value, represented in the computer by an integer denoting intensity or colour and it is the array of integers that is stored and transmitted. It is these integers that are acted upon by the 'tools' of computer graphics packages, computational operations that assign or change the values of these pixels in order to display them in visual form. These values represent a range of qualities, such as colour, saturation, brightness or opacity, which can be changed to give different effects. The story is told of the first images of Mars transmitted from Mariner IV being stored on magnetic tape as integers, printed out on paper as sets of numbers and coloured in by scientists with different crayons for each number. Scientists and crayons have been replaced by computer software and hardware, but the principle is unchanged; computer graphics is indeed 'painting by numbers'.

As with painting or photography, the artist ultimately needs to have some understanding of how the medium and the tools – paint, emulsions, brushes, lenses – interact with and influence each other. In working with digital images in which the basic elements are assigned values, the artist has to come to understand the ways in which the computational tools manipulate, transform and process those values. The medium being worked with is not paint or emulsion, but a set of mathematical values and relationships which can be represented visually. This means that the images can be created and transformed in ways which often have no direct counterpart in other media. Fortunately, it is not necessary to understand the underlying mathematics to appreciate the possibilities it offers, or to use the computer-based tools.

Constraints

The exciting possibilities of working in a new medium should be considered in the context of the constraints it imposes and the ways in which it contrasts with other media which may be more appropriate for different purposes. The lack of physical and kinaesthetic involvement with the medium can be considered to be a limitation of IT in the visual arts. The craft skills requiring dexterity and delicacy of touch in working with different and difficult materials are absent in using computer graphics. Although there are advantages in being able to produce visual effects without fine motor skills and hand–eye co-ordination, the pleasure and purpose in working with physical materials in order to develop control and texture need to be explored in other ways. The digital image has a sense of distance from its creator; a painting bears the visual 'autograph' of the artist, whereas a digital image may share the 'allographic' qualities of the notation of a musical score or play which is interpreted and performed by others (Mitchell 1994: 50–1).

Just as word processing and desktop publishing allowed writers to focus on format, often to the detriment of content, so the accessibility and ease of use of many of the computer graphics techniques can encourage speed and quick decisions, rather than considered thought and preparation in visual composition and structure. There can also be a tendency to rely on the ease of production of effects rather than experimentation, leading to uniform accuracy and lack of distinctive 'signature' (Scrimshaw 1988).

Many of the criticisms of IT and its mechanistic production of images could be heard as echoes of the protest in the nineteenth century against the new-fangled technique of photography. This also began as a medium for observation and mimicry, before developing its own distinctive ways of representing meaning.

The production of images

IT enables the production of images in a variety of ways: making marks, digitising an image created in another medium, manipulating and transforming the image or representing information in visual forms not 'seen' before.

Making and capturing an image

Traditional mark-making techniques of the artist – such as sketching, painting, spraying, smudging, blending and using pens and brushes of different shapes and sizes with different types of papers and canvases – are imitated in computer graphics by the tools available to make marks on the screen. Brushes, crayons, spray guns and paint pots can be selected and directed by using a mouse or digitising pen to produce 'digital brush strokes'. (See Figures 9.2 and 9.3.)

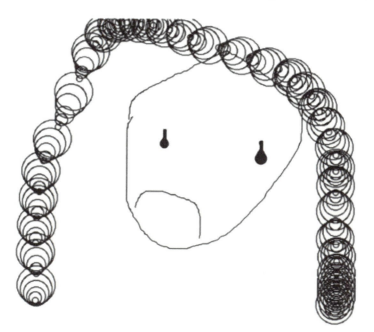

Figure 9.2 Katie: picture drawn by a 4-year-old girl working with Kidpix on a PC. The effects were produced by using the mouse as: a brush tool with a 'spring' pattern for the hair; a 'dripping paint' pattern for the eyes; and a pencil tool with a thin line for the outline. (This is an example of children's work produced at the University of Brighton.)

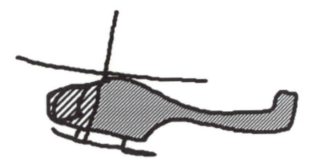

Figure 9.3 Police helicopter: picture drawn by a 7-year-old boy working with ClarisWorks on a Macintosh. He used a thick brush for the outlines and filled in the areas with a pattern selected from a palette of patterns and colours. (This is an example of children's work produced at the University of Brighton.)

One of the features of 'making marks' with a graphics program is the ease with which corrections, alterations and refinements can be made. Most packages have the facility to 'rub out' or undo the effects, thus allowing experimentation and exploration without having to start from the beginning each time. As in editing text in a word processor, marks need not be final, but are always open to development as ideas become clearer or change.

The devices used to control these tools, such as the mouse, however, can be clumsy and not suited to fine motor control. Electronic painting or drawing directly on the screen is a useful technique, but limited in the effects it can produce in originating an image. It may be more appropriate to produce the original image with other media – such as pencil, paint, textiles, photographs, found images – and capture it using a scanner, digital camera or video still camera. These will code and represent the image as pixels, providing the digital data for storage, transmission, display and further manipulations. There have been a number of developments in the market for scanners and digital cameras, bringing down the price and therefore enabling primary schools to consider them appropriate IT resources.

A digital camera takes pictures, but stores the information, not on film, but in a digital form on disk. This can then be transferred to the desktop computer, saved to disk and loaded into a graphics package like any other saved image. The obvious advantage of a digital camera is that it is easily portable to the locations where the children wish to take their 'photographs'. The quality of the image is not as high as that on photographic paper, but these digital images have potential, as will be discussed later. (See Figure 9.4.)

A scanner can 'read' information from a source, such as a picture or object, which is then digitised and stored on the computer. Scanners can also be hand-held, but are usually of the 'flat-bed' type, looking like a small photocopier. (See Figure 9.5.)

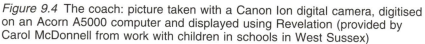

Figure 9.4 The coach: picture taken with a Canon Ion digital camera, digitised on an Acorn A5000 computer and displayed using Revelation (provided by Carol McDonnell from work with children in schools in West Sussex)

Images produced by other people can be captured for further development by a number of means. Picture files can be made available to a wide audience through distribution on disk, CD ROM or over the Internet. Although at present allowance still needs to be made for possible incompatibility between systems and formats for the transmission of pictures, they can, theoretically, be loaded into the user's graphics package and used as a starting point for further work.

Manipulating and transforming an image

The making of marks and the production of the image on the screen is only the first stage of the process of using the potential of IT. Having produced an image from the initial data, which could be drawn from a variety of sources, from mouse marks to scanner or satellite, the distinctive contribution of the computer

Figure 9.5 Polaroid photograph scanned and digitised on an Acorn A5000 (provided by Carol McDonnell from work with children in schools in West Sussex)

is the processing power that it has to enhance, manipulate and transform the visual image, altering or abstracting the relationship between its elements. These computational operations act upon the pixels, changing values and relationships in order to produce a variety of visual effects.

Some are used as 'filtering techniques' to change the appearance of the image by emphasising or omitting particular features or qualities. Changes in figure and ground, positive and negative, tone-scale, opacity, highlighting, colour transformations and diffusion are examples of effects used to alter the appearance of the image. Children could therefore experiment with the consequences of colour substitutions, blurring and blending of colour margins, altering the opacity of elements to give 'ghostly' effects or tracing the outline of figures and patterns. Such techniques are similar to those of photography – from dodging and burning, to coloured lenses and different types of paper – but offer greater variety and new possibilities. (See Figures 9.6a–9.6d.)

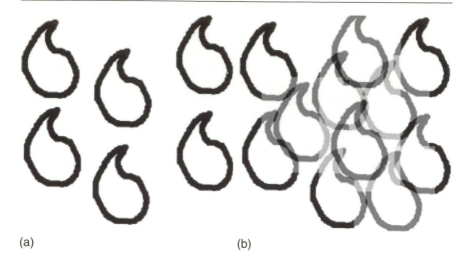

(a)   (b)

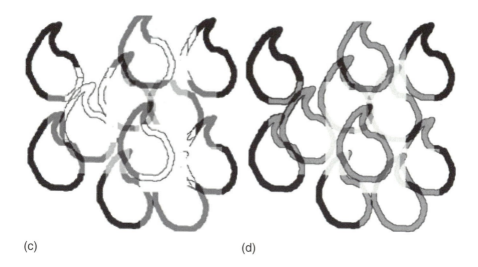

(c)   (d)

Figure 9.6a First of a series of 'drop' images, produced working with Revelation on an Acorn A7000. The 'drop' was painted with a brush tool, selected and copied.

Figure 9.6b The 'blend' tool was used to create greys, from the blending of the black and white elements in the selected area.

Figure 9.6c The 'trace' tool was used to give the traced effect in selected areas.

Figure 9.6d The 'outline' tool was used to highlight the edges, creating a different effect from the trace.

It is, however, the processes of electronic collage and transformation that gives access to techniques not easily available using traditional methods. Elements of the image can be selected and then cut, moved, copied, distorted, sheared, stretched, flipped, rotated and scaled to create a range of effects. Such adjustments can be explored and considered, rejected and erased or developed and refined, the stages being printed or saved along the way to reflect the development and working through of ideas and techniques. (An example of collage and transformation work is Figure 9.7.)

A key feature of working with digital images is the opportunity to explore and refine ideas, undo 'mistakes', leave trails and use elements of transformed data as starting points for new images. Techniques with such a range and level of sophistication used to be available only through specialist and costly equipment. The hardware and software available in most primary schools today will enable young children to make a start with these processes.

New visual representations

IT can code visual images in a digital form for storage, display and transformation. It can also generate visual images from non-visual sources, such as mathematical relationships and represent them in a variety of forms.

An immediate application of this facility is seen in the presentation of data as graphs as discussed in Chapter 7. The visual expressions of the fractal geometry developed by Benoit Mandelbrot are extraordinary and unpredictable, echoing the chaotic and asymmetrical forms of nature. The breathtaking pictures of the landscapes of Venus reported in newspapers and magazines were not captured as photographs, but constructed from the digital information sent from radar scans. Scanners can be situated in satellites to look at the planets and stars, or in microscopes to look at the structure of organisms and molecules. They can provide data on variations in light, sound, heat and atomic vibration, which are used to build digital models. These models can in turn be represented visually, producing images – of planets, human bodies or molecules – which could not be realized in any other way.

The spatial relationships between elements in a three-dimensional object can be mapped and coded digitally, enabling the visualisation of projections and movements around and through these objects. Designers can use computer-aided design applications (CAD) to help them visualise their 3-D products, whether they be tea cups, racing cars or city skyscrapers. The virtual reality (VR) of flight simulations and arcade games generates images of existing, new and imaginary worlds by modelling relationships in different dimensions: virtual landscapes, skies, structures and interiors can be created from mathematics instead of marks.

Classrooms may not yet have the more sophisticated applications which collect, store and produce these images, but the children have access to them throughout their general culture – on television screen, in print, on CD ROM, over the Internet and in computer games. They need to be able to make the links between the work that they themselves do within the digital medium, and the developments that are possible in the commercial world.

Communicating to others

Display

Digital images are usually displayed on a screen or by a printer, in each case the quality of resolution and colour balance often being in direct proportion to cost. High-quality devices used in the commercial or research world are not available to primary schools and children are often disappointed by the colours and textures in the printed product of their work on screen, particularly in comparison with paint and photographic prints. It is important, therefore, that the discrepancies and contrasts are discussed and understood, in order to appreciate the nature and structure of digital images and the ways in which their purpose differs from that of fine prints and high resolution photographs.

The ephemeral nature of the screen display with its low resolution and limited colours could be seen as constraining and a disadvantage in comparison with a high quality photographic print. If, however, the inherent qualities of a digital image are recognised – its discrete structure and its potential for transformation, multiplicity and transmission for further interaction – they can be used to advantage to create and develop images appropriate to the medium. Pictures produced for the screen which can be copied and transmitted across the World Wide Web for a variety of purposes in a version which may never be final, will have a very different character and quality from those produced as unique fine art or photo-journalism. Many photographers are now exploring the qualities of the low-resolution, pixellated world in expressing their ideas. (See Figures 9.8a, 9.8b.)

The world of the screen – television, video and computer – is a familiar element of the child's culture in our society. The advent of digital television promises a range of different reasons to interact with the screen, from home shopping to video on demand and customised news. The representation and understanding of visual meaning through the screen will be an important element in the development of literacy in the 'information age'.

Ownership, audience and purpose

Issues of display are not limited to the physical quality of the product, but are also about broader questions of the ownership, audience and purpose of digital images.

The electronic way in which the image is stored means that it can be copied many times without any degradation or deterioration and communicated all over the world, to be used and developed by others. Which image, therefore, is the

Figure 9.7 'The fruits go to the woods', a poster produced as part of the 'Big Breakfast' project. The underlying story is based on the songs 'If you go down to the woods tonight', 'Bananas in pyjamas are coming down the stairs' and 'She'll be coming round the mountain'. The fruits and photographs were scanned, selected, scaled and copied; the krispies were scattered on the mountain and used as paint; the mountain in the background was produced by selecting a section of another picture of a mountain and using the selected motif as paint; the word 'woods' was tilted and then reflected in the stream. This work was produced by 9-year-old boys using Photoshop and Macintosh computers, at Glebe Middle School, Southwick.

Figure 9.8a A Polaroid photograph was scanned and digitised on an Acorn A5000. (Figures 9.8a and 9.8b were provided by Carol McDonnell from work with children in schools in West Sussex.)

Figure 9.8b Using the package Revelation on the Acorn, an element of the image was selected, enlarged and worked on to develop the contrast in the shapes and shades, and to produce effects in the sky.

original? When is it finished? Who owns it? How can provenance and value be ascribed to it? How can it be copyrighted? Is interaction with and development of the source image seen as collaboration or interference?

A distinctive feature of working with such images is the emphasis on the transforming process and the potential for transmission, rather than the capture and printing as in photography. Mitchell refers to this process as 'electrobricollage' (Mitchell 1994: 7) and describes digital images as 'fragments of information that circulate in the high speed networks now ringing the globe and that can be received, transformed and recombined like DNA to produce new intellectual structures having their own dynamics and value' (p. 52).

The boundaries between originators and audiences, producers and consumers of images become blurred. Instead of trying to mimic the processes of traditional paint, photography and print, perhaps visual images should be produced not only to explore the digital medium, as described above, but also to extend notions of audience and collaboration. Virtual galleries and museums, whether in the classroom or on the Web, would not only make pictures available for viewing, but also offer them for further transformation and transmission. An example of a discussion of such galleries and museums can be found on the World Wide Web (see Figure 9.9).

VISUAL LITERACY IN THE 'INFORMATION AGE'

I often quote a statement made by Picasso, which is thought-provoking and challenging: 'Art does not evolve by itself, the ideas of people change and with them their mode of expression' (Picasso 1923/1975: 264). The artistic presentation of ideas can affect a range of senses – through images, text, sound and movement – and I have argued that IT can make a distinctive contribution to such modes of expression (Loveless, forthcoming). We do not, however, express ourselves in isolation, equipped only with media and techniques. We live in a cultural context in which we are influenced by the ideas and systems of others, which we can in turn develop or challenge.

IT should be seen not just as equipment requiring particular technical skills, but also as part of our culture in which the collection, organisation, analysis and communication of information plays a central role. The notion of 'IT capability' in the National Curriculum encompasses this wider understanding of the appropriate use of IT (DfE 1995b). It is important for teachers to have a critical understanding of the context in which children experience IT in their learning and the ways in which the 'ideas of people change'. If we are educating children to be active participants in an information society, what forms of literacy will they require? How will they read and construct meaning from visual information and how will they approach opportunities to use IT purposefully and appropriately? (See Chapter 11 for a discussion of 'new literacy'.)

The use of IT poses interesting challenges to notions of visual literacy. Allen (1994) argues that traditional art pedagogy has been limited in its view of visual

text continues on p. 138

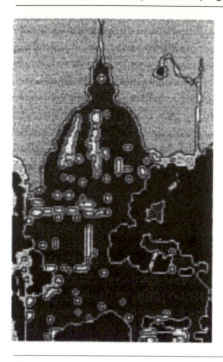

Museum Resources

'How to' articles and other resources meant to guide those who are just starting out.

- Virtual Museums and Schools
- Exploring Virtual Museums – This is an interactive WWW page which introduces the visitor to the concept of a 'virtual museum' and suggests sites to visit, providing links to facilitate the exploration.
- How to Build the School Museum – Step by Step – A guide to the careful and thoughtful development of a school museum.
- Staff Development for Virtual Museum Building – A comprehensive and detailed guide to provide a ten hour, five session course to teachers (and students) which will equip them with museum-building and planning skills. Developed and tested at the Bellingham Public Schools (the site of this link).
- Home Sweet Home: WWW Pages Which Deliver – Eighteen design tenets for the development of HTML pages which function smoothly and quickly to deliver information in an attractive yet efficient manner.

This page has been visited 1457 times since January 1, 1996

Building Virtual Museums

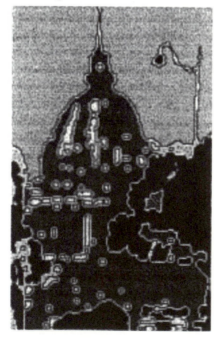

This page was constructed by Jamie McKenzie. It may be copied and used by non-profit institutions for staff development purposes so long as credit is given.

Sections

- Exploring Home Pages
- Exploring Museums
- Hot Metal (HTML) Resources
- Student Centered Learning
- Virtual Museum Article

A virtual museum defined . . .

A virtual museum is a collection of electronic artifacts and information resources – virtually anything which can be digitized. The collection may include paintings, drawings, photographs, diagrams, graphs, recordings, video segments, newspaper articles, transcripts of interviews, numerical databases and a host of other items which may be saved on the virtual museum's file server. It may also offer pointers to great resources around the world relevant to the museum's main focus.

Exploring Home Pages

Most schools and districts offer little more on their home pages than photographs of the school, a list of staff and a few student works. A good home page would do at least three things:

- 1) Point internal users to good outside information resources
- 2) Point external and internal visitors to good internal curriculum resources
- 3) Introduce external visitors to the school

Here are some examples of school home pages which offer more than just the basics:

- Alaska – University Park Elementary
- Walker Elementary
- Rice School
- School Home Pages A listing of all WWW school sites nationwide
- Mankato Schools Check out the Cyberfair!
- Cyberspace Middle School
- Discovery Middle School Includes MIDLINK Magazine
- Smoky Hill HS
- Los Alamos HS
- Science Academy of South Texas Much of this site is under construction, but the framework of ideas is impressive.
- Back to index

Exploring Museums

We cannot find any school sites which provide what we intend to build, but there are sites which possess many of the features we associate with virtual museums. We expect that students and staff will 'beg, borrow and steal' the best of these features and invent school versions to support a student centered curriculum.

- Acropolis – Visit this ancient site and wander through temples and graceful columns. Be prepared for large graphics.
- Bellingham Antique Radio Museum – This special collection museums goes global with a well designed WWW site.
- Field Museum – Dinosaurs & Masks
- Franklin Institute – Long renowned for its wonderful 'hands on' science exhibits, the Franklin Institute is leading the pack of virtual museums with multimedia and superb online resources.
- High Museum – Excellent collection of paintings and photographs.
- Palaeolithic painted cave at Vallon – Pont-d'Arc. Startling and dramatic images from the recently discovered cave. Brilliant photographs. Excellent text.
- Native American Resources – Culture, Art, Education, Texts Related to Native American Issues, Video Resources, Related Museums, & Government Resources.
- New Mexico Museum of Natural History and Science
- Ontario Science Center
- Paleontology (California Museum of)
- Sea World Animal Database
- Smithsonian – This site leads you to some very good national collections.
- Treasures of the Czars – The museum provides outstanding visuals.
- WebMuseum – An extensive collection with hundreds of excellent paintings along with quite interesting biographical and interpretive sketches.
- Whales – Rich collection of resources and projects to support the study of whales.

Hot Metal (HTML) Resources

- A Beginner's Guide to HTML

- Crash Course in Writing WWW Documents
- Home Page Design
- Introduction to HTML
  Back to index

Student Centered Learning (HTML) Resources

- Using WWW for Constructivism
- Constructivist Readings
- Back to index

Virtual Museums are the Future

Unlike most school research projects, virtual museums provide persistent, ongoing 'change, activity, and progress' (American Heritage Dictionary definition of 'dynamic'). The collection process is never-ending. Students may continue their work over several years, and even after they leave their elementary school to begin work at the virtual museum housed at the middle school, they can return for 'electronic' visits and note the expanding collection. Multi-age classes may focus upon the same challenge for several years running without fear of repetition.

Students can actually see the 'fruits' of their inquiry. They become 'knowledge builders' rather than mere consumers. Museums are also fine vehicles for multidisciplinary studies, as the collection may include everything from music and art to science and politics and mathematics. The driving research question for the Asian Rim museum (Which culture would you pick if your family were to live abroad for a year and why?) naturally steers students to look at a broad range of factors which bridge the disciplines. Virtual museums offer multi-sensory opportunities appealing to a variety of learning styles and multiple intelligences. One can see a Picasso. One can see and hear Tori Amos perform 'Cornflake Girl.' While it is difficult to touch or taste, the same would be true of a conventional museum. Virtual museums have great advantages over textbooks – bringing vitality, color and motion to student exploration.

- Full Text of Museum Article
- Back to index

This page has been visited 533 times since January 1, 1996.

Figure 9.9 Building virtual museums: an example of a page on the World Wide Web, which is part of an on-line magazine, From Now On, presented by Jamieson McKenzie. The location of this set of linked pages is: http://www.pacificrim.net/~mckenzie. The underlined headings are hypertext links to other pages of information and images. This material was taken from the WWW in August 1996.

literacy and has not acknowledged the role played by the moving image and popular culture in children's approach to visual meanings. In using IT, children have shown their ability to draw upon and extend a wide range of strategies in visual communication. They have appropriated a range of influences – such as television, film, computer games, fashion, literature and music – and incorporated them into ways of working in which the boundaries between the classroom, the street and the home are challenged.

Children in the Glebe Middle School, West Sussex, participated in a project in which they used IT to support their term's work on nutrition under the theme 'The Big Breakfast'. They were observed to use nine elements in producing a visual image with a powerful computer graphics application. They demonstrated the interaction between narrative, content, audience, colour, text, design, affect, interpersonal ways of working and attitudes to IT. The facilities of the graphics package enabled them to manipulate and refine their designs in a positive and collaborative way, developing a range of successful strategies for using complicated techniques within a purposeful activity. Their visual literacy – the ability to construct meaning through visual images – was supported by a broader ability to combine narrative, a sense of audience and cultural symbols (Hobin and Cornish 1995, Loveless and Hobin 1996).

Communication in our society and culture is becoming increasingly visual – from the printed page to video-conferencing, from diagrams to advertising. Visual literacy and media literacy are closely linked and IT plays a significant role in these modes of communication. There is, however, a mythology beginning to surround children's use of IT and their interaction with the world of the screen: computer, television and film. The press and television reflect and fuel the concerns of parents and teachers trying to understand the ways in which IT has an impact on modern childhood. There is anxiety and suspicion about children having access to images and values which might be considered inappropriate, whether they be 'shoot-'em-up' games or pornography. Heppell asserts that some people use a deficiency model of children using computer games and multimedia technology. They claim, he says, that these activities limit children's ability to concentrate and follow a line of argument, without considering the 'emergent capabilities and new expectations' of the children. But his view is, 'Games can provide a challenging problem solving environment where players observe, question, hypothesise and test. Games can offer a vehicle for collaborative endeavour and, crucially, they have changed the climate of expectation that surrounds children's computing experiences' (Heppell 1994: 158). (See also chapter 2.)

There is also anxiety about the role IT plays in education and about the perception that children will 'learn better' with access to computers. Sefton-Green (1994) highlights a common, uncritical view that IT promotes learning and progress, a view that makes no reference to the complex interactions between machine, user and context. It is true that adults, both in school and in the home, often have the view that children have expertise and knowledge of the technology that is more advanced and intuitive than their own. But they are often unaware of the ways in which children use the technology, or some of the difficulties that they might encounter in the loneliness of their technologically advanced bedroom (see Sanger 1996).

It is important, therefore, that teachers begin to develop an informed and critical view of the cultural context in which children and adults approach the use of IT. They need to be aware of the discussions, misgivings and enthusiasms that surround children's experience of IT in the visual arts and the effects these have on expectations and practical outcomes.

The role of the teacher

In order to develop an understanding of the potential of IT in teaching and learning in the visual arts, teachers need to address the ways in which the curriculum and pedagogy can be affected by its presence in the classroom.

The visual arts curriculum should reflect the knowledge, skills and concepts required in learning the subject. This chapter has discussed ways in which IT can support and extend this curriculum. It can be considered as a medium for visual mimicry and manipulation. It can give access to images of works of practitioners in the arts through virtual museums and galleries on the World Wide Web and CD ROM. It can also provide the opportunity to reflect on the development of artistic processes by comparing its potential for visual expression with other media and techniques. Learners need to develop an understanding of the appropriate use of IT in particular situations. This requires insight into the nature of the task, the potential of IT to contribute to the activity and the skills and techniques needed to solve the problem.

The ImpacT Report, a research project carried out for the Department of Education and Science in the UK, reported that the effective use of IT in classrooms having a positive impact on children's achievements was influenced by a range of factors. These included 'pupil access and opportunity, teacher characteristics and abilities and school and local educational authority support' (Watson 1993: 4). The presence of the IT itself was not sufficient for learning. Teachers who demonstrated effective use of IT were not only confident in the use and management of the resources themselves, but were also clear about their philosophy and pedagogy in the subject itself, aware of the knowledge and processes required and the learning demands of the domain.

In addition to an understanding of the contribution that IT can make to art, teachers must also consider the ways in which visual literacy is developed in the broader context of the use of IT in the 'information society'. There is ongoing educational debate about the nature of this entity (Neiderhauser 1996) and the range of 'literacies' needed to handle, understand and communicate information in a variety of forms (Baker *et al.* 1996). The 'information society' is often characterised as one in which technology provides access to a great store of information and allows it to be analysed and represented and then communicated to a wide audience. Literacy in the information age requires not only the skills to operate the technology, but also the ability to identify and structure a line of enquiry and to analyse and present the synthesis of the information retrieved and used in solving the problem.

A broader, critical view of literacy with IT, beyond the acquisition of skills, is needed in order to be able to understand and question its contribution to education and the contexts in which it may be used appropriately. Street (1993) describes an 'ideological' model of literacy which is situated in a social and cultural context, as more useful than an 'autonomous' model in which literacy is seen as a set of separate competences to be transferred to different situations. Beynon (1993) and Matthews (1992) emphasise the importance of teachers' critical understanding of the impact of IT in education. Both authors address teachers' assumptions about gender and the ability to use computers, and also discuss deep-seated beliefs about the nature of human and artificial intelligence. The images and expectations of IT that are held in our society are wide ranging and powerful, both extending and constraining people's experience and teachers need to consider how these are reflected and acknowledged in classroom practice.

The presence of IT raises particularly challenging issues for pedagogy. Teachers have to address their confidence in technical skills; the organisation of often limited resources; the management of learning activities appropriate to cognitive and social needs; and the evaluation and assessment of the quality of learning experiences for the pupils. In addition to considering the organisation and management, teachers need to reflect upon their own theories and beliefs about teaching and learning in the visual arts in order to understand the teaching roles and styles adopted and implemented in the classroom. Research into the roles demonstrated by teachers and learners in classrooms indicates that teachers do alter their ways of working with IT. The roles change over time as the task progresses, shifting from that of technical adviser and demonstrator to manager and facilitator through to consultant and co-learner (Fisher 1993, Fraser et al. 1988, Hoyles and Sutherland 1989, Loveless and Hobin 1996).

An effective teacher knows when and how to intervene in order to build and dismantle the 'scaffolds [to] help children to learn how to achieve heights that they cannot scale alone' (Wood 1988: 80). The presence of IT can challenge teachers to reflect upon their own strategies of interaction and intervention and to consider the complementary roles played by the learner, the teacher and the computer at different times in different contexts.

Practical considerations for teachers

How can teachers approach the use of IT in the curriculum in order to provide useful and effective experiences for the pupils? A philosophical understanding of the contribution it can make to the visual arts needs to be supported by practical planning and the organisation of appropriate activities.

Planning must be grounded in the learning intentions for the curriculum area and must provide pupils with opportunities to discuss the advantages and disadvantages of using IT to develop these visual processes. IT must be used alongside other media in order to give the pupils insight into its possibilities and limitations by contrasting and combining traditional and computer art, using each as both starting points and finished products (See Figure 9.10.)

Making marks with pens, pencils, charcoal and paint can be compared with

Starting Point

Observation of water in the school pond and in puddles

Learning Intentions

What do we want the children to learn?

* how to develop their perceptual skills
* creative, imaginative and practical skills to express ideas and feelings, record observations and design and make images
* the use of a variety of materials, tools and techniques
* how to respond to ideas, methods and approaches used in different styles and traditions
* how to discuss the ideas and methods of their peers

Competences

What do we want the children to do?

* observe & record
* develop ideas in sketchbooks
* work with materials for collage & paint
* take and work from photographs
* select and use IT equipment & graphics techniques
* generate pictures, save, retrieve, edit and print
* use selection and transformation tools in graphics package
* experiment with visual elements to make images
* communicate meaning for a chosen audience
* discuss and evaluate their work

Knowledge

What do we want the children to know?

The potential for the communication of ideas and meaning through visual language using a range of media, tools and techniques

The differences in the nature of the media used

Equal Opportunities

awareness of certain children in groups, particularly boys and girls in IT groups

Time span

Over four weeks with other activities

Experience

How can we use and build on the children's past experience?

Framework

* Observations, sketches, notes & discussion
* Presentation of materials for –
  collage, painting, digital images, photographs
* Organisation of groups for 'workshops'
* Display of 'Work in Progress' for discussion
* Exhibition and discussion of images

Ways of Learning

* Observation
* Practical experimentation
* Presentation
* Discussion
* Evaluation

Resources

* Ponds, puddles, trays – the sea?
* sketchbooks
* collage materials – variety of papers, foil, tissue, net
* painting materials – papers, paints, variety of brushes
* Computer & colour printer
* Graphics package
* camera and film
* examples of artists' work – Monet, Hockney, Homer, Mitchell

Outcomes/Audiences

Display of images to express ideas about water using photographs, collage, paint and computer graphics

Presentation to class, year group and school

Digital images shared with link school by e-mail

Opportunities for Assessment

* spontaneous observations
* planned observations during activities
* discussions with the children during and after activity
* looking at range of images
* self assessment of IT skills
* self assessment in discussion and evaluation

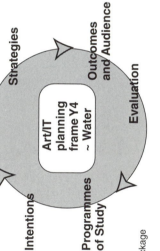

Figure 9.10 An example of a planning statement for an art activity in Year 4. The chosen theme was 'Water' and the development of IT capability was incorporated into the learning about media, display and audience.

the effects of computer tools such as the brush or spray can. The computer tools can be used to reproduce and interpret images produced in other media, or used as starting points for further development. A portrait can be composed directly on to the computer screen or the sweeping lines of a first attempt with the mouse can be developed with other materials such as string prints or wire. Colours can be substituted and changed and the quality of the coloured light on the screen and the coloured pigment on paper can be compared. The facility to select areas of a computer image for moving and copying can be used to explore printing, pattern and collage, developing ideas of texture, for example, with weaving, embroidery and clay. (See Figure 9.11.)

I drew some circles on the back of my photo copy and rotated them to get this effect

Figure 9.11 Rotated rings. Concentric rings were drawn by a Year 6 boy on to a photocopy of a photograph. They were cut and rotated to give the distorted effect. This was developed further into a 3D spiral of the photograph. (This example was provided by Carol McDonnell from work with children in schools in West Sussex.)

The classroom organisation should reflect the children's opportunities to work in a variety of media over a period of time in a range of activities. In a busy and crowded classroom, not all children can use computer graphics in every task. Their access to these facilities should be planned over time to give them the experience of experimenting, deleting mistakes, changing and refining ideas, saving and printing work in progress and producing a final outcome which can be shown to an audience. Displaying work daily on a 'work in progress' board in the classroom provides the children with the opportunity to discuss their ideas, techniques, comparisons and extensions in order to evaluate their work and consider ways forward.

The teacher therefore plays a variety of roles in this process. Planning requires identification of the learning demands of the activity: the knowledge, concepts and skills required. The resources need to be organised and their use demonstrated and modelled. The activity itself must be 'choreographed' and managed, from the groupings of children to the differentiation of the task for different cognitive needs and abilities. Support, interaction and intervention must be appropriate and opportunities provided for the teacher and the children to evaluate and assess the quality of the learning experience in order to inform future planning.

The arrival of IT in the classroom does not guarantee quality learning for the children. It can be effective, however, when learners and teachers have insight into the contribution it can make to the nature of the problem, whether that be communicating, handling, modelling, controlling, monitoring or measuring information. In the visual arts, IT has the potential to be a tool that mimics, processes and manipulates images; a resource that provides access to and participation in the work of others; and a catalyst in the development of new ways of expressing a visual language. It is the *interaction* of the facilities of IT, the children's ability to explore and extend their visual ideas and the teacher's pedagogy that can improve the quality of teaching and learning.

At the beginning of this chapter attention was drawn to the three elements of visual education: perception, use of materials as media, and knowledge and understanding of the language of art. Can IT support the development of visual literacy? The last word has been left to an observer of the children working in the Glebe School Project, illustrated in Figures 9.1 and 9.7. "The children's approach to the work and their finished posters were startling in their visual sophistication. This is a medium with which they engage, work with ease and express their ideas with a freshness and liveliness."

(Hobin and Cornish 1995)

Chapter 10

Computers in the classroom: some values issues

Michael Bonnett

Introduction: some questions

It is clear that computers have the potential to be an immensely powerful influence in the classroom, making new things possible in new ways, offering new opportunities and making new demands on both teachers and children. But while few would dispute the power and efficiency of computers to store and manipulate information, it is quite another matter to claim, as advocates do, that their introduction will enhance the quality of children's work, their learning, their motivation. These claims are not straightforward to assess because they raise the question: What is to *count* as quality in these regards? That is to say, what is to be *valued* here in educational terms? We need to reflect on the relationship between what computer use offers and the broader educational purposes that primary teachers may have. I would like, therefore, in this chapter to set out some important dimensions of decision-making that may be in danger of being insufficiently thought through under current pressures to incorporate IT into the school curriculum.

There are many aspects to this. But at the heart of the issue lies one central point: ways of generating, storing and processing ideas and information are never neutral. In the same way that, only in the world of the sales brochure can one find a car which is both the most powerful and the most economical, both the most commodious and the most sleek, so computer programs – along with other ways of structuring children's learning – each necessarily facilitate some kinds of activity at the expense of others. They reflect certain motives or values. Now this simple fact raises a very important area of concern: are the central values that are embodied in certain kinds of IT application really compatible with those of the classroom context into which they are being imported and the superordinate educational values of the teacher? This is an issue that frequently is not explicitly explored; nevertheless, because of the interactive – and therefore potentially involving – nature of computer-aided learning, the answer may be very important. It may be at least as important as assessing the qualities of, say, a human helper in the classroom, or the values (e.g. regarding gender or race) embedded in the books in the reading corner. Indeed, as we shall see, some kinds of computer program may actually inhibit teachers from properly exercising professional judgement over the character of their children's learning.

Allied to this set of concerns is another broad issue. It would be naïve to suppose that the kinds of interaction children experience in the classroom do not affect their view of life outside it. Indeed there would be little point to teaching if there were no such transfer. This brings us up against a further important question: how might the values implicit in IT in its various forms affect pupils' perceptions of 'good' thinking and their general outlook on the world around them? This becomes a particularly pressing issue with the increasing cumulative presence of IT across the curriculum.

In the very early days of computers in schools, it was not uncommon to encounter the following sort of observation:

> We are at the outset of a major revolution in education, a revolution unparalleled since the invention of the printing press. The computer will be the instrument of this revolution . . . By the year 2000, the major way of learning at all levels, and in almost all subject areas, will be through the interactive use of computers.
>
> (A. Bork 1980, quoted in Crook 1994: 3)

It is always perilous to make sweeping predictions, and with the turn of the millenium there is still little sign in schools that reality is about to catch up with Bork's vision. It is also interesting to consider the reasons put forward for the limited diffusion of computer use in schools compared with such early prognoses. Often they revolve around essentially technical and practical problems such as ignorance of, and lack of confidence in, the use of IT; unreliability of hardware and software (often at crucial teaching moments!); broad stereotyping of IT in terms of early unsophisticated software, the expense of maintaining or upgrading. But a focus on the issues mentioned previously raises another possibility. To what extent might teacher unease and the resulting lack of penetration of IT be the product not simply of resource problems or feelings of lack of expertise, but of some – often tacit, but maybe very real – conflict of values? That is to say, some teachers' intuitive reluctance to embrace IT may sometimes result from a perception that the kind of learning they value is incompatible with the kind of learning that interaction with IT promotes. It seems to me that this is an important dimension to the use of IT in schools and the issues it raises will be a focus of this chapter.

A way forward

When a new piece of equipment is introduced into schools as something with which pupils should acquire a familiarity, initially there may be a temptation to start with the equipment and look to see how other aspects of the curriculum can be adjusted to accommodate it. Computers in schools is a case in point. In the revised National Curriculum, besides effectively elevating IT to the status of a separate subject with its own separately documented Programme of Study and Level Descriptions, there is the continuing requirement to extend its use into all areas of the curriculum (with the exception of PE). Under such pressure the danger of simply attempting to 'fit in' yet another area of activity into the curriculum without giving due thought to its relationship to the areas into which it is to be 'fitted', is strong. An extreme version of this approach is provided by Crook (1994: 6) when he speaks of the need to define 'the optimal *computer* environment for supporting innovation as effortlessly as we can' (my emphasis). Fortunately, as other chapters in this book testify, more productive approaches can be explored. As in the rest of this book, in this chapter I want radically to reverse the order of starting with the 'equipment' and will begin, instead, by trying to identify educational needs.

Central to education is the quality of thinking and understanding that children develop. We need therefore to begin by identifying the different aspects of this quality as a prerequisite to considering what, if any, contribution IT might make to their development. Of course this strategy immediately brings us up against a variation of the fundamental question from which this chapter took its start: how are we to define 'quality' in respect of children's thinking and understanding? There are many ways in which this can be done – not least in terms of the subject-related abilities that are set out in the National Curriculum. However, for present purposes, I want to take as a point of reference a threefold classification of thinking quality which radically cuts across traditional subject boundaries.

The intention here is not to dismiss the importance of subjects, but to highlight some broader and perhaps more fundamental considerations relevant to the development of children's thinking and understanding than a subject orientation commonly invites. In particular I hope to provide an illustration of how values lie at the heart of issues of thinking quality and how these need to be identified and properly acknowledged if: (a) true integration of IT with other areas of the curriculum is to be achieved, and (b) the possible effects on children's thinking of the values embedded in IT itself – i.e. of becoming 'computer literate' – are to be sufficiently understood. But first, I must sketch the main dimensions of quality in thinking and understanding which will form the framework for this discussion.

Aspects of thinking quality

It is possible to classify thinking in myriad ways. I have already alluded to the subject-based classification, but there are others reflected in the use of terms such as 'logical' and 'intuitive', 'critical' and 'creative', 'inductive' and 'deductive', 'convergent' and 'divergent', 'analytic' and 'holistic'; 'higher order' (such as problem-solving) and 'lower order' (such as information acquisition). No doubt each of these is useful in certain contexts. But there is, I think, another set of distinctions, gaining in currency, which leads us to address some particularly important issues with regard to the introduction of IT into the curriculum. Different writers have used different terminologies and for convenience I will refer to them under the headings of *rational-calculative, authentic,* and *poetic.* (See, for example, Bonnett 1978, 1991, 1994, Cooper 1983, Heidegger 1966, Standish 1992, Taylor 1991)

Rational-calculative thinking is the sort that we engage in when we are concerned to order things in a way that enables us to *use* them. This instrumental motive involves defining things through imposing a system of categories upon them so that they can be 'summed up' in thought and are thus set up to be managed and controlled in line with whatever purposes we might have in mind. Thus we classify entities as 'chairs' and 'tables', 'fruits' and 'vegetables', 'dentists' and 'doctors' according to the functions they serve. Today, this kind of thinking is extremely pervasive. Indeed, many commentators have suggested that this instrumental element has come to dominate modern rationality as a whole. We constantly seek to evaluate, predict, control, our environment the better to exploit it. And in the process, increasingly, individual things become seen as *instances* of general categories ('a chair' rather than this unique chair) and come to derive their meaning and their value from the place we give them in our chains of calculative reasoning: our theories, our explanations, our experiments, our plans.

For example, we may view our jobs, cars, furniture, and acquaintances, according to our needs and aspirations and our theories about what will best serve these. We manipulate our social and natural environment (e.g. we engineer plants and animals) to serve our purposes more efficiently. It sometimes seems as though little remains sacred if it stands in the way of this sort of progress. Indeed, it has been argued that our ability and inclination to reason in this calculative way distinguishes western culture from others, that it is a central feature of our technology and consumerism.

Clearly, rational-calculative thinking is the sort of thinking that enables us to 'get things done' and its success in this regard is highly seductive. Few of us would lightly forgo many of the products of this kind of thinking, which even at a basic level range from on-the-shelf food to potable water, and anaesthetics. In comparison, thinking which has no obvious practical outcome is in danger of appearing pointless. In a society preoccupied with economic growth and material welfare, there is a strong tendency for the values of efficiency and mastery celebrated by rational-calculative thinking to become elevated to an impregnable position.

Now a number of criticisms have been raised with respect to this kind of thinking, particularly its highly manipulative stance. I shall return to these presently. For the moment let us consider one less frequently voiced: preoccupation with the publicly agreed categories, procedures and standards through which rational-calculative thinking is articulated holds out a serious danger of encouraging a depersonalised kind of understanding. That is to say, this sort of emphasis can encourage thinking that is technically correct in terms of public standards, but lacking personal significance. For example, for her age, a child may be able to reproduce a perfectly adequate technical account of how light is focused by a lens, but see no *personal* point to, or value in, this knowledge. She may be able to explain the socially accepted reason for a moral rule, but feel no personal commitment to it. She may be able to evaluate a poem or story or some historical character or event through the estimations of others more knowledgeable, but feel untouched by what she knows.

The importance of a subjective dimension to thinking and understanding is highlighted by the idea of *authenticity*. Authentic thinking refers to the idea of relating what is learnt to one's *own existence*, to seeing how it should affect one's outlook and one's actions – in a way that properly acknowledges the element of personal responsibility that each of us has for how we live our lives (Bonnett 1994, Cooper 1983). It refers then to the need for learners personally to evaluate what they learn so as to achieve a degree of authorship of their understanding.

Clearly there will be different levels to this depending on the particular content. For example, the depth of personal significance that should attach to someone's learning, say, basic sentence construction or number bonds presumably will be of a different order from that which should attach to their learning, say, about the First World War. With the latter, simply to learn the statistics would be pointless if one were not affected by the conditions under which this war was fought, could not empathise with the courage, the fear and the suffering, etc. That is to say, for such learning to have an *educative* quality, it needs to evoke a rich subjective response on the part of the learner. Here, then, the development of the learner's own perspective on what is learnt is paramount and is seen as the source of personal meaning in education. The idea of authentic learning underlines the way in which proper understanding requires interpreting material in the context of one's own concerns, and in this way having them enlarged and refined.

This idea that there is an important subjective aspect to learning is taken further, but in a somewhat different direction, in the notion of *poetic thinking*. In contrast to calculative thinking, which attempts to define and order things, poetic thinking attempts to be receptive to things themselves in their individual and particular qualities. Instead of adopting the mental stance of standing back and subjecting things to rational scrutiny, it attempts to participate in and celebrate things in their 'here and now', responding to them in some more direct way.

Contemplation of an artwork, astonishment at the sublime subtlety of a flower in the grass, direct involvement in a dramatic role, piece of music, novel or poem, wonder at the dimensions of the galaxy or variety and beauty of organisms in a drop of pond water, responding creatively to materials such as paint, wood or clay, with which one is working – these are all examples of poetic thinking. At its heart is an emotional involvement in the thing itself. This provides insights which cannot be adequately captured in statements or be contained by rational categories – and therefore cannot be reduced to bits of information or 'data'.

Poetic thinking represents an orientation that is non-instrumental, yet of the greatest importance in understanding and appreciating our world. Consider, for example, how the image of an oil-covered bird can affect our sense of what risks it is appropriate to take with the environment. What is valued in this kind of thinking is celebration of the experience itself and the fundamentally receptive orientation towards the environment which is involved, with its intuitive sensing of harmony and discord.

Clearly it would be wrong to assume that these three dimensions of thinking are mutually exclusive, or that any specific example of 'real' thinking will be 'pure' in terms of them. Much is hybrid and frequently it will be a matter of emphasis. Nonetheless we can begin to see that, qualitatively, there are some basic distinctions to be drawn. One important consequence of doing this is to highlight the difference in emphases between that kind of thinking which primarily seeks to collect information and construct rational explanations and that kind of thinking which simply wishes to reveal things as they are – to be open to the many-sidedness of things with no further end in view.

Further, it is clear that, at the level at which we are now considering thinking quality, we are not merely dealing with purely intellectual or cognitive capacities, but *broad ways of relating to the world*, which include attitudes, dispositions and emotions. We are dealing, not with sets of neutral procedures or processes, but highly value-laden stances to life. It will be important, therefore, to assess the extent to which the use of IT in schools reinforces any of these values and the potential ramifications of this both in terms of subject area compatibility and any wider effects on children's conception of 'good' thinking and, consequently, their outlook on the world.

Of course, we should not simply assume here that in the classroom issues of differing values will always involve outright conflict. Occasions when promoting one set of values, *of itself,* is to actively undermine another may be comparatively rare. Perhaps it is possible to switch from one frame of mind to another without 'interference'. More commonly, perhaps, the conflict lies in terms of *priorities* in a situation of limited time and resources, where the likely practical effect of devoting more attention to one set of values or qualities, is to diminish the influence of another.

Software and values

In an article written some years ago Peter Scrimshaw spoke of the essential modifiability of the computer in terms of the growing range of software with which it may be loaded and the variety of input and output devices with which it may be connected. He suggested that in many ways the computer is best viewed as a species of very primitive creature characterised by an incredibly fast rate of mutation and with an ever growing number of sub-species that between them can already thrive in almost any educational habitat.

(1989: 105)

A central aspect of this adaptability is the software available. This determines the rules in terms of which a computer interacts with its environment: processes inputs and produces outputs. It therefore provides an important focus for our evaluation. But notwithstanding the protean character of computers suggested by Scrimshaw, in the educational context two constants needs to be recognized from the outset. Firstly, any piece of educational software will embody either a theory of learning, or – as in the case of so-called 'content-free' software such as word processors – a set of values concerning effective means and desirable outcomes. These are often not made explicit, but they are there nonetheless, for it is impossible to structure children's activity in any purposive way without them. Now the fact that such theories and values are rarely made explicit does not diminish their influence – quite the contrary – for as long as they remain invisible they remain more freely operative, being protected from critical evaluation. It is thus essential that they are revealed and analysed in relation to the teacher's own goals.

This latter point leads to the second constant: *the computer represents only a part of the learning environment.* The general learning culture of the class, the teacher's expressed expectations, the learner's motives and understanding of what is possible, required, etc. are crucial influences. So too, is the context in which children are engaging with the software. For example, setting up a database is potentially a very different kind of engagement from interrogating a pre-formed database constructed on someone else's categories. Thus in considering the different generic kinds of software available, it will be important to keep such aspects of this larger learning context in mind.

There is now a wide range of IT software to be found in schools. In what follows, I shall try to illustrate the kinds of value issues facing teachers by focusing on two basic types: (a) 'open' applications such as word processors, databases, spreadsheets, paintboxes, which the learner uses as a tool; (b) computer-assisted learning systems which present tasks and provide feedback, sometimes dubbed 'computer as tutor' programs. With the above threefold classification of thinking quality in mind, let us begin by looking at the computer used as a tool.

Computer as tool

Undoubtedly the most common software in UK schools is that which turns the computer into a tool. In response to the requirements of the National Curriculum, word processors, databases, spreadsheets, graphics and 'paint' applications are increasingly becoming naturalised in the primary classroom. In one way or another, they each represent an extremely powerful and flexible means of organising and reorganising data and in this way encourage children to encounter, explore and construct, patterns and relationships that would otherwise be very time-consuming to produce or simply beyond their capacity unaided. It would be hard to dispute, for example, the liberating potential of word processing to organise and reorganise thoughts swiftly, and to undertake routine tasks such as correcting spelling and producing good quality copy (see Chapter 8). Similarly, the capacity of databases for storing and retrieving information in ways that can exhibit and generate significant patterns, thus enhancing a principled understanding of it, seems beyond doubt.

Clearly such potential is to be greatly valued in schools. It encourages progress beyond the mechanics of writing or storing information to an engagement with *meaning*. It facilitates experimentation, hypothesising, previewing and reviewing the ways in which relationships can be developed and expressed. Importantly, it enables the pupil actively to *do* things to and with material. Compared to tutoring software, such applications hold out the potential for being relatively open vehicles for children to express and construct their own thoughts and ideas and to discern meaning – i.e. patterns of relationship – on a scale previously impossible to achieve. Clearly, then, the possibilities for both rational-calculative and authentic learning are greatly enhanced.

In what ways, then, might a conflict of values occur with regard to this use of computers? Some have made the point that providing, say, word processing facility to children, of itself does not *guarantee* that any of the valuable possibilities of redrafting etc. will occur (see, for example, Jessel 1992). A tool can be used in a variety of ways and there is evidence to suggest that unless teachers provide a context for the use of word processing in which the value of procedures such as redrafting are embedded or are made explicit, they will not occur. Instead there may be a preoccupation with presentation, or speed of completion. While such outcomes are clearly not without value in their own terms, it is questionable that they should be reinforced at the expense of attending to others. (Any more than would the production of a pastiche of other's ideas made possible by the convenience of being able to scan in or download text from other sources.)

But of course it is true that this does not represent a conflict of value at the level of *principle*, only at the level of *practice*, i.e. the situation could be rectified if the practice were to be adequately contextualised and structured. Nonetheless, there is perhaps an issue concerning the amount of time for hands-on experience that is practicable and its incursion into time available for other activities. Even if the resources were available, could word processing be allowed simply to replace long hand? If not, why not? What are the values involved here? These are questions that we will need to face up to as word processors (perhaps voice-activated) become the dominant form of written communication outside the school.

The case, however, may stand a little differently when it comes to some other applications. Let us return to databases. Their very considerable virtues have been noted above, but let us now ask a simple question: what *happens* to things in the process of putting them into a database? What kind of thinking is involved and what values are being reinforced? Here, perhaps, we are presented with a paradigm example of rational-calculative thinking being asserted at the price of the poetic.

Central to the whole concept of a database is the attempt to fix or define things in terms of a set of pre-specified categories. These determine the way in which data can be entered and stored – and thus the way in which data is *sought* (collected). That is to say, from the outset a highly preset orientation towards things is established: one is invited constantly to view things from the point of view of how they will 'fit' a certain blueprint or schema. And this schema itself is highly manipulative, in that it has been constructed with a certain set of 'ulterior' purposes in view, namely the sorts of operations one is likely to wish to perform on the stored data, the way we wish to *use* it. In other words, some notion of an *end-product* decides what the database will accept and in what form.

This is easily illustrated by the kinds of databases frequently set up in primary schools: say on 'mini-beasts' or plant life in the local environment. There is, of course, no *one* way in which these are structured, but there is no avoiding the fact that in order to use them children are compelled to view things as instances of defined abstract categories – i.e. as specifiable *objects* – rather than in terms of the manifold and in many ways *in*definable uniqueness of the things themselves. What happens to the subtle presence of a wild flower when it has become subsumed in a database? Receptive engagement with the here and now is eschewed. This is even worse in the case of some very primitive databases still used in primary schools which restrict even the terms in which the child can describe an object (say, using only 'green', 'brown', and 'black', etc., as colours) – limiting still further the child's expressed view and therefore their interpretation of what is significant.

Now from one point of view there is nothing whatsoever wrong with the objectification of things. It simply reflects – albeit in heightened form – analytic scientific thinking which is renowned for its effectiveness. To develop it in the classroom is a perfectly legitimate endeavour. The value issue surfaces when we acknowledge that the manipulative attitude being reinforced here can have broader repercussions if it is in any way encouraged to set the standard for 'good' thinking as a whole. Again, there is perhaps no reason why in principle this should happen, but there are two reasons why in practice, it may. First, the sheer increase in ease and power to store and manipulate data made possible by current generation databases is not likely to be lost on pupils who are increasingly encouraged to use them. We all tend to like what we can do well and to see the virtues in what we like. Enhanced pleasure and confidence in this way of relating to the world, unchecked, holds out the danger of further underwriting the dominance of calculative thinking. Second, in the context of a broader social and intellectual climate outside the school which itself encourages an instrumental ethos, the danger of this happening must be compounded. And the possible repercussions in terms of a child's attitudes are large.

To what extent, for example, is it desirable that we increasingly come to view nature in this manipulative way – as a set of objects to be catalogued and interrogated? Could this not all too easily become the precursor to seeing the environment exclusively as there to be managed, controlled and used, i.e. to viewing it essentially as a *resource*? Again, perhaps there is no necessary logic to this train of development, but historically, it is a familiar one – reflected today in the funding of *applied* science and the research and development budgets of large corporations. And of course, such a frame of mind does not confine itself to the physical world. To what extent is it desirable to encourage viewing people as objects in this way, to pigeon-hole them as being of certain types such as 'middle-class' or according to some function, as with 'labour' or 'customer'? We must remain sensitive to the current pressure to, yet total inadequacy of, attempting to understand the human situation in morally neutered quasi-scientific and instrumental terms, and to the danger of being unable to recover a more holistic appreciation of things once the analytic attitude has taken a hold and done its work.

It is not, of course, that such object-orientated perspectives have *no* place in the development of thinking; the question is: should they assume the *central* place? Some would urge that 'database mentality' must be strongly countered by a sense of the poetic, the power of metaphor to break the mould of imposed categories, to enhance more open ways of relating to the world, which enable a contact more directly participative and celebratory. Here a space is preserved for awe, wonder, mystery and the inspiration of things themselves – coloured, as it were, with no ulterior motives.

Related to this is a further consideration. The materials stored in databases and in CD ROM titles can easily take on a spurious authority: if it's not there it's unimportant, beyond the pale, or doesn't exist. Clearly any such resource represents a *selection* reflecting, amongst other things, certain values and what was available at the time of compilation. This may seem too obvious to be worth stating, but as children are encouraged to view such resources as sources of knowledge – and perhaps because of their power and convenience, increasingly the *main* source of knowledge on a topic – it would be very understandable for them to lose sight of this element of selection, assuming they were ever made aware of it in the first place. At least with books there are some simple indicators of what one is getting and what is missing (such as comparative size, scanning relevant pages, etc). Because with CD ROM titles information is not arranged linearly and can be accessed in a variety of ways, rapid judgements on content are far less easy to make. It is also hard to assess the ways in which the information web predetermines the cognitive links made by the user: the extent to which it robs children of the opportunity to build their own knowledge through an alternative set of cognitive links.

Also the potential richness of the resource (a CD ROM disk can hold the equivalent of 250,000 typed A4 pages, e.g. a complete 21-volume encyclopaedia) and the ease with which its contents can be accessed may result in a kind of information overload. It may encourage a substitution of genuine knowledge (which involves authentic understanding) by a plethora of data. Volume of content does not equate with richness of experience. As A. N. Whitehead once put it, 'A merely well informed man is the most useless bore on God's earth.' He went on to warn against the acquisition of myriad disconnected, 'inert', ideas.

> Let the main ideas that are introduced into a child's education be few and important, and let them be thrown into every combination possible. The child should make them his own, and should understand their application here and now in the circumstances of his actual life.
>
> (Whitehead 1932: 2–3)

One of the chief dangers of information overload is that it can, at one and the same time, inhibit authentic thinking and seduce us into believing that all we need to solve our problems is yet more information. Many have pointed out that there is a serious sense in which we, both as individuals and as a culture, need to 'catch up' with what we in some sense already know. We need to evaluate and decide our stance towards it and thus make it our own. Resources as potentially content-rich as CD ROM have the potential to undermine this priority. Their use will need therefore to be carefully (though not necessarily rigidly) monitored by the teacher.

Thus if the teacher is to exert professional judgement over children's learning there is a need to be aware of whatever principles of selection may have been operative in the compilation of published resources. He or she also needs to be alert to any invited associations which the way data is accessed and presented may encourage. Again this problem is likely to be accentuated in the context of CD ROM, where the very volume of the resource and flexibility of format are likely to shroud these underlying principles.

Let us now return to the previously voiced concern about abstraction from the reality of things themselves. It perhaps gains further force when we think of some other kinds of software. It is not possible to pursue the point in depth here, but reservations arising from a proclivity to deal in abstractions are well illustrated, perhaps, by the grossly over-simplified pictures of the world offered by simulations and the entirely different quality of contact with the medium provided by a paint/graphics package compared with applying 'real' paint.

Take the latter example for a moment: is it irredeemably Luddite to feel that something important is in danger of being lost? To pursue this would lead us to questions concerning the underlying value of art in the curriculum: for example, what is the relative importance of the manipulation of images compared to a creative response to things and materials? What is the balance to be struck between them and how are they best brought into relationship? The anxieties which underlie such questions would seem to be entirely understandable in a situation where resources and time are necessarily limited. Here the practical consequence of introducing IT might be to supplant one kind of art with another which celebrates significantly different values (see also Chapter 9).

Similarly, the seduction of the simplified world of simulations and the sheer convenience of their availability at the press of a key is not to be underestimated when teachers are under pressure to extend children's thinking. Can the same quality of excitement and wonder that children can feel at witnessing seeds germinating in a jam jar be generated by computer simulations now available? When one can simulate the effects of changing variables in a matter of minutes rather than days or weeks, with the capacity of a CD ROM title to simulate a complete field trip in the convenience of a corner of the classroom, what price a sense of direct sensual engagement with the environment? What price authentic and poetic understanding when a principled patterning of material and ideas is so easily at hand? (See also Chapter 2 for a discussion of the value of adventure game and simulation software.)

It may seem at this point that the discussion has become thoroughly negative. If so, I must emphasise that this is not the intention. I have been at pains to acknowledge the truth of many of the claims made on behalf of 'computer as tool'. But at the same time the fundamental issues of value raised by the increased presence of IT in schools needs to be recognised, especially at a time when the calculative outlook is potentially being reinforced by the extended place that has been given to science and technology in the primary curriculum. The issue of how to achieve a proper balance between the calculative and the poetic is a large one. To assume that the introduction of IT into the classroom won't affect it, would be naïve in the extreme.

Computer as tutor

Elsewhere in this book the point has been made that computer tutoring programs have so far made very little impression in UK schools. Nonetheless, owing to strong interest in the US and increasing commercial pressures over here there may be something of a renaissance around the corner. Because of this, and the fact that such software illustrates in a particularly strong way some of the potential tensions I have been exploring in this chapter, I will spend a little time considering it. (See McFarlane 1995a, for a comprehensive review of recent studies.)

At its most basic this kind of software provides instruction by setting tasks (e.g. asking questions, giving commands) and giving feedback on the child's response according to whether it matches a pre-specified correct answer. If correct, the child moves on to a further task, if not, the child has another go or is given the correct answer. More sophisticated programs (known as 'integrated learning systems') attempt to assess the individual pupil's response and on the basis of this provide an appropriate task to move her on in her learning. That is to say, there is an attempt to provide automated diagnosis of learning difficulties and prescription of remedies.

As previously mentioned, in the early thinking about IT in education this notion of the *computer as tutor* was prominent, and gave rise to the spectre of classrooms where teachers became increasingly redundant as the computer took over as the prime source of educational instruction. If it is true that the aspirations of the producers of this kind of software have now become more modest, this does not detract from the fact that there are still important issues raised by the more limited ways in which it can be introduced into children's learning.

Consider it in relation to what I have called rational-calculative thinking. Clearly such a use of the computer could be seen, at the very least, to release the teacher from mundane consolidation work. Insofar as structured practice is a necessary part of learning and the computer provides a more interesting and stimulating context for it than, say, a book of exercises, this would seem to be worthwhile – though issues of relative cost-effectiveness are also relevant. Certain further issues begin to emerge, however, when we look beyond simple reinforcement programs to those that attempt to diagnose and to prescribe. Here the authority of the teacher could clearly become an issue since it would seem entirely proper that a teacher as professional would wish to know the basis upon which diagnosis of a child's learning in her class is being performed – and to be uncomfortable if this information is not forthcoming. For various technical and commercial reasons this may not be easy to ascertain. Now to the extent that this is the case, clearly an incipient, but important, set of concerns are raised regarding: (a) the value of teacher authority and the opportunity to exercise professional judgement; (b) the values and theories implicitly built into the program by the software designer; (c) the relationship between the criteria of diagnosis used by the computer and the larger context within which the child's understanding is being developed *and is itself to be understood.*

> Because children's behaviour and children's learning is so various and complex, it is highly unlikely that any one simple framework of understanding, any single model of learning, will give us the 'position' from which we will be able to understand everything we see.
>
> (Drummond 1993: 81)

The truth in this observation raises a clutch of important questions. How can the computer respond intelligently to the wealth of previous experience – a significant amount of which is tacit – which may inform the child's response? And how can it make adequate provision for the child to *make* that response? Until, at the very least, the computer is able to read 'free' input as contrasted with some form of multiple choice input, there seems to be no possibility of this. On the contrary, given the particularity of each child's experience and learning style, there would seem to be a good chance of dissonance with the broader learning context.

This in turn sets in train a further serious reservation: the danger of reinforcing a passive mentality which seeks only the 'right' answer, thus stifling children's motivation to seek out underlying reasons or to produce answers that are in any way divergent. In John Holt's (1990) terms the object of learning can too readily become simply to please the teacher (computer) regardless of under-standing (since the pupil's personal web of understanding is in constant danger of being overridden or disrupted). And unlike an aware teacher, it is hard to see how a computer could become sensitive to this undesirable development. As long as this is the case, any claims made on behalf of such software to the effect that it enhances children's thinking and understanding must be viewed with considerable suspicion and the place of computer as tutor must be strictly limited to structured practice or 'drill and skill' functions.

The whole issue of genuine interactiveness is brought into even sharper relief when we start to consider the exercise from the point of view of developing authentic understanding. While it is perfectly conceivable that a child may be introduced to something during the course of working with tutoring software which stimulates them to think more deeply in the way required by authentic learning, this will be largely a matter of chance and there is no way of capitalising on it if it should occur. Such understanding often needs to be elicited, indeed provoked, by a sensitive interlocutor. Indeed, it requires a dialogue which is itself essentially *poetic* in character, the teacher attempting to listen for what is incipi-ently present in the unique here and now engagement of pupils – the questions and the possibilities inherent in their current thinking.

Here the teacher has to be both accepting and demanding, so that the child is provoked into acknowledging deeper possibilities and into pursuing them in a way that is consistent with his or her own engagement – his or her own sense, however embryonic, of what is *needed*. Often, clear unambiguous answers to questions will not represent the best way of enhancing such engagement. Sometimes carefully tailored replies that require the child to puzzle, to reflect, to explain, to personally evaluate, will be far more productive. It is hard to see how the essentially formulaic basis of tutoring software could ever invite or replicate this kind of open yet demanding dialogue. For the same reason, it is hard to see how, given that a teacher intervenes to facilitate such an exchange, tutoring systems could ever take it up and extend it, for they could not achieve continuity with what had occurred. Parallel considerations apply to introducing collaborative learning in this context. This sort of consideration seems consistent with independent evaluation, which shows the positive effects of such systems on basic numeracy, but not in language skills – the former presumably being more formulaic (Underwood *et al.* 1996).

Here then, we see that it is of the highest importance that the quality of learning promoted by such tutoring software is properly acknowledged. Only in this way can we ensure that it is used in appropriate contexts and that the convenience and overt structure that it provides do not seduce us into allowing it simply to supersede learning that celebrates other values, ones which would be considered by many to be more central to education.

Summary and conclusion

If I have seemed to dwell on points that are critical of IT it is because I feel that no good purpose is served by ignoring real problems. Many teachers' incipient sense of apprehension at the burgeoning of IT in schools cannot simply be dismissed as due to lack of proper experience coupled with a perverse Luddism. It cannot be doubted that fundamental issues of value are raised by the increasing presence of IT in the classroom. I have suggested that these arise at two levels: first – at the macro-level, when it is seen as part of a larger consolidation of calculative thinking in the primary curriculum that occurred with the raised status of science and technology; and second – at the micro-level, when the qualities of thinking encouraged by particular kinds of software are made explicit and their possible ramifications for children's attitudes are considered.

Clearly we cannot simply assume that IT will neither disrupt the teacher's values as expressed in the broad culture of the classroom, nor the values which orientate particular curriculum areas. This chapter has attempted to be suggestive rather than in any sense definitive and the examples considered are merely illustrative, not exhaustive. But it seems to me indisputable that true integration of IT into the ongoing work of the primary school classroom requires the honest attempt to address explicitly a set of interrelated value questions. These could be framed as follows:

1 What are the teacher's central educational values, in terms of which he or she attempts to organise learning and develop the culture of the classroom?
2 What are the values inherent in different areas of subject matter?
3 What order of priority of values should hold in different teaching situations?
4 What values are embedded in the software actually available to the teacher and to what extent are these compatible with responses to points 1–3 above?
5 In what specific regards can compatible software enhance such values compared with its non-use? (i.e. How can the use of IT improve on alternatives?)
6 What, if any, reorientation of values might the use of IT incur?

It is not, of course, that such issues are unique to the introduction of IT into the classroom; parallel considerations are raised by many published resources used by teachers. However, they are issues which the sheer power and potential interactiveness of computers move almost into another league. At a time when central government and commercial pressures to increase computer use in schools are effectively in tandem, it is of the utmost importance to ensure that IT remains the servant of education rather than a hijacker of the enterprise. If this can be achieved the truly enormous potential of IT to enhance the educational experience of children in primary classrooms has a chance of being realised.

Chapter 11

New technologies: multimedia and going on-line

Angela McFarlane

Why all the fuss?

Technologies, especially computer-based technologies, tend to attract a fanatical following. This is even true in the field of computer use in education, although the fanatics may be in a minority. These followers voraciously devour every new advance, savouring the technical wizardry and ever faster and more complex performance of the latest hardware and software. Going further than McLuhan's 'The medium is the message', for some, the medium is all there is. Perhaps techno-fever has never been so great as it is today in response to multimedia, the combination of any three of text, images, sound, video or animation in one package. The enthusiasm is especially great where the delivery of multimedia is envisaged over the Internet (the Net) or its more recent incarnation, the World Wide Web (WWW). Here, via telephone lines for the most part, millions of computers all over the world are linked. Anyone can set up a computer with his or her choice of material in any medium, and connect it to the Net. Everyone with Net access, i.e. with a computer, a modem and a service provider, can then access this information and even add to it. This idea has taken a hold in our collective cultural imagination to such an extent that every newspaper, feature film and most sizeable organisations appear to have established their own 'web site', and the URL (the address of these sites) with its instantly recognisable format (e.g. http://webpagesr.us/) has become so commonplace that puns playing on it are used to advertise beer.

There is no doubt that the combination of high resolution images, digital stereo sound, animation, and video (of sorts) with text that multimedia can offer is a powerful one. But why is everyone apparently so excited? After all, educational television producers have been combining all these media in one package for at least a generation. Furthermore, as video taping is positively encouraged through the night-time broadcasting of such productions, apart from equipment and a television licence, these programmes are free to schools.

There are three features of multimedia (as distinct from multi-media, a combination of a book with audio or video cassette for example) that make it very different from anything which has preceded it. Firstly, true multimedia is put together in a hypertext environment. That means the information is presented in a series of chunks, each linked to one or more other chunks in such a way that you do not have to view them in a predetermined sequence. For example, imagine you are viewing a screen showing an exploded diagram of a car engine, with a short accompanying text about the principles of internal combustion in which some words are in bold. By clicking on the emboldened words, you will be taken to a screen with more information on a related topic. For example, the name Daimler might appear and the related screen might tell you more about him and his other inventions. The parts of the engine might be 'buttons' or 'hot links' as well, so clicking on one of these might take you to a detailed description of the spark plug, including an animation of the ignition sequence. These subordinate screens might also have hot links which take you further on, or back to the original screen as you choose. (For a more detailed description of the possible structures of hypertexts see Scrimshaw 1993, ch 12.) Hypertexts, which include graphics, sound animation or video as well as text, are also known as hypermedia.

The second, exciting, feature of multimedia is that the publication of such material on CD ROM, which has a very high capacity and can store enormous amounts of information, including material via the WWW, provides access to a wealth of information otherwise inaccessible in the school or home. Potentially, everything ever published and much more that has never been available before, is accessible.

The third, and perhaps most exciting feature of all is that authoring tools are freely available which enable even primary school pupils to create their own multimedia. This opens up an entirely new way of presenting a child's thoughts to an audience, and even to herself.

Multimedia in school

Combined with the massive capacity of optical storage media, or the high speed telecommunications link, the potential of multimedia begins to exceed anything previously known. Children in school can have access to satellite images, the contents of the Berkeley Palaeontology Museum in California, Beethoven's fifth symphony in full digital stereo, complete with annotated score telling them everything they ever wanted to know about the composer, the music and the instruments it is played on. All this at the click of the mouse button. Such limitless potential must surely be a good thing for education?

The very nature of multimedia, vast, non-linear and readable only through a computer screen, means that it is very difficult to assess the scope and quality of a title or source without spending considerable time on it. There is no equivalent to picking up and flicking through a book, an action that will give an experienced teacher a clear view of coverage and relevant target group. However, there are a number of indicators which can be helpful. Additionally there are strategies which can make the use of multimedia a powerful and effective teaching tool.

This is especially so when the skill and knowledge development it encourages is recognised by the teacher, and the assessor!

Recognising good educational multimedia

The first point it is essential to absorb is that although reference is commonly made to multimedia as though it were in some fundamental way homogeneous this is a very dangerous assumption. Books, cinema, television or any other communication medium have features which make them universally recognisable, and this is true to some extent of multimedia, although the definitions are far more flexible. However the assumptions made about these common features may be very misleading. For example to say that using multimedia will improve children's education is as seductive as saying that using books will improve children's education. It is easy to gain ready acceptance of the latter assertion, and even of the first. However if you then suggest that the books are all either comics and so-called 'adult' literature the assertion is quickly shown up as flawed. The value of the books, as with the value of the multimedia, is inherent in the selection and arrangement of its content as much or more than in the fundamental nature of the medium.

The criteria teachers use to decide which books are suitable for the classroom and how they can best be used are skills which have a 500-year history, albeit a highly varied one. The evaluation of multimedia is more problematic, not least because of the time and specialised equipment needed even to view all the material, and the variety of access routes to it, which appear on a CD ROM or an on-line database. It would therefore be helpful to devise some generic criteria and strategies for choosing and using multimedia in teaching. Given the enormous variety in style and content of this medium, this goal is only achievable in a limited sense. The criteria for assessing a multimedia simulation of a field study are so different from those that are valid for a multimedia database of *The Times* that common desirable features will be few.

It is still costly to create a CD ROM title, so most multimedia titles are not intended to appeal first and foremost to a school audience. They must sell widely to justify the initial investment in development, and the most likely perceived market is the home. In order to appeal to the home user the title will be well produced, colourful, engaging and entertaining, all desirable in an educational resource. The trade-off here is that subject content is often simplified to cater for the non-specialist user, with subsequent loss of depth and, perhaps more important to young children, accuracy. It can be rather like offering an encyclopaedia of home medicine as a text for a medical student. Multimedia encyclopaedias can be especially disappointing in this respect. Most of them are based on single volume print sources, of themselves of limited value. As a result, often time-consuming searches for information can yield only a few lines of text on a given topic.

Further, the selection and arrangement of the content on a title destined for the home will not have been made with any school curriculum in mind. Thus much material on a disk may have little or no relevance to the topic being taught. Additionally the very nature of multimedia, arranged as it usually is in a hypermedia environment, invites the user to explore and investigate this extraneous material. I do not wish to address here the inherent value of this exploration for its own sake, which may be considerable. It is, however at odds with the objectives of the teacher restricted by the very precise demands of the curriculum as currently taught in UK schools. Children studying content that is not on the syllabus can be seen to be wasting time when the demands of the curriculum are that they study a defined body of content in a restricted time. Teachers wishing to use titles designed for the home, even where they carry a large 'educational' label, will need to be aware that they will need to take the time to identify exactly what material on the disk relates to the topics under study, and devise strategies for ensuring that students using the disk spend their time engaged with these rather than any other areas.

There are, by way of contrast, a relatively small number of CD ROM disks that have been produced with the classroom in mind. Here there is more chance that the content will match the degree of depth and accuracy that is required. However there is still a problem that children may be drawn away from the topic designated. Buttons to link to other parts of the material, colourful icons and navigation aids are after all designed to entice the user to 'click and see' even here. It is in the nature of the medium to invite users to explore, make discoveries, create personal cognitive links and so create their own knowledge. It is this essential nature of hypermedia that makes it so rich in potential as an educational tool. This user-orientated perspective is, however, at odds with the syllabus-centred, possibly teacher-centred culture which the National Curriculum sustains in the primary classroom. Here the teacher defines the specific learning objectives, which for the most part must reflect a statutory curriculum.

With the increasing body of content available in the form of multimedia, and (where this is available over the Internet) the relative low cost of that compared to print media, we may be forced to rely more and more in the future on multimedia as the publication medium in which we receive our educational resources. Unless we find strategies for resolving the tensions between the user-oriented culture of hypermedia and the mostly syllabus-oriented culture of the classroom, the use of multimedia will remain problematic. We currently have educational systems throughout the world which rely heavily on grading children on their knowledge of a pre-defined body of content, with some passing acknowledgement of their skills in manipulating and applying that knowledge. Whether this remains valid at all in a world where the body of information available is growing so rapidly, and access to it is also increasingly easy, is a separate if highly important issue. One thing is more certain however: that method of assessment is likely to disadvantage the child who has spent a significant time browsing hypermedia. Her skills in locating, interpreting, analysing and communicating, developed as she went along, may go unnoticed because she has not retained a memory of the precise details of the Roman conquest. This is yet another example of an important question for teachers that is brought into clear focus by the use of IT. We have to ask which criteria are ultimately the more important in the world the pupil will inhabit.

Developing information-handling skills

Given the increasing availability of vast information sources, I want to address here the very important issue of developing children's ability to use such sources intelligently. I will then go on to discuss how this bears on the availability of electronic information sources.

As with the development of skills related to using text to develop thinking (see Chapter 8 of this volume) there is nothing new *per se* in the skills related to good information-handling. It is vitally important here, as elsewhere, that teachers do not abandon their otherwise entirely sound critical faculties in the face of IT. It is also important to remember that we know a lot about effective teaching and learning that remains valid in the context of new technologies and new methods of presenting information.

The Schools Curriculum Council suggested a nine-step framework for researching information as follows:

- Decide what information is needed.
- Look for the information.
- Select individual resources.
- Retrieve information.
- Process information.
- Record information.
- Review the task.
- Present the information.
- Evaluate the task.

A document produced by the Cambridgeshire Schools Library Service for in-service courses, poses these steps as questions making their underlying meaning more explicit. These are:

- What do I need to do? (Formulate and analyse need.)
- Where could I go? (Identify and appraise likely sources.)
- How do I get the information? (Trace and locate individual resources.)
- Which resources shall I use? (Examine, select and reject individual resources.)
- How shall I use the resources? (Interrogate resources.)
- What shall I make a record of? (Record and store information.)
- Have I got the information I need? (Interpret, analyse, synthesise and evaluate.)
- How should I present it? (Present and communicate.)
- What have I achieved? (Evaluate.)

Though not to be regarded as a rigid linear sequence, these nine steps can be used to structure information retrieval exercises for children from an early age. This kind of activity is described in the National Curricula for children in Key Stage 2, aged 8 to 11. The series of questions are easily understood by children and can help to make the process explicit to them. Here, as with the development of comprehensive literacy as discussed in Chapter 8, it is important to share with children the nature of the task they are undertaking, and to help them understand that they are not simply learning about volcanoes, or the Victorians, they are actually learning a way of finding out, of studying, of creating their own knowledge – a way of learning.

The nine steps are a way of representing a skill set which some of us, who succeed in the education system, have usually acquired by inference. Many children in the past have managed in the school system without mastering these skills, only to fail in further or higher education (Clark 1990). In the current school system however, these skills must be well developed by GCSE level, and even more than before we cannot afford to fail children by leaving them to work out the process for themselves.

As I have said, the skills behind effective information retrieval and evaluation are not inherently different whether the sources are electronic or paper based. They way they are applied can alter, however, and the weighting might be different. I want now to look at each of the steps in turn and discuss how access to large repositories of information, on CD ROM or through the Internet, affect the process at each stage.

Although the steps are presented as a list, this is not a strictly linear procedure. At the evaluation stage, the child may decide more information is needed, and having retrieved some information, she may go back and search for some more and so on. However the steps should all be in the process somewhere, often more than once.

Deciding what information is needed

Deciding what you want to know about, and reminding yourself (or being reminded) while searching is perhaps even more important with electronic media than with paper. Multimedia can be very distracting, as it is often designed to invite the child to explore the information it contains by browsing. Screens are often very visually stimulating, with invitations to just click and go off to look at a fascinating animation, or hear a story. Of course well-designed books can be seductive in this way too. (For example, I rarely go to my cherished leather-bound *Shorter Oxford English Dictionary* and manage to check only the word I opened it to investigate.) However, the non-linear nature of multimedia makes it very easy to get lost, especially if you follow the commands to 'click here' or just give in to the inviting appearance of an interesting button. This often leads to frustration among teachers, who find that children using multimedia may spend a lot of time off-task. For this reason it is helpful to use titles designed for use in school, which are likely to concentrate on material that needs to be covered.

Looking for the information

Electronic sources should make this stage of the process easier because they facilitate active indexing; this allows you to search for any topic by using the search facility to locate relevant words in the text, or related images, video clips, etc. However there are two caveats to this. First, not all multimedia published on CD ROM has a search facility. Many titles are arranged so that you have to explore and locate the information you want by browsing. This is time-consuming and may be unproductive: key facts the child has decided she wants may not have been included, or may simply be in part of the vast network of information she has not had time to access. Even when you know something you want is on one of this style of CD ROM titles, you may be unable to relocate it easily – which is really infuriating. Second, and this applies particularly to on-line services, the number of apparently relevant pieces of information turned up by a search can be vast. Because sources may be offered simply because the search term appears in the text somewhere, they may in fact be irrelevant in the current context. An Internet search I made before a trip to Madrid, to find out about the city layout, turned up over 18,000 'hits', the majority of which were about football and included the words 'Real Madrid'.

Effective electronic searching can be extremely powerful, but children need to be shown how to use it intelligently. The Internet is not a good place to start learning. It is vital that children have developed a sound grasp of using inclusive and exclusive searching, and the nature of the subset of the database as a whole that they get as a result of such a search. They also need to be able to execute searches in several stages to refine the selection of sources they choose to examine in more detail. These skills can be built up, beginning with sorting exercises in reception classes. Questions such as, Can I have the red toys? Can I have the toys which are red *and* have wheels? – an exclusive search that excludes the toys which do not match both search terms, red *and* with wheels. Can I have the toys which are red *or* blue? – an inclusive search that includes the toys which have either red or blue coloration. These queries begin to build searching skills. The use of cards with descriptions of objects can come next, with searches being made by one child at the request of another. Alternatively, in Year 3 simple computer-based databases can be introduced. However, it may be necessary to refer back to cards to help children build a mental model of the database in the computer, which remains abstract and rarely seen as a whole. Until this mental model, which includes the consequences of selecting a subset through a search, is well established, the child is unlikely to be in control of her quest for information.

Selecting individual resources

It is important here to encourage children to use a range of resources on and off the computer, and to make informed choices about which to retrieve. It may be necessary to impose a limit, for example, to the number of pages which can be printed off from electronic sources, both to encourage discrimination and to prevent horrifying printing costs.

Retrieving information

Electronic sources should make retrieval easy. It is possible to print any page from an on-line source, although images may not print. CD ROMs designed for educational use often have very generous copyright conditions, which allow copying or printing of all material for use within the school. This is not always so however, and some titles may not support printing at all. It is possible to 'grab' a screen from any electronic source, but be aware that this may infringe copyright. As mentioned above, encourage children to be selective. There may be a temptation simply to hit the print button with little consideration of the value of the source.

Processing information

At this stage the selected sources are examined more closely, which may be done at the computer or away from it. Where computer access is restricted it makes sense to arrange for children to print their selection and use this print-out, alongside other relevant selected sources, to examine more closely. At this stage it is useful to introduce the question of how reliable the source of information is. Sources will often disagree – which is the more credible? On-line sources should be more up-to-date than print, but may be less accurate. Remember that no one referees or edits the Internet! CD ROM sources can be very disappointing on the point of accuracy, of language as well as content. The strong editorial skills which ensure accuracy in the print world are seldom applied in the multimedia one, it seems. This may be due at least in part to the fact that it is difficult for the editor to be certain she has checked every section of a branching structure, or that the person programming it has used the latest version of the data provided, or that every link button leads to the place it was meant to.

Recording information

Using a word processor makes it much easier to build up a record of related information in a systematic way. New information can be grouped with related material as it is found, and the existing records amended if a more secure piece of information supersedes it.

Reviewing the task

This step involves synthesising the child's own version of the findings she has made, and includes evaluation and analysis. Again, the use of the word processor makes it easier to experiment with the text until it expresses the ideas and views the child wishes to communicate. (For a discussion on how this process contributes to the whole basis of rational analytic thinking see Chapter 8.) It is also possible to introduce at the reviewing stage the concept of indicating where you have used a few sentences or phrases from a book, a Web site, or even another child, and to say where they came from; likewise an image or soundfile. In this way the distinction between legitimate use of information sources and 'copying' can be learned.

Presenting the information

It is possible to present a synthesis of the information as straight text, or with images, in a word processor or desktop publishing package. However, simple authoring tools such as Magpie on the Archimedes, Hypercard on the Apple, ToolBook on the PC or Hyperstudio on all three platforms, mean children can combine information they have found or created in the whole variety of media to make their own multimedia. (See Chapter 8 for a discussion of this.)

Evaluating the task

This stage is where you all sit down and talk over what has been done.

Surfing the superhighway

I have referred above to some of the advantages and drawbacks of information sources available on-line. I would now like to look at this in more detail.

It is important to remember that anyone can publish anything he likes on the Internet, which makes it extremely powerful and gives a public voice to the individual in a way never before possible. It also means that when viewed as an information source, it needs to be approached with caution. The drawback most frequently referred to is the availability of information unsuitable for children, particularly that of a pornographic nature. Another problem less news-worthy but equally important when organising a child's learning, is that a great deal of it is dross! There are good reasons why print media producers use editors. These highly skilled people make sure that the information we receive is well written, that facts are substantiated, that material is organised logically. We know when accessing a print source what its likely worth is, and how accurate it is likely to be. In the case of newspapers we know that a *Daily Star* headline will offer a rather different perspective from that of the *Guardian*. The *Reader's Digest* has a reputation for verifying all facts with a number of sources before going to print.

Time magazine employs well-respected writers in a variety of fields to present an informed interpretation of current affairs. But anyone can and does put anything on the Internet.

Fortunately, there are some solutions on offer to schools to help increase the chances of finding useful material on the Internet. The RM Internet for Learning and BT's Campus World offer schools access to an edited subset of the Internet. They have created a collection of references to material which is likely to be of interest to schools. It is possible to range further, but certain restrictions have been applied to searching to reduce the chances of finding sexually explicit material, for example. Unfortunately this also prevents you using words such as 'breast' as a search term, and therefore excludes you from information on breast cancer, treatment, screening, etc. This simply serves to highlight the difficulties of censorship: how to protect the young and vulnerable without restricting their freedom. As with other material there is no easy answer, but on balance it is surely better to take the safer option when children are browsing for themselves. It is always possible for teachers to use a wider access to locate relevant materials and then use the access software to 'book mark' them for children.

In fact the 'book mark' process is essential if effective use of on-line sources is to be made by young learners. Simply browsing endlessly, in an unstructured way (so-called 'surfing'), is ultimately extremely frustrating, especially when the child has made decisions concerning the type of information she wants. It is often better to use on-line sources to provide experiences and information not otherwise available, which can be located by the teacher and 'book marked' so it can be accessed directly by children. An example of this relates to the popular topic of volcanoes. There is some basic information on volcanoes available on the World Wide Web, although at the time of writing it did not compare favourably with a good book. However, what you can do is access information on any current eruptions, and possibly even see a video clip. You can also 'post' questions to an expert vulcanologist. (It is interesting that the language of paper is used here, typing in a question or information to a Web site is commonly referred to as 'posting'.) With luck you will also get an answer, not immediately but maybe in a day or two. The vulcanologist might be in California, and asleep when you send the question!

This opens up the third topic I want to address here: electronic mail (E-mail).

E-mail

E-mail may not be perfect, but it is pretty useful and I am one of the world's women who love to 'natter on the net'. It is claimed that many women who have otherwise eschewed the use of computers are seduced by the facility E-mail offers to network with friends, and through conferencing – where many users contribute to an ongoing discussion over a period of time – form new contacts. Just as women use the telephone more than men, women may eventually outnumber men in the world of E-mail (see Spender 1995). One interesting gender-related facet to emerge in one primary school experimenting with E-mail was that the boys acted as technicians – happily logging on and downloading messages – but it was the girls who engaged with the content and substance of the messages (McFarlane 1995b). The boys liked the toys, the girls liked to communicate.

The use of the word 'natter' really does an injustice to the level of communication that E-mail will support. Nattering suggests idle chat, but most of my E-mail is far from that (although idle chat has its place!). E-mail gives me a relatively cheap and easy way to keep in contact with colleagues in other countries, we can even work on joint writing tasks on-line. I have been able to approach various experts in the UK and beyond to help me locate information about their work. The speed of reply makes this easier than writing a letter or sending a fax; people usually type in some acknowledgement as soon as they get the message. It is also less intrusive and cheaper than telephoning; famous professors do not always come to the telephone, and if in another country may not be awake! A good E-mail system means that you can compose your message and then only use the telephone line for the short time it takes to send the message.

Well that is all very nice for me in the rarefied world of academe, but the really exciting part is that children are beginning to share this kind of experience too. As I discussed in Chapter 8, technologies are increasingly available to children and E-mail is no exception. It is possible to send questions to a variety of experts through the WWW, or directly by E-mail. Many educational organisations set up postboxes to handle such queries. It is also possible to E-mail other children to share information, or just to be 'pen pals'. This kind of contact opens up all kinds of audiences to the child, giving them rich stimulus for writing and broadening their concept of the world beyond school and the people in it.

The nature of the language of E-mail, and its implications for judgements on literacy is raised in Chapter 8. It is recognised that E-mail makes use of a form of language which has much in common with speech; it uses a 'chat' mode (Sharples 1985). An example of this is that E-mail messages, even from people you have not met, never begin Dear Madam, or even Dear Miss Jones. 'Dear Mary' is a form used very occasionally, usually by the British, but 'Hello there', or 'Hi Mary' would be more usual. Signing off is likely to be equally informal with 'Best wishes', or simply the name of the writer. The body of the text is likely to be less formal than is usual on paper too. I often refer to my E-mail messages as electronic postcards, which is for me the nearest paper-based genre. Of course it is possible to send and receive more complex compositions, usually by 'attaching' them to the E-mail so they are retrieved and read off-line, which changes their nature somewhat. This is much more like receiving a fax: the transmission is fast but you may take more time to consider and compose a reply.

The informal mode of writing in E-mail brings the writer closer to the reader, which can give children a much stronger sense of audience, and of the person or people they are writing to. Another good feature of E-mail is that you can send the same message to a number of people at the same time. This helps a group of schools collaborating on a project to keep one another up to date. The child writing also has very direct control over what she sends and when, and to whom. The teacher may then becomes less directly involved in the process as leader and evaluator. An interesting example of this is reported in the NCET study (NCET 1991) where children collaborated by E-mail to compose poetry. The children themselves took on the role of critical review of each other's work, not the teacher. However, the teacher still plays a fundamental role in facilitating co-operative work, as experience in a small group of primary schools in Cambridgeshire and the surrounding counties demonstrated in an alternative project. Here pupils could contact other schools, since they were provided with a modem and an E-mail subscription. Each school determined what kind of contact it wanted to initiate, and for what purpose. The teachers and Year 6 pupils involved came up with several good ideas, but the experience eventually left them feeling very frustrated. Questions broadcast to other schools often went unanswered and responses to other people's questions, which might have involved some data gathering, went unacknowledged. It seems that a culture of E-mail use did not become established, and some basic so-called 'netiquette' was broken. 'Netiquette' refers to a culture rather than a set of rules; for example users are expected to check their messages regularly, and to offer a response, even if it's only, 'Sorry I can't help!'

In this case, where everyone concerned was new to the system, it might have been more successful if the teachers involved had communicated between schools first, to agree on some suitable topics for communication and collaboration among the children, and establish a consensus on the objectives of the exercise. The NCET project gave a taste of the kind of communication schools can use their E-mail for successfully. It represented a very diverse set of activities and communications: from pen pals to poets, child field scientists reporting back to 'base' at the school, from child expert on local dialect to 'expert' writer guiding story-writing; they were all there, 'nattering on the net'.

In 1988 I witnessed a fascinating exchange of information by E-mail between children in an Education 2000 school in Letchworth, Hertfordshire and a school in Japan. Because this was a special project, supported by Apple, they had very sophisticated equipment, which meant that they could send each other copies of drawings. An agreed set of questions about everyday life were swapped by pairs of pupils, and to overcome the problems of language, the pupils each drew pictures to illustrate what kind of house they lived in, who was in their family and so on. These were then exchanged the next day. This year I watched a group of primary children from Cambridgeshire conduct a video conference with some classmates who had gone on a visit to Canada. They shared information, often visual, on what they were doing. These children are the pioneers, enjoying experiences which may become everyday practice for all of us in time.

Summary

Multimedia is widely available through the medium of CD ROM, and via on-line services which also support electronic mail. These new technologies present enormous opportunites and challenges to all of us, in school and beyond. This chapter seeks to explain something of the nature of these new technologies. It examines the ways in which they differ from what is already familiar, how they can be harnessed to help achieve current teaching and learning objectives, and how they act against and might ultimately change some of those objectives. There is also an in-depth look at information-handling skills: how they can be made explicit, and developed, through practice in using electronic information sources.

. . . and where might we end up?

Angela McFarlane

Changing technology, changing schools?

It is not difficult to find references to the need to change our educational system. As we approach the third millennium there is an emphasis on the one hand for a need to improve 'basic' numeracy and literacy by teaching children more rigorously, and on the other to produce more independent learners capable of using information sources to construct their own knowledge. In both cases it is possible to find supporters of IT who feel that the 'right IT' in the classroom will do the job, that given enough exposure to IT all ills will be cured. But can it ever be that simple? Even if our schools were not severely hampered by shortages of suitable computers, software and services and our teachers were all well trained in the effective use of IT, would the revolution then happen automatically?

Predicting the likely impact of technology on education is a risky business, the history of which is littered with heroic failures. Take, for example, Uzanne, quoted in Kuhn and Stannard (1996): 'With the coming of the New Media, the need for print on paper will rapidly diminish. The day will soon arrive when the world's literature will be available from The Automatic Library at the mere pressing of a button.' This sounds like another World Wide Web fan – except Uzanne was talking about the New Medium of wax phonograph cylinders, in a book called *The End of Books* published over one hundred years ago in 1894! Seymour Papert (1980), the father of LOGO, painted a vision of a society liberated by interactions with environments such as LOGO, ultimately moving away from formalised schooling to a more generalised learning culture which would permeate the home. Nearly twenty years has seen little evidence of this happening, and although turtle graphics LOGO has become very common in schools it has rarely impacted on the fundamental culture of the school or home.

Technological visionaries of one kind or another have been promising us, among other things, that schools and the rest of our world will be unrecognisable in five, ten or twenty-five years. For the vast majority of us, not surprisingly, the world is changing, but by a process of evolution rather than revolution. Certainly primary schools of the present day are very different places to work in than schools of 1980, but those changes have more to do with politics and legislative change than with technology. But how much has the way pupils are taught, the degree to which pupils take control of their own learning and develop the skills of independent intellectual activity, actually changed? For it is in these fundamentals that IT has always been hailed as the irresistible agent of change, rather than the precise nature of curriculum content, or frequency of pencil and paper testing.

Perhaps it is too easy to underestimate the inertia inherent in the school establishment – its innate ability to absorb and assimilate technological change without fundamentally changing its nature. With that thought in mind I shall proceed with caution as I attempt to highlight current trends which might lead to a greater impact on schools, and the effects these might have on the culture of learning.

Portable computers

Central provision of computers is unlikely ever to extend to the allocation of one computer per child. By the time they are cheap enough for that, the children will be coming to school with their own for the most part and, as with calculators today, the school will make provision for those who do not have one. These computers will be portable and personal in nature, with their own selection of software and data on them. The children will use them as freely as they do paper notebooks today. The school may continue to provide a small number of computers as they do at present, which are more powerful or have better visual displays or sound capability perhaps than the children's own machines (although the portables are catching up fast on all technical fronts). These school computers may be used for on-line and other multimedia access, or (this being the most likely), for specific educational software that will not run on the children's own machines. Ironically this may be because the only software specifically designed to support active learning will only run on outdated machines, as the educational software industry collapses to be replaced by purely commercial sources. The school may also provide access to services such as printing or battery recharging.

The NCET Portables Evaluation (Stradling *et al.* 1994) looked at 118 projects where portable computers were used in schools. The model of provision included a very wide range of resourcing, from providing eight machines for a class to making a computer available to each child. The computers themselves also varied from palmtops to full desk-top equivalents. The results of these studies were generally very positive, and are documented throughout this volume. However, none of these projects actually changed the culture of the school fundamentally. For that it is necessary to look further afield, to the now world-famous Melbourne Ladies College (MLC) in Australia. Here, in 1989, Year 7 pupils were each provided with a personal computer. The object was to 'have students *do* learning for themselves, with the aid of the computer' (Spender 1995: 111). The machines were loaded with Logo Writer and database software initially, as tools to help the girls to create their own knowledge. Other software has been made available as required.

The results have changed the nature of the school. In order to facilitate the active learning the teachers observed taking place, the formal timetable was to a large extent abandoned. The idea of ringing a bell and making children do something else when they were engrossed in a problem-solving activity was so incongruous that the idea of the forty-minute lesson was abandoned. Also, formally arranged desks and chairs were a constraint and impeded the collaborative group-work the computers were being used for, so they went. Visitors described huddles of girls, sometimes on the floor, working through a task. As tasks grew to incorporate wider subject areas than traditional boundaries, teachers began to work as expert consultants rather than controllers of learning. An interesting example of boundary-crossing was the way some children began to use French in a Maths context – the first time the French teacher had ever known children to use French voluntarily outside a French lesson.

The overall verdict is that children in the project at MLC are more pro-active in their learning, and there is no loss of the social or creative experience that some fear is the inevitable result of a computer-rich culture. (See Spender (1995: 110–20) for a synopsis of the MLC project.) It is interesting to note the similarities between the classroom environment the personal computer initiative at MLC has fostered and that of the highly child-centred UK primary classroom currently so besieged by political opinion. It would be foolish to lose sight of the fact that the cultural changes seen at MLC, although mediated through the personal computer, actually came about because the school was willing to change. It wanted to pursue the potential of a different kind of learning, which the computers could be used to support. Simply handing out computers will not bring about such changes to the school culture, no matter how desirable the changes are.

Multimedia and going on-line

The issues surrounding the use of multimedia and on-line services in school are addressed at length in Chapter 11. Here I want to look at how realistic the prospect of having these things widely available in schools actually is. Access to technology is largely determined by costs, and these are a result of the size of the market. UK schools are estimated to spend some £25 million a year on IT, but even so they do not form a big enough force to drive technical development. This is led by a global market, and is currently perceived as driven by domestic sales. Pundits are predicting that 1996 sales of home computers in the USA will be found to have outstripped those of television sets. These computers will all be multimedia computers, because no one in this market is selling anything else now. Thus the price of these computers will drop, and schools will benefit as a result.

Once the computer is acquired, on-line access to text-based data on the Internet and E-mail can be a reality for any school. A fast modem, which is what is needed to connect the computer to a telephone line, can cost as little as £100, and subscription to a service provider £10 a month; these are 1996 prices and are likely to continue decreasing. Call charges are a worry for schools, as they are hard to monitor or control. However, recent developments in Cambridgeshire are an indication that this problem may resolve itself. The County Council IT Department is an on-line service provider. Its computer is connected to a telephone line via the local cable company. Schools in the county who use the same cable service get calls to another user free, so there are no E-mail call charges. If the promised explosion in provision of on-line services to the home comes about, access to radio and television programmes as well as the World Wide Web and E-mail will be both affordable and easy to operate through a television or computer. However, true multimedia on-line requires a faster telephone line than normally provided. Currently these are prohibitively expensive for primary schools, but fierce competition between providers may soon alter that too.

There is occasionally speculation in the popular media that on-line provision will ultimately replace CD ROM, which will prove to be an intermediate technology. Whether or not CD ROM will provide the publishing format for large local storage of information may be in doubt, although once a technology has a hold in the market it is difficult to dislodge even if something technically superior comes along. The DOS operating system on IBM-PC compatibles must be the prime example of this. Anything that improves on CD ROM will have to remain compatible with it so that people can still play the titles they have. I am in little doubt that some form of local storage of large volumes of information will remain popular. Sources which are accessed frequently, and contain information which does not change or date rapidly, will be cheaper to acquire and handier to access via CD ROM for the foreseeable future. Certainly for school users a CD ROM is more reliable; you know where it is (in theory) and that it will be the same each time you use it. The Web page you used last year, or even yesterday, may no longer be there, or may well have been edited. Add to that the uncertainties of accessing a remote computer over which you have no control (it may be switched off), over a telephone line which can be unreliable or unavailable, especially when calling overseas, and expensive to use, and the reliability of a source on CD ROM seems to secure its future, in schools at least.

Software

Application software such as word processors, spreadsheets and databases get easier to use, more powerful and cheaper as time goes by. However, they are not designed for use in schools, but for the home and the office. As pointed out in every related chapter of this book, that means these packages may not be ideal for schools. The high cost of development of powerful, robust application software tailored to the needs of schools is so high that we are in danger of losing the few companies who still address this market. After this schools will have little choice in the matter.

As well as application software, and content-rich resource software such as that found on CD ROM, there has been a resurgence of interest in educational software which actively tutors the child. Foremost among these has been the ILS or integrated learning system. The most fully developed ILS systems are ones where individual learners are presented with a question, usually a multiple choice item or one requiring a numerical answer, and their response is recorded. Management software compares the student's response to the correct response stored in the system, the student is given instant feedback on the judgement, and an automated selection of the next item, often from a vast bank of material, is made. This selection is based at least in part on the information stored about the learner's earlier responses. Not all products currently marketed as an ILS actually do all this, in particular not all have the diagnostic and prescriptive facilities offered by the more complex systems, or the individualised task assignment, and are therefore not ILSs in the full sense.

Since 1992 a number of these systems have been independently evaluated (Underwood *et al.* 1996). The most significant findings are that the most important variable is which system is being used; it is a grave mistake to assume that the term ILS implies comparable products. With a good ILS the best that can be expected is independently verifiable learning gains in numeracy, which may be very impressive, but not in language. Also the system which has proven most effective is very expensive. Given these outcomes it seems unlikely that schools of the future will be full of children in headphones, sitting at computer terminals, logged in to today's lessons.

Teacher development

There is an adult-, usually teacher-, dominated culture in all but the most 'progressive' schools, even where the most child-centred approach to learning prevails. It is the teacher who decides what is to be studied, when and how – increasingly within a statutory framework. If the teacher decides that the learning experiences she offers will not change, no software introduced into her classroom will be able to do this on its own. However, if the teacher is open to the possibility of using IT for change, and willing to pursue new approaches to teaching and learning that the use of various software packages support, then – and only then – the presence of the software can facilitate a change.

One thing is certain, unless the desperate lack of teacher expertise (documented in Chapter 1) is addressed, IT will never have a significant impact on the culture of the classroom. Teachers who are uncomfortable with computers, and who fail to see how they can be used to enhance learning, simply do not use them. One-day awareness courses are clearly inadequate to address this huge skill gap, yet this is the most commonly experienced form of in-service training. Indications are that waiting for successive cohorts of newly trained teachers to slowly bring a new level of expertise into schools will be unlikely to help either. Trainee teachers spend most of their time in school, so who will teach them about IT? The teachers who are there already often look to the student for help in this area. The apparent lack of multimedia authoring in Initial Teacher Training referred to in Chapter 11 is an example of the way the experiences of newly trained teachers are lagging behind the developments in leading-edge schools.

I feel that there is a serious cultural issue at the heart of this problem. Teachers who have no experience of using IT as learners have difficulty appreciating what a powerful learning tool it can be. Additionally the imposition of the IT components of the National Curriculum left some teachers feeling that the computer was something they had to use, to satisfy the 'computer bits' in the curriculum. IT was not presented, as it could have been, as a tool to help teachers and children achieve some of the more difficult objectives they already had.

If there is to be a change in the school culture, to create an environment which supports the development of children as active learners, and to cultivate an understanding of the skills and processes at the heart of authentic learning, and a mastery of the appropriate use of IT to support it, two things at least must happen. First, teachers must be given the support they need, not just additional resources but time and assistance to develop their own understanding and to apply this new knowledge to their planning and teaching. Second, the formal assessment systems must be adapted to give children credit not simply for regurgitating information, but for demonstration of their independent problem-solving and study skills.

The starting point for this book was a desire to try to make the role that IT can play in supporting authentic learning more explicit to teachers and student teachers. Although it would be unreasonable to expect any teacher to be routinely doing all the things we describe in this book, every teacher should be willing to try at least one that is new to them – not because the statutes demand it, or because the children like computers (not all do anyway!), or because parents expect it, but because they are prepared to see if it really does help the children in their care to understand and take control of their own learning.

Appendix of software

Software referred to in Chapter 2: Developing children's problem-solving: the educational uses of adventure games

Software	*Supplier*
Animal Rescue The Worst Witch Crystal Rain Forest ArcVenture	Sherston Software Ltd Angel House, Sherston, Malmesbury Wiltshire SN16 0LH
Albert's House Number 62, Honeypot Lane	Resource Exeter Road, Wheatley, Doncaster, Yorkshire DN2 4PY
Darryl the Dragon Dinosaur Discovery Flowers of Crystal Granny's Garden SpaceX	4Mation 14 Castle Park Road, Barnstaple, Devon EX32 8PA
Exploring Nature CD ROM	Usborne Books
Lemmings	Psygnosis Ltd
Discworld CD ROM	(Sony Electronic) Kentish Town Road, London NW1

Software referred to in Chapter 5: IT and thinking skills in humanities

Examples of software currently available and useful for humanities, Key Stages 1 and 2, are given here.

Data handling

'Junior Pinpoint' (Longman Logotron) [Acorn] and [PC]
Very flexible and easy to use data-handling package enabling children to set up and edit an appropriate format for the recording of data. Ready-made historical datafiles can also be purchased, e.g. 'Ancient Civilisations', 'British Monarchs', 'The Victorians' and 'Britain since 1930'. More sophisticated historical databases are likely to become available, such as 'Victorian Crime and Punishment' (based on a register of Victorian prisoners) (see Multimedia CD ROM below).

'Picturepoint' (Longman Logotron) [Acorn]
Simple data-handling for younger children which leads into 'Junior Pinpoint'.

'Keynote' and 'Key Datafiles' (Anglia) [Acorn] and [PC]
Ready-made datafiles include 'Time Travel', 'Ancient Egyptian Times', 'Viking World', 'Tudor Times' and '19th Century Biographies'.

Desktop publishing

Many different programs are available, and the most important consideration is to adopt one that can be used across the whole curriculum (and ideally across the whole school, i.e. one with varying levels of complexity) so that teachers and children can become thoroughly familiar with one package and use all of its features to best advantage.

'PenDown DTP' (Longman Logotron) [Acorn]
This offers a wide range of levels.

'First Page' (Longman Logotron) [Acorn]
and
'NewSPAper' (SPA) [PC]
These are both good packages for children's communication of their historical understanding by combining text and images in an attractive and vivid way.

Chronology

'Time Traveller' (LDA Multimedia) [Acorn]
A timeline program which has prepared databases for the Victorian period and for Britain since 1930. Especially effective in allowing comparisons to be made between different kinds of event (e.g. economic, political) on parallel timelines, and providing an effective stimulus for discussion of cause and effect, if well used.

'Time Lines' (Soft Teach) [Acorn] and [PC]
Flexible timeline package which can incorporate pictures drawn, scanned or taken from video. Also text entries from the sample databases provided can be copied into other word processing programs.

'Ancient Greece' (Chalksoft) [Acorn]
gives the user a timeline along which to travel back to the principal eras of Greek civilisation.

'Chronicle' (SCET) [PC] and [Mac]
Enables text, graphics, sound and video images to be incorporated into a time-line. Designed to be compatible with the 'PictureBase' resources on CD ROM (see below), so that images and text from those collections can be used in the construction of timelines.

'Ancient Greece' (Chalksoft) [Acorn]
and
'Time Detectives – The Victorians' (Sherston) [Acorn]
Two examples of information-rich 'adventure games' which offer useful time-lines as a way into the program for children.

Overlay keyboard

'Touch Explorer Plus' (NCET) [Acorn]
A simple program which allows teachers to design overlays to produce questions or information on screen when children explore, say, historical pictures and maps by touch. Two ready-made overlays supplied with the program offer the plan of an Elizabethan cottage, and the changing plan of a Victorian street over three decades.

Simulations

'Landmarks' series (Longman Logotron) [Acorn] and [PC]
These are simulations for various periods: Ancient Egypt, Elizabethans, Victorians, and the Second World War, in which we are conducted by a contem-porary figure who can respond to our questions and help us to find evidence and solve puzzles. Adults often find the process frustrating, but children are usually highly motivated and can learn a great deal of information, which they can carry into complementary tasks.

'Arcventure' series (Sherston) [Acorn]
'Arcventure I: The Romans'
'Arcventure II: The Egyptians'
'Arcventure III: The Vikings'
'Arcventure IV: The Anglo-Saxons'

These 'adventure games' combine the simulation of an archaeological dig, which can familiarise children with some of the skills of handling and interpreting evidence, with travel down timelines to an imaginative reconstruction of past time; in this they can interrogate the historical inhabitants of their archaeological site about the objects they have found. Highly motivating pieces of software backed by well-researched detail.

Multimedia CD ROM

'Anglo-Saxons' (Research Machines/British Museum) [PC]
Authoritative and attractive, offering a lot of scope for interactive searching, but lacking facility to download images.

'Frontier 2000' (Cambridge Software House) [Acorn] and [PC]
The timeline is comprehensive and offers good interactivity.

'Picturebase: Victorian Britain' (AVP Computing) [Acorn] and [PC]
Clear text and pictures, with a notepad facility, but interactivity would depend on the structure of tasks set by the teacher.

'Photobase' series (Longman Logotron) [Acorn] and [PC]
'Decades' series (TAG Developments) [Mac]
Both of these draw on enormously rich pictorial archives, but are lacking in documentation, so that carefully structured tasks would be required from the teacher.

'World of the Vikings' (TAG Developments) [Mac] and [PC]
Research database useful for teachers in background reading and preparation. 'Evidence Boxes' excellent for children.

'Victorian Crime and Punishment' (Longman Logotron) [Acorn]
A sophisticated historical database and package designed to run with 'Junior Pinpoint'; it is based on the register of inmates of a Victorian gaol – complete with prisoners' photographs!

'*The Times* Exposures' (News Multimedia Ltd) [Mac] and [PC]
Collections of news photographs from *The Times* on themes such as 'Britain since the 1930s' and 'How Things Change' (100 years of change in everyday life). A rich variety of visual evidence which can be downloaded and printed out, but with little supporting text, though some nice facsimile documents. A good resource around which the teacher can structure tasks.

'Information finder: World Book Encyclopedia' (World Book Childcraft) [Mac] and [PC]
Excellent resource but it needs fairly good reading skills, and is only appropriate to upper end of Key Stage 2.

'Oxford Children's Encyclopedia' (Oxford University Press) [PC]
Offers a good search facility which encourages children to refine their searches, and a notepad to incorporate text into their own work.

'Kingfisher Children's Micropedia' (LDA Multimedia) [Acorn] and [PC]
Offers a second level of entry for younger children or poor readers.

Bibliography

Adams, A. (1990) The Potential of Information Technology within the English Curriculum, *Journal of Computer Assisted Learning*, 6, pp. 232–8

Allen, D. (1994) Teaching Visual Literacy: Some Reflections on the Term, *Journal of Art and Design Education*, 13, 2, pp. 133–43

Assessment of Performance Unit (APU) Science Reports, 1988, London: HMSO

Assessment of Performance Unit (APU) Science Reports, 1989, London: HMSO

Atkinson, S. (ed.) (1992) *Mathematics with Reason*, Sevenoaks: Hodder & Stoughton

Baker, D. A., Clay, J. and Fox, C. (1996) *Challenging Ways of Knowing in English, Maths and Science*, London: Falmer Press

Bastide, E. (1992) *Good Practice in Primary Religious Education, 4–11*, London: Falmer Press

Beare, R. (1992) Software Tools in Science Classrooms, *Journal of Computer Assisted Learning*, 8, pp. 221–30

Beynon, J. (1993) Epilogue. Technological Literacy: Where do we all go from here?, in H. Mackay and J. Beynon, (eds) (1993) *Computers into Classrooms: More Questions than Answers*, London, Washington DC: Falmer Press

Beynon, J. and Mackay, H. (1993) *Computers into Classrooms: More Questions than Answers*, London: Falmer Press

Black, P. (1993) The Purposes of Science Education, in R. Sherrington, (ed.) *ASE Primary Teachers' Handbook*, Hemel Hempstead: Simon and Schuster Education

Blackmore, M. (1992) The Liverpool Scene: New Students' Experiences, Knowledge and Attitudes towards Information Technology, *Ditte 1*, Coventry: National Council for Educational Technology

Blaye, A., Light, P., Joiner, R. and Sheldon, S. (1991) Collaboration as a Facilitator of Planning and Problem Solving on a Computer-based Task, *British Journal of Developmental Psychology*, 9, pp. 471–83

Blyth, J. (1994) *History 5 to 11*, London: Hodder and Stoughton

Blythe, K. (1990) *Children Learning with LOGO*, Coventry: National Council for Educational Technology

Bonnett, M. (1978) Authenticity and Education, *Journal of Philosophy of Education*, 12, 1, pp. 51–61

Bonnett, M. (1991) Developing Children's Thinking . . . and the National Curriculum, *Cambridge Journal of Education*, 21, 3, pp. 277–92

Bonnett, M. (1994) *Children's Thinking*, London: Cassell

Booth, L. R. (1984) *Algebra: Children's Strategies and Errors*, Windsor: NFER–Nelson

Bourne, R. (1995) *Differentation: Taking IT Forward*, Coventry: NCET

Brosnan, T. (1989) Teaching Chemistry using Spreadsheets – 1: Equilibrium Thermodynamics, *School Science Review* 70, 252, pp. 39–47

Bruner, J. (1966) *Towards a Theory of Instruction*, Cambridge, Mass.: Harvard University Press

Bruner, J. (1988) ch. 1.1 in *Computers in Education 5 to 13*, Milton Keynes: Open University Press.

Bruner, J., Jolly, A. and Sylva, K. (eds) (1976) *Play: its Role in Development and Evolution*, Harmondsworth: Penguin Books

Campbell, J. and Little, V. (eds) (1989) *Humanities in the Primary School*, Lewes: Falmer Press

Cavendish, S. and Walters, W. (1994) Spreadsheets, in J. Underwood (ed.) *Computer-based Learning*, London: David Fulton

Clark, N. J. (1990) 'Why wasn't I taught this stuff years ago?' Using a Computer to Assess and Improve Study Skills, *Journal of Computer Assisted Learning*, 6, pp. 174–89

Cockcroft Report (1982) *Mathematics Counts*, London: Department of Education and Science

Cole, G. (1993) Getting Down to Graph Roots, *Times Educational Supplement*, 26 March

Cooper, D. (1983) *Authenticity and Learning*, London: Routledge and Kegan Paul

Cooper, H. (1995) *The Teaching of History: Implementing the National Curriculum*, London: David Fulton

Copley, T. (1994) *Religious Education 7–11: Developing Primary Teaching Skills*, London: Routledge

Crompton, R. (ed.) (1989) *Computers and the Primary Curriculum 3–13*, London: Falmer Press

Crook, C. (1987) Computers in the Classroom: Defining a Social Context, in J. Rutkowska and C. Crook (eds) *Computers, Cognition and Development*, Chichester: Wiley

Crook, C (1994) *Computers and the Collaborative Experience of Learning*, London: Routledge

Curriculum Council for Wales (1993) *IT in National Curriculum History: Guidance and Case Studies for Teachers at Key Stage 2 and Key Stage 3*, Cardiff: CCW

Davis, J. (1986) *Artefacts in the Primary School* (Teaching History Series no. 45), London: Historical Association

DES (Department of Education and Science) (1988a) Report of the Committee of Inquiry into the Teaching of English Language, *Kingman Report*, London: HMSO

DES (1988b) *English for Ages 5 to 11*, London: HMSO

DES (1989) *Science in the National Curriculum*, London: HMSO

DfE (Department for Education) (1995a) *Art in the National Curriculum*, London: HMSO

DfE (1995b) *Information Technology in the National Curriculum*, London: HMSO

DfE (1995c) *Mathematics in the National Curriculum*, London: DfEE (Department for Education and Employment)

DfE (1995d) *Science in the National Curriculum*, London: HMSO

DfE (1995e) *Survey of Information Technology in Schools*, London: HMSO

DfEE (1995) *Superhighways for Education: the Way Forward*, London: HMSO

Dunne, E. and Bennett, N. (1990) *Talking and Learning in Groups*, London: Macmillan

Driver, R. (1981) Pupils' Alternative Frameworks in Science, *European Journal of Science Education*, 3(1) Jan.–March, pp. 93–101

Drummond, M. J. (1993) *Assessing Children's Learning*, London: David Fulton

Egan, K. (1990) *Romantic Understanding: the Development of Rationality and Imagination, Ages 8–15*, London: Routledge.

Elliott, C. P. (1988) Spreadsheets in Science Teaching, *School Science Review*, 70 (251), pp. 87–93

Eraut, M. and Hoyles, C. (1988) Groupwork with Computers, ESCRC-InTER

Occasional Paper, InTER/3/88; University of Lancaster and *Journal of Computer Assisted Learning*, 5(1), pp. 12–24

Fisher, E. (1993) The Teacher's Role' in P. Scrimshaw (ed.) (1993) *Language, Classrooms and Computers*, London and New York: Routledge

Fisher, R. (1987) *Problem-solving in Primary Schools*, Oxford: Basil Blackwell

Flavell, H. and Tebbutt, M. (1995) *Spreadsheets in Science*, John Murray

Fraser, R., Burkhardt, H., Coupland, J., Phillips, R., Pimm, D. and Ridgway, J. (1988) Learning Activities and Classroom Roles with and without the Microcomputer, in A. Jones and P. Scrimshaw, (eds) (1988) *Computers in Education 5–13*, Milton Keynes and Philadelphia, Pa: Open University Press

Friedler, Y. and McFarlane, A. E. (1997) Data Logging with Portable Computers, a Study of the Impact on Graphing Skills in Secondary Pupils, *Journal of Computers in Mathematics and Science Teaching*, 16(2)

Frost, R. (1995) *IT in Primary Science*, London: IT in Science

Frost, R., McFarlane, A. E., Hemsley, K., Wardle, J. and Wellington, J. (1994) *Enhancing Science with IT*, Coventry: National Council for Educational Technology

Geographical Association and National Council for Educational Technology (1989) *Geography through Topics in Primary and Middle Schools*, Sheffield: NCET and GA

Goodfellow, T. (1990) Spreadsheets: Powerful Tools in Science Education, *School Science Review* 71 (257) pp. 47–55

Hall, J. and Rhodes, V. (1988) *Microcomputers in Primary Schools*, London: Educational Computing Unit, King's College, London

Hall, N. (1989) *Writing with Reason*, Sevenoaks: Hodder & Stoughton

Harris, B. (1994) The Future Curriculum with IT: Implications for Science Education, *School Science Review* 76, 275, pp. 15–25

Healey, L. and Sutherland, R. (1991) *Exploring Mathematics with Spreadsheets*, Oxford: Basil Blackwell

Heidegger, M. (1966) *Discourse on Thinking*, New York: Harper & Row

Heppell, S. (1994) Multimedia and Learning: Normal Children, Normal Lives and Real Change, in J. Underwood, (1994) *Computer Based Learning: Potential into Practice*, London: David Fulton

HMI (1960) *Science in Secondary Schools*, London: HMSO

HMI (1985) *Science 5–16: A Statement of Policy*, London: HMSO

Hobin, J. and Cornish, S. (1995) 'Big Breakfast', a MacroMedia Director presentation of the work of the Glebe School Project, in S. Worden (ed.) *Digital Creativity, the CD-ROM, Proceedings of the Computers in Art and Design Education (CADE 95) Conference*, University of Brighton, April 1995

Hodgkinson, K. (1986) How Artefacts Can Stimulate Historical Thinking in Young Children, *Education 3–13*, 14(2)

Holt, J. (1990) *How Children Fail*, 2nd edn, Harmondsworth: Penguin Books

Hoyles, C. and Sutherland, R. (1989) *Logo Mathematics in the Classroom*, London: Routledge

Huber, L. (1988) ch. 5.2 in *Computers in Education 5 to 13*, Milton Keynes: Open University Press

Hunter, P. (1988) The writing process and word processing, *Microscope Special: Writing*, pp. 3–8

Jackson, A., Fletcher, B. and Messer, D. (1986) A Survey of Microcomputer Use and Provision in Primary Schools, *Journal of Computer Assisted Learning*, 2, pp. 45–55

Jared, E. and Thwaites, A. (1995) What is your Favourite Colour?, in J. Anghileri (ed.) *Children's Mathematical Thinking in the Primary Years*, London: Cassell

Jenkins, E. W. (1995) Central Policy and Teacher Response? Scientific Investigation in the National Curriculum of England and Wales, *International Journal of Science Education*, 17(4), pp. 471–80

Jessel, J. (1992) Do Children Really Use the Word Processor as a Thought Processor?, *Developing Information Technology in Teacher Education*, 5, pp. 23–32

Katterns, S. and Haigh, N. (1986) The Effective Teacher and Computers, *Journal of Computer Assisted Learning*, 2(3), pp. 147–68

Keeling, R. (1987) 'Grasshopper', Newham Software

Kent, A. and Phillips, A. (1994) Geography through IT, in B. Marsden and J. Hughes (eds) *Primary School Geography*, London: David Fulton

Kimber, D., Clough, N., Forrest, M., Harnett, P., Menter, I. and Newman, E. (1995) *Humanities in Primary Education: History, Geography and Religious Education in the Classroom*, London: David Fulton

Kuhn, S. and Stannard, R. (1996) *IT in English: Review of Existing Literature*, Coventry: National Council for Educational Technology

Layton, D. (1973) *Science for the People*, London: George Allen & Unwin

Leron, U. (1988) On the Mathematical Nature of Turtle Programming, in D. Pimm (ed.) *Mathematics, Teachers and Children*, London: Hodder & Stoughton

Lipinski, J. M., Nida, R. E., Shade, D. D. and Watson, J. A. (1986) The Effects of Microcomputers on Young children: an Examination of Free-play Choices, Sex Differences and Social Interactions, *Journal of Educational Computing Research*, 2 (2)

Lodge, J. (ed.) (1992) *Computer Data Handling in the Primary School*, London: David Fulton

Loveless, A. (1995) *The Role of IT: Practical Issues for Primary Teachers*, London: Cassell.

Loveless, A. (forthcoming) The Visual Arts and New Technology in the Classroom, *Computers in the School*

Loveless, A. and Hobin, J. (1996) Visual Literacy and New Technology in Primary Schools: the Glebe School Project, *Technology and Teacher Education Annual 1996, Proceedings of SITE 96*, seventh international conference of the Society for Information Technology and Teacher Education (SITE), Charlottesville, Va.: Association for the Advancement of Computing in Education, pp. 1057–60

Lynch, W. (1991) *Planning for Language, Teaching and Learning with Computers*, Coventry: National Council for Educational Technology

McFarlane, A. E. (1995a) *Integrated Learning Systems: a Critical Review of the Literature*, Coventry: National Council for Educational Technology

McFarlane, A. E. (1995b) Old boys' network?, *Times Educational Supplement*: 23 June

McFarlane, A. E. and Jared, E. (1994) Encouraging student/teacher confidence in the use of information technology, *Computer and Education* 22(1/2), pp. 155–60.

McFarlane, A. E., Friedler, Y., Warwick, P., and Chaplain, R. (1995) Developing an Understanding of the Meaning of Line Graphs in Primary Science Investigations using Portable Computers and Data Logging Software, *Journal of Computers in Mathematics and Science Teaching*, 14 (4) pp. 461–80

McMahon, H. (1990) Collaborating with Computers, *Journal of Computer Assisted Learning*, 6, pp. 149–67

Marsden, B. and Hughes, J. (eds) (1994) *Primary School Geography*, London: David Fulton

Martin, A. (1994) *Teaching National Curriculum History with IT* (Occasional Paper no. 4), London: Historical Association

Matheison, K. (1993) *Children's Art and the Computer*, Sevenoaks: Hodder & Stoughton

Mathematical Association (1992) *Computers in the Mathematics Curriculum*, Leicester: Mathematical Association

Matthews, B. (1992) The Social Issues in Information Technology, *Journal of Information Technology for Teacher Education*, 1(2), pp. 201–13

Mellar, H., Bliss, J., Bookan, R., Ogborn, J. and Tompsett, C. (eds) (1994) *Learning with Artificial Worlds: Computer Based Modelling in the Curriculum*, London: Falmer Press

Metz, M. (1988) Chairs for Bears, in D. Pimm (ed.) *Mathematics, Teachers and Children*, London: Hodder & Stoughton

Mitchell, W. J. (1994) *The Reconfigured Eye*, Cambridge, Mass. and London: MIT Press

Moyles, J. R. (1989) *Just Playing? The Role and Status of Play in Early Childhood Education*, Milton Keynes: Open University Press

NCET (1989) *History in the Headlines*, Coventry: National Council for Educational Technology

NCET (1990) *Rewriting History: An Inset Guide to Using Text Handling in History*, Coventry: National Council for Educational Technology

NCET (1991) *On-line Electronic Mail in the Curriculum*, Coventry: National Council for Educational Technology

NCET (1992) *Evaluation of IT in Science*, Coventry: National Council for Educational Technology

NCET (1994a) *CD ROM in Primary Schools*, Coventry: National Council for Educational Technology

NCET (1994b) *Enhancing Science with IT*, Coventry: National Council for Educational Technology

NCET (1994c) *Primary Science Investigations with IT*, Coventry: National Council for Educational Technology

NCET (1995) *Science Information Sheet: Spreadsheets*, Coventry: National Council for Educational Technology

Niederhauser, D. S. (1996) Information Age Literacy: Preparing Educators for the 21st Century, *Technology and Teacher Education Annual 1996, Proceedings of SITE 96*, seventh international conference of the Society for Information Technology and Teacher Education (SITE), Charlottesville, Va.: Association for the Advancement of Computing in Education, pp. 415–18.

Ofsted (1996) *Subjects and Standards 1994/95*, London: HMSO

Ogborn, J. (1992) Modelling with the Computer at all Ages, *Portugaliae Physica*, 21 (3/4), pp. 93–114

Osborn, P. M. (1987) Spreadsheets in Science Teaching, *School Science Review*, 69 (246), pp. 142–6

Papert, S. (1980) *Mindstorms: Children, Computers and Powerful Ideas*, New York: Basic Books

Peacock, G. (1993) Word-processors and Collaborative Writing, in J. Beynon and H. Mackay (eds) (1993) *Computers into Classrooms: More Questions than Answers*, London and Washington, DC: Falmer Press.

Peacock, M. and Breese, C. (1990) Pupils with Portable Writing Machines, *Educational Review*, 42(1), pp. 41–56

Picasso, P. (1923) Picasso Speaks the Arts (New York) May. Reprinted in H. B. Chipp (1975) *Theories of Modern Art*, Berkeley, Los Angeles, Calif. and London: University of California Press

Primary Science Review, 20, December 1991

Primary Science Review, 40, December 1995

Potter, F. (1987) Language Reading and IT: A Need to Extend the Work of the Microelectronics Education Programme, *British Journal of Educational Technology*, 18.

Rowland, T. (1994) *CAN in Suffolk*, Cambridge: Homerton College

Sanger, J. (1996) Screen Based Entertainment Technology and the Young Learner, a contribution to the Seminar 'Multimedia literacy: developing the creative uses of new technology with young people', The Central School of Speech and Drama and Arts Council of England, 29 January 1996

Scaife, J. and Wellington, J. (1993) *Information Technology in Science and Technology Education*, Milton Keynes: Open University Press

Schools Curriculum & Assessment Authority (1995) *Key Stages 1 & 2 Information Technology: the New Requirements*, London: SCAA

Scrimshaw, P. (1988) Computers in Art Education: Threat or Promise?, in A. Jones and P. Scrimshaw (eds) (1988) *Computers in Education 5–13*, Milton Keynes and Philadelphia, Pa.: Open University Press

Scrimshaw, P. (1989) Educational Computing: What Can Philosophy of Education Contribute?, *Journal of Philosophy of Education*, 23(1), pp. 103–11

Scrimshaw, P. (ed.) (1993) *Language, Classrooms and Computers*, London: Routledge

Sefton-Green, J. (1994) Catching Up with the Kids, Lighthouse Conference presentation, Hurstpierpoint College, 1 October 1994

Sharples, M. (1985) Paper presented during the NALEC meeting held at the Cheshire Language Centre, North Cheshire College, Warrington, 2 March

Shawyer, G., Booth, M. and Brown, R. (1988) The Development of Children's Historical Thinking, *Cambridge Journal of Education* 18(2), pp. 209–19

Smart, L. (1996) *Using IT in Primary School History*, London: Cassell

Southall, R. (1992) The World of Data Handling and its Place in Primary Education, in D. Lodge (ed.) (1992) *Computer Data Handling in the Primary School*, London: David Fulton

Spender, D. (1995) *Nattering on the Net: Women, Power and Cyberspace*, Melbourne: Spinifex Press.

Standish, P. (1992) *Beyond the Self*, Aldershot: Avebury

Stradling, B., Sims, D. and Jamison, J. (1994) *Portable Computers Pilot Evaluation Report*, Coventry: National Council for Educational Technology

Straker, A. (1989) *Children using Computers*, Oxford: Basil Blackwell

Street, B. D. (1993) *Cross Cultural Approaches to Literacy*, Cambridge: Cambridge University Press

Suffolk County Council (1995) *Making Use of IT in Science*, Suffolk County Council

Swatton, P. and Taylor, R. M. (1994) Pupil Performance in Graphical Tasks and its Relationship to the Ability to Handle Variables, *British Educational Research Journal*, 20(2), pp. 227–45.

Taylor, C. (1991) *The Ethics of Authenticity*, London: Harvard University Press

Taylor, R. M. and Swatton, P. (1990) *Assessment Matters, No. 1: Graph Work in School Science*, London: HMSO

Terry, C. (1984) *Using Micro-computers in Schools*, London: Croom Helm

Underhay, S. (1989) Project Work: Adventure Games, in R. Crompton (ed.) *Computers and the Primary Curriculum 3–13*, Lewes: Falmer Press

Underwood, J. D. M. and Underwood, G. (1990) *Computers and Learning: Helping Children Acquire Thinking Skills*, Oxford: Basil Blackwell

Underwood, J. D. M. *et al.* (1996) *Integrated Learning Systems: a Report of Phase II of the Pilot Evaluation of ILS in the UK*, Coventry: National Council for Educational Technology

Watson, D. M. (ed.) (1993) *The ImpacT Report, an Evaluation of the Impact of Information Technology on Children's Achievements in Primary and Secondary Schools*, London: DfE and King's College London

Webb, L. (1993) Spreadsheets in Physics Teaching, *Physics Education*, 28, pp. 77–82

Wharry, D. and Richardson, R. (1988) *Teaching and Learning with Robots*, London: Croom Helm

Whitehead, A. N. (1932) The Aims of Education, reprinted in *The Aims of Education and Other Essays* (1966), London: Ernest Benn

Wiegand, P. (1993) *Children and Primary Geography*, London: Cassell

Wood, D. (1988) *How Children Think and Learn*, Oxford: Basil Blackwell

Woolnough, B. and Allsop, T. (1985) *Practical Work in Science*, Cambridge: Cambridge University Press

Index